CISTERCIAN STUDIES SERIES : NUMBER EIGHTY-TWO

BEDE THE VENERABLE
(673-735)

ON THE SEVEN
CATHOLIC EPISTLES

THE COMMENTARY
ON THE
SEVEN CATHOLIC EPISTLES

of

CISTERCIAN STUDIES SERIES : NUMBER EIGHTY-TWO

BEDE THE VENERABLE

Translated by

DAVID HURST
Monk of Portsmouth Abbey

CISTERCIAN PUBLICATIONS
Kalamazoo, Michigan
1985

This translation has been made from the critical Latin edition prepared by David Hurst, OSB, and published in the series Corpus Christianorum, Series Latina, 121: *Bedae Venerabilis Opera*, pars II : *Opera exegetica* (Turnhout: Brepols, 1983)

Published by Cistercian Publications
WMU   Kalamazoo, Michigan 49008

Available in Britain and Europe from
A.R. Mowbray & Co Ltd
St Thomas House   Becket Street
Oxford OX1 1SJ

The work of Cistercian Publications is made possible in part by support from Western Michigan University

Library of Congress Cataloguing in Publication Data:

Bede, the Venerable, Saint, 673-735.
    The commentary on the seven Catholic Epistles of Bede the Venerable.

(Cistercian studies series ; no. 82)
Translation of: In epistolas VII Catholicas.
    1. Bible. N.T. Catholic Epistles—Commentaries.
I. Hurst, David, OSB. II. Title. III. Series.
BS2777.B4213 1985   227'.907   84-7755
ISBN 0-87907-882-0

Printed in the United States of America
Typeset by Gale Akins, Kalamazoo

I pray you, noble Jesus, that as you have graciously
granted me joyfully to imbibe the words of your
knowledge, so of your gracious goodness you
will also allow me to come at length to you,
the fount of all wisdom, and in your
presence to dwell forever.

From *A History of the English
Church and People*

TABLE OF CONTENTS

FOREWORD

HARDLY ANY PLACE in the Christian world was farther from Rome in the late seventh century than recently-converted Northumbria, the northernmost kingdom of what today is known as England. Yet neither the great distance nor the tremendous difficulties of travel at that time prevented Benedict Biscop from making several trips to Rome, as well as to centers of monastic culture on the continent. On these journeys Benedict Biscop developed a conception of the monastic life that was largely based on the Rule of St Benedict, and he also brought back to Northumbria stone masons, glass makers, and even a singing master—John the Chanter, who had been Archchanter of St Peter's—to teach the monks of the far north to sing in the roman style. Then, too, Benedict Biscop brought back things: sacred vessels, vestments, religious paintings, relics, and a great many books, dealing especially with biblical and theological subjects. All of these ideas, talents, and goods, especially the books, Benedict Biscop put to use in founding, in about 674, a monastery at Wearmouth (modern Monkwearmouth in the county of Durham), which was to become one of the great centers of monastic learning of the late seventh and eighth centuries.

In about 679, upon Benedict Biscop's return to Wearmouth from one of his roman journeys, a boy of seven was presented by his family to the monastery as an oblate. The lad's name was Bede, and he spent the rest of his life as a monk, at first at Wearmouth, and later at a second house established by Benedict Biscop at Jarrow, five miles away.

Bede made use of the great library assembled by Benedict

Biscop to become, in the words of Dom David Knowles, 'the
most learned man in Western Europe'.[1] He read, and wrote,
in a wide variety of fields—natural science, mathematics and
astronomy (applied to vexed questions of the day concerning
the calendar), grammar, rhetoric, geography, history, hagio-
graphy, theology, and above all interpretation of the Scriptures. Bede's earliest scriptural commentaries were devoted to
the book of Revelation, the Acts of the Apostles, and the
catholic epistles. He later wrote commentaries on the gospels
of Luke and Mark, along with a collection of gospel
homilies, and commentaries on Genesis, Proverbs, Tobit, the
Song of Songs, as well as works on various historical books
of the Old Testament.

How the title 'Venerable' first came to be attached to
Bede's name is a matter of pious legend, but already in 835, a
hundred years after Bede's death, the council of Aachen
described him as *'venerabilis et modernis temporibus doctor
admirabilis Beda'*. There was a local cult of Bede in the north
of England throughout the Middle Ages, though it was not
until 1899 that Leo XIII decreed that May 27th should be
observed as the feast of the Venerable Bede, given the title
Doctor of the Church,[2] the only Englishman to be awarded
this title, and the only Englishman we meet in Dante's
Paradiso.

Bede combined his great learning with sanctity and a
personal charm which still shines through his writings,
though he speaks but little of himself in his works. He saw
himself always as a learner and a teacher, and in the
conclusion of his well-known *History of the English Church
and People,* he tells us:

> I have spent all my life in this monastery, applying
> myself entirely to the study of the Scriptures; and,
> amid the observances of the discipline of the Rule
> and the daily task of singing in the church, it has
> always been my delight to learn or to teach
> or to write.[3]

Bede's words here show the importance he attached to his study of the Scriptures, and of his works listed just following this passage, over eighty percent are exegetical. Although today Bede is remembered chiefly for his historical works (and generally speaking only these have previously been translated), during the Middle Ages his reputation was founded mainly on his scriptural commentaries, which were read and copied in monastic centers throughout Europe. Cyril Smetana has recently shown the great importance that Bede's commentaries and exegetical homilies had in the collection of homiletic materials assembled by Paul the Deacon as part of the carolingian liturgical reform. Bede's contribution forms almost a quarter of the entire anthology, exceeding even the number of selections taken from Augustine, Jerome, or Gregory the Great. Smetana attributes this dominance of Bede's work in Paul the Deacon's homiliary to the theological depth and thorough orthodoxy of Bede's ideas and to the admirable clarity of Bede's style.[4] (Presumably Bede, a native speaker of Old English, developed this Latin style from the books that Benedict Biscop had collected, but Bede's style often seems to have greater clarity and precision than that of his patristic models.) In addition to these factors, one might suggest another cause of Bede's popularity with medieval readers, namely, his balanced concern with both the historical sense of the Scriptures and with deeper, allegorical meanings contained beneath the literal sense. Bede emphasized the necessity of basing his interpretations solidly on the historical sense (*Commentary on Genesis;* CC 118A: 3, 29/31), but at the same time he felt the need of going beyond the literal sense of a passage, of 'stripping off the bark of the letter to find a deeper and more sacred meaning in the pith of the spiritual sense' (Preface to his *Commentary on Ezra and Nehemiah;* CC 119A: 237, 13/15). Furthermore, in reading Bede's commentaries, one is aware of being guided by a teacher who always has a marvelously sane and practical concern with his readers' efforts to grow in the spiritual life. This concern is perhaps especially evident in the commentary here translated, since the catholic epistles so often lend themselves to pastoral and spiritual interpretation.

It is fitting that this first volume of Bede's scriptural commentaries made available in English should be the work of Dom David Hurst, who has devoted much of his fruitful scholarly career to Bede's commentaries and exegetical homilies. The long-needed critical editions of these works have now nearly all been published in the *Corpus Christianorum* series, and the majority of these texts were edited by David Hurst—from his edition of Bede's *Homilies on the Gospels* (CC 122), published in 1955, to his just-published edition of the text here translated (CC 121). The many years that Father David has spent in such close association with Bede's commentaries and homilies, first as an editor and now as a translator, have given him an unrivaled knowledge of Bede's thought on the scriptures and on Bede's relationship to his sources, as well as an admirable feel for Bede's style.

Lawrence T. Martin

The University of Akron

NOTES TO THE FOREWORD

1. David Knowles, *Saints and Scholars* (Cambridge: Cambridge Univ. Press, 1962) p. 14.

2. Herbert Thurston, 'Bede,' in *The Catholic Encyclopedia* (New York: Robert Appleton Co., 1907) Vol. 2, p. 385.

3. *Bede's Ecclesiastical History* V, 24, ed. Bertram Colgrave and R.A.B. Mynors (Oxford: Clarendon Press, 1969) p. 567.

4. Cyril L. Smetana, 'Paul the Deacon's Patristic Anthology,' in *The Old English Homily and its Backgrounds,* ed. Paul E. Szarmach and Bernard F. Huppé (Albany: State University of New York Press, 1978) pp. 79-80.

INTRODUCTION

THE SEVEN BRIEF LETTERS of James, 1 and 2 Peter, 1, 2 and 3 John, and Jude, usually given at the end of the New Testament just before the book of Revelation, have never received the same attention from exegetes as has been given to the four Gospels and the Letters of Paul. Throughout the christian centuries commentaries on them have been, comparatively, rate. During the early patristic period, Augustine, bishop of Hippo in North Africa, composed a commentary on 1 John. Given the deep theological content of this Letter, it is understandable why Augustine must have chosen it for exposition.

For some reason now difficult to fathom Bede chose the final part of the New Testament, the book of Acts, these seven Letters, and the book of Revelation, when he first began his attempts at written exegesis of the books of sacred scripture early in the eighth century.[1] For the Letters of Paul he was content to piece together extracts from the writings of Augustine to form a lengthy commentary. Eventually Bede was to expound the meaning of a number of the books of the Bible. But these first efforts of his were unique in that he was more inclined then than later to follow a literal interpretation of the text. The heavily allegorical meaning that he was to adopt later on in explaining the various books of scripture is not nearly so noticeable in his early commentaries. Here allegory and symbolism which are to be found in practically all the exegetical writings of scriptural commentators before Bede's time are employed, but not to the extent that Bede was to make use of later on when he had become a more experienced elucidator of the meaning of the sacred texts.

Bede's reputation as a scripture scholar, in fact, has generally been that of a clever compiler of the insights of previous exegetes rather than that of a thinker of any originality. To some extent this is true. Bede's commentaries have the appearance of being nothing more than a kind of collage of passages gleaned from preceding writers. In his exegesis of these seven Letters from the New Testament this quality of his work can be seen particularly in his exposition of 1 John, where he has borrowed extensively from Augustine's work. An examination of the content of the material contained in the interpretation of the other six Letters will reveal occasional passages—sometimes with no indication given of the author, a standard practice of the time—from other writers, Cyprian, Ambrose, Jerome, and Gregory the Great. The practical and pastoral nature of Bede's approach to the books of the Bible is, however, always apparent. In the ninth century the Englishman Boniface was sending letters back to his native land asking for copies of Bede's commentaries to use in his mission of converting the Germans to Christianity.[2] And the simple, catechetical nature of Bede's explications, very much suited to a people to whom he refers several times as uneducated and but recently exposed to christian teaching, is obvious to one reading the examination of the meaning and application of the biblical message.

The need for a synthesis of what has been formerly thought out, not only in matters affecting religion but in all branches of human knowledge, makes itself felt from time to time. Cicero was successful in condensing the diffuse philosophical writings of Plato and making them usable for the practical roman mind of the West. Jerome also made much of the work of Origen available to those whose principal language was Latin, not only through translation but also by simplifying and condensing Origen's theological ideas. In fact, these seven scriptural Letters themselves, prescinding from any commentary on them, relied heavily on the Old Testament and on preceding New Testament books and sought to make former religious thought pertinent to a new and changed external situation. This midrashic mode of religious thinking is built into the canon of the Bible, as is the quality of *paideia,* instruction by the example of admirable individuals or groups who had lived earlier. Bede often uses as models of proper conduct characters mentioned in the Letters and other persons cited in the scriptures.

We should also note that there is a distinctive humane approach to matters regarding religion distinguishable in the writings of Bede. He is quite insistent, for instance, that in the life to come after death God will be an exacting, though fair and just, judge of the actions of every human being; still he states time and again that mankind cannot live a completely sinless existence here on earth, that sins and faults, even serious ones, will be committed, but that the effect of these failures can be mitigated by sincere confession, penance, and acts of charity and forgiveness towards others. The rewards of striving to live a blameless life here and now, and especially the inexpressible happiness that awaits the good person in the after life, he stresses far more than fear of punishment for wrongdoing. This positive and joyful attitude is also apparent in later cistercian writers such as Bernard of Clairvaux and Aelred of Rievaulx. All of their writings have a particularly benevolent character. There should be no reason for surprise, then, that the first Cistercians, who were very conscious of this human aspect of religion, were aware of the importance of the scriptural commentaries of Bede.

In the twelfth century, manuscript copies of this work of Bede were in the libraries of Cîteaux and Clairvaux (and are still preserved respectively in the Public Libraries of Dijon and Troyes in France) and at the Cistercian houses of Beauprés and Vaucelles (now respectively at the Bibliothèque Nationale in Paris and the Bibliothèque Publique of Cambrai).[3] Despite differences of national and regional castes of thought that emphasize this or that aspect of religion, there is a remarkable continuity in the development of religious thought. Perhaps an english translation of one of the earliest of Bede's scriptural commentaries will help manifest this continuity.

The english translation of this work has been made from a new Latin edition of the commentary on these seven Letters from the New Testament prepared for the series, *Corpus Christianorum.*

D.H.

NOTES TO INTRODUCTION

1.   For the dates of the composition of these earliest biblical commentaries of Bede see M. L. W. Laistner, *Expositio Actuum Apostolorum et Retractatio* (Cambridge, Massachusetts: The Mediaeval Academy of America, 1939) xiii-xvii; *A Hand-List of Bede Manuscripts* (Ithaca, New York: Cornell University Press, 1943) 20-31.

2.   *MGH Epistolae* III. English translation in E. Emerton, *The Letters of Saint Boniface* (New York: Columbia University Press, 1940) 133-34, 167-68.

3.   The shelf-numbers of these manuscripts are given by Laistner, *Hand-List,* 31-36.

ABBREVIATIONS

EDITIONS CITED

CC	Corpus Christianorum
CSEL	Corpus Scriptorum Ecclesiasticorum Latinorum
GCS	Die Griechischen Christlichen Schriftsteller der ersten Jahrhunderte
MGH	Monumenta Germaniae Historica
PL	Patrologia Latina
TU	Texte und Untersuchungen zur Geschichte der altchristlichen Literatur

Scriptural citations have been given according to the enumeration and nomenclature of *The Jerusalem Bible*. Psalm citations are given by Hebrew enumeration with Vulgate enumeration in parentheses.

AUTHORS AND WORKS CITED

Ambr.	Ambrose, Bishop of Milan (340-397)
Exp. Luc.	*Commentary on the Gospel according to Luke*
De fide	*On Faith*
De paen.	*On Repentance*
De spir.	*On the Holy Spirit*
Aug.	Augustine, Bishop of Hippo (354-430)
Civ. Dei	*The City of God*
Enarr. in ps.	*Commentary on the Psalms*
Ep(p).	*Letter(s)*
In Ioh. ep.	*Commentary on the First Letter of John*

Serm.	*Sermons*
Bede	Bede the Venerable (673-735)
Act. Ap.	*Exposition on the Acts of the Apostles*
Bened.	Benedict, abbot of Monte Cassino (480-544)
RB	*Rule for Monks*
Cassiodorus	Cassiodorus, founder of Vivarium (480-575)
In ep. apost.	*Commentary on the Letters of the Apostles*
Cypr.	Cyprian, bishop of Carthage (c. 210-258)
Hab. virg.	*On the Dress of Virgins*
De zelo	*On Jealousy and Envy*
Eusebius/Rufinus	Eusebius, Bishop of Caesarea (264-340)
Hist. eccl.	*Church History* (in the Latin translation of Rufinus of Aquileia [345-410])
Greg.	Gregory the Great, Bishop of Rome (540-604)
Hom. ev.	*Homilies on the Gospels*
Moral.	*Morals, Commentary on Job*
Reg. past.	*Pastoral Care*
Innocentius I	Innocent I, Bishop of Rome (reigned 401-417)
Epistola ad Decentium	*Letter to Decentius*
Isid.	Isidore, Bishop of Seville (c. 560-636)
Etymol.	*Etymologies*
Jer.	Jerome, monk (340-420)
Adv. Jov.	*Against Jovinian*

Comm. Eccl.	*Commentary on Ecclesiastes (Qoheleth)*
Nom. Hebr.	*Interpretation of Hebrew Names*
Vir. ill.	*On Famous Men*

Plin.
   Nat. hist.

Pliny the Elder (AD 23-79)
   Natural History

Virg.
   Aen.

Virgil (BC 70-19)
   Aeneid

BEDE THE VENERABLE

COMMENTARY ON THE SEVEN CATHOLIC EPISTLES

PREFACE

JAMES, PETER, JOHN, JUDE wrote seven Letters which church tradition calls catholic, that is, universal. Although in the list of the apostles Peter and John are accustomed to be ranked as more important, the Letter of James is placed first among these for the reason that he received the government of the church of Jerusalem,[1] from where the source and beginning of the preaching of the Gospel took place and spread throughout the entire world. The apostle Paul also shows respect for this see when in naming him he says, *James, Cephas, and John, who appeared to be pillars.*[1] Or at least[2] because he sent his Letter to the twelve tribes of Israel who were the first to become believers, this one rightly ought to have been placed first. Rightly were the Letters of Peter placed second, because he wrote to the elect newcomers,[2] who in Greek are called converts,[3] that is, he wrote to those who were converted from paganism to Judaism and from Judaism to the grace of gospel election. Rightly were the Letters of John placed third, because he wrote to those who came to believe from the gentiles, since neither by race nor by belief had they been Jews. Accordingly, many church writers, among whom is Saint Athanasius, head of the church of Alexandria, assert that his first Letter was written to the Parthians.[4] The Letter of Jude rightly has been placed last, because although this also was an important tribe,[5] nevertheless he is of lesser importance than the aforesaid apostles; or because the Letter of James was written first, then Peter's, after them John's, therefore up to now they retain the order

[1] refers to backnotes   1. Ga 2:9   2. 1 P 1:1

3

in which they were written. For it is clear that blessed James suffered martyrdom in the thirtieth year after the Lord's passion,[6] Peter in the thirty-eighth, that is, in the final year of Nero,[7] and he wrote in his second Letter, *I am convinced that the laying aside of my mortal body*[8] *may be quick, according to what our Lord Jesus Christ made known to me by revelation.*[3] From that it is evident that he wrote this Letter just before his passion, while James had gone home to the Lord some years previously; but in fact it is not fitting that his Letters, which he wrote to the same churches, be separated from one another. In turn, John wrote his Letters along with his Gospel after a further interval of time, when having returned from exile after the slaying of Domitian he found the Church disturbed during his absence by heretics, whom he attacks in his Letters and calls antichrists.

NOTES TO PREFACE

1. Since the name James occurs several times in the New Testament, there was considerable discussion by early writers as to just which of them composed this Letter. In choosing to identify him with the James who was the first bishop of Jerusalem, Bede was following a work of Saint Jerome, *De viris illustribus* 2 (ed. E. C. Richardson [Leipzig, 1896] TU 14:7, 16/17). This is a collection of short biographical sketches of outstanding persons of the first christian centuries, beginning with Saint Peter and ending with himself, inspired by a similar work from classical antiquity. Taking as his authority an earlier church writer, Hegesippus, he equates the James who wrote this Letter with the first to preside over the church of Jerusalem. That one of those named James was the first bishop of Jerusalem is implied but not definitely stated in Ac 12:17, 15:1-20, 21:18. Bede discusses the matter at some length in his comment on Ac 1:13.

2. Latin *certe*. While the adjective *certus* usually means 'definite', the adverb form, besides meaning 'definitely', also is used by Bede to indicate an alternate idea or possibility of interpretation, and so is given in the lexicons to mean 'at least'.

3. Latin *proseliti*

4. This statement that 1 Jn was written to the Parthians I have not been able to find among the writings of Saint Athanasius. However, Saint Augustine (*In Ioh. ep.; PL* 35: 1977-78) and Cassiodorus (*In ep. apost.; PL* 70: 1369-70 D) both say that it was written to the Parthians. Ancient Parthia lay to the south of the Caspian Sea, and presumably was regarded as an entirely pagan area.

5. Judah

6. Jer., *Vir. ill.* 2; TU 8: 23.

7. Ibid. 1; 6, 28/29.

8. Latin *tabernaculi*

5

COMMENTARY ON JAMES

1:1 JAMES, a servant of God and of our Lord Jesus Christ, to the twelve tribes which are in the dispersion, greeting. About this James the apostle Paul said, *James, Cephas, and John, who appeared to be pillars, gave to me and Barnabas the right hand of fellowship, as we were among the gentiles, they however among the circumcised.*[1] Therefore, because he had been ordained an apostle for the circumcised, he took care both to teach those present from among the circumcised by speaking to them and also to encourage, instruct, rebuke and correct the absent by letter. *To the twelve tribes,* he says, *which are in the dispersion.* We read that after blessed Stephen was slain by the Jews, *a great persecution broke out at that time in the church which was at Jerusalem, and all except the apostles were dispersed throughout the districts of Judea and Samaria.*[2] Therefore he sent a letter to these who were dispersed, who suffered *persecution for righteousness' sake,*[3] and not only to these but also to those who, having received the faith of Christ, were not yet taking care to be perfect in works, as the following parts of the Letter assert, and even to those who were persevering in separation from the faith and, more than this, were eager to persecute and disturb it among the believers, as far as they were able. All these, then, were in dispersion because of different calamities, exiles from their native land and harassed by their enemies in countless slaughters, deaths and hardships wherever they were, as church history amply demonstrates. But we read also in the Acts of the Apostles that they had already been

1. Ga 2:9   2. Ac 8:1   3. Mt 5:10

7

dispersed far and wide by the time of the Lord's passion, for
Luke says, *For there were living at Jerusalem devout Jews
from every nation which is beneath the sky;*[4] quite a few of
these nations are even given by name when there follows,
*Parthians and Medes and Elamites and those who live in
Mesopotamia,*[5] and so on. Therefore, he encourages the
righteous not to fall away from the faith in temptations, he
reproves sinners and advises them to refrain from sinning and
to make progress in virtues lest what they had received as
sacraments of the faith might turn out to be for them not
only fruitless but also a cause of damnation; he advises
unbelievers to do penance for killing the saviour and for
other wicked deeds in which they were involved before
heavenly punishment descending either invisibly or even
visibly strikes.

**1:2 My brothers, think it complete[¹] joy when you have
encountered different temptations.** He begins his advice
with the more perfect that he may in due course come to
those whom he saw to be less perfect, in need of correction
and of being brought to the height of perfection. And it
should be noted that he does not say simply, 'rejoice', or
'think it a joy', but, *think it complete joy,* he says, *when you
have encountered different temptations.* Think it worth
complete joy if it happens that you undergo temptations on
account of your faith in Christ, *This is a grace, if anyone
on account of his consciousness of God undergoes [temptations], suffering unjustly,*[6] as Peter says; and as his fellow
apostle Paul, *The sufferings of this time are not worthy [of
being compared] with the future glory which will be
revealed in us;*[7] and all the apostles *went joyful from the
presence of the council since they were counted worthy
of suffering insult for the Name of Jesus.*[8] We ought therefore to be saddened not if we are tempted but if we have
been overcome by temptations.

4. Ac 2:5   5. Ac 2:9   6. 1 P 2:19   7. Rm 8:18   8. Ac 5:41

1:3 Knowing that the testing of your faith works patience.
For this reason, he says, you are being tempted by adversities,
that you may learn the virtue of patience and that through
this you may be able to show and test that you have in your
heart a firm faith in the future reward. What Paul says,
Knowing that tribulation works patience, patience proof,[9]
ought not to be considered contradictory to this passage
but rather in agreement. For patience works proof, because he whose patience cannot be overcome is proven
perfect. This also is taught here thoroughly in what follows,
when it is said:

1:4 Let patience have a perfect work. And again, *the testing
of faith works patience,* because that love of reasoning causes
the faithful to be trained through patience, that through it
the degree of the perfection of their faith may be tested.

**1:5 If anyone of you, however, stands in need of wisdom,
let him beg it from God, who gives to all abundantly and
does not reproach, and it will be given to him.** All saving
wisdom, indeed, must be begged from the Lord, because, as
the wise man says, *All wisdom is from the Lord God and
was always with him,*[10] and no one is able to understand and
be wise of his own free will without the help of divine grace,
although the Pelagians argue a lot [about this]. But here
particularly he seems to be talking about that wisdom
which it is necessary for us to use in temptations. If anyone
of you, he says, is not able to understand the usefulness of
temptations which befall the faithful for the sake of testing,
let him beg from God that there be given him the realization
by which he may be able to recognize with what great kind-
ness the father chastises the sons whom he carefully makes
worthy of an eternal inheritance. And he says advisedly,
who gives to all abundantly, so that no one, aware of his own

9. Rm 5:3-4   10. Si 1:1

frailty, may lack confidence in being able to obtain what he requests, but rather each one should recall that *the Lord has heard the desire of the needy,*[11] and as the same one says elsewhere, *The Lord has blessed all who fear him, the lowly with the greater.*[12] But since many people request many things from the Lord, which however they do not deserve to receive, he adds in what way they ought to make their request, if they want to get their wish:

1:6 Let him beg, however, in faith, in no way hesitating, that is, let him, by living well, show himself to be worthy of being heard when he begs. For anyone who remembers that he has not obeyed the Lord's commands rightly loses hope that the Lord pays attention to his prayers. For it has been written, *The prayer of one who closes his ear that he may not hear the law will be detestable.*[13] **For he who hesitates is like a wave of the sea which is tossed and carried about by the wind.** Anyone who hesitates about attaining heavenly rewards because his consciousness of sin pricks him, at the onslaught of temptations easily abandons the position of faith by which in peace and quiet he appeared to serve God and he is carried away at the will of the invisible enemy as if by a blast of wind through different kinds of errors of vices.

1:8 The double-minded man is indecisive in all his ways. *In all his ways,* he says, in adversities and in prosperity. The man, however, is double-minded, who both bends his knee to entreat the Lord, sends forth words of entreaty, and yet because his consciousness[14] accuses him within, he lacks confidence in being able to obtain what he requests. The man is double-minded who wishes both to rejoice here with the world and to reign there with God. Likewise the man is double-minded who in the good he does looks not for reward inwardly but for approbation outwardly. Hence it is

11. Ps 10:17 (Vulg. 9:38)   12. Ps 115 (113):13
13. Pr 21:13, 28:9   14. *conscientia*

well said by a wise man, *Woe to the sinner entering the land by two ways.*[15] A sinner enters the land by two ways indeed when he both shows that what he seeks by his work is God's approbation and the world's in his thoughts. All such as these, however, are indecisive in all their ways, because they are both very easily discouraged by the adversities of the world and ensnared by prosperity, so that they turn aside from the way of truth.

1:9—10 Let the humble brother, however, glory in his exaltation. He says that it is fitting for you to *think it complete joy when you have encountered different temptations,*[16] because everyone who endures adversities humbly for the Lord will receive from him proudly the rewards of the kingdom. **But let the rich man** glory—is understood from the previous part of the verse—**in his humility.** It is clear that this has been said by way of mockery, which in Greek is called irony. So, he says, let him remember that his glory, in which he takes pride about his wealth and looks down on or even oppresses the poor, must come to an end, that having been humbled he may perish for ever with that rich man clothed in purple who looked down upon the needy Lazarus.[17] **For he will pass away like the blossom of hay.** The blossom of hay is pleasing both to smell and to see, but very quickly it loses the grace of its beauty and sweetness, and therefore the present happiness of the wicked which cannot be long-lived, is most properly likened to it.

1:11 For the sun has risen with its heat and has dried up the hay, and its blossom has fallen off. He refers to the sentence of the very strict judge, by which the temporal loveliness of the condemned is in the end consumed, as the heat of the sun. Yet the elect also flourish, but not like hay. For *the righteous will flourish like a palm tree.*[18] The righteous

15. Si 2:14   16. Jm 1:2   Lk 16:19-21
18. Ps 92:12 (91:13)

flourish for a short while, *for they will quickly dry up like the hay and they will soon wither like the plants of herbs.*[19] The righteous flourish like trees because their blossom, that is, their very sure hope, waits for everlasting fruit, and their root, that is, charity, remains fixed and immovable. Because of this, indeed, the wise man says, *Like a vine I have brought forth fruit and my blossoms a sweet smell.*[20] Accordingly, Naboth, a righteous man, preferred to die rather than have the vineyard of his fathers turned into a garden of plants.[21] To change the strong works of the virtues, which we have received from the teaching of the fathers, for the short-lived pleasure of the vices, is in truth to convert the vineyard of our fathers into a garden of plants. The righteous, however, wish to lay down their life before preferring to choose earthly over heavenly goods. Hence it is well said of them in the psalms that they will be *like a tree that has been planted beside streams of water, which will give its fruit in its time,*[22] and so on. But what of the unrighteous? **And the loveliness of its appearance has vanished,** he says, **so too the rich man will languish in his ways.** He is talking not about every rich man but one who trusts in the uncertainty of riches. For in contrasting a rich man with a humble brother, he has shown that he was speaking about that sort of rich man who is not humble. For even Abraham, although he was a rich man in the world, nevertheless received a poor man after his death into his bosom, a rich man he left in torments.[23] But he did not leave the rich man because he was rich, which he himself also had been, but because he had scorned being merciful and humble, which he himself had been; and on the contrary, he did not receive Lazarus because he was poor, which he himself had not been, but because he had taken care to be humble and innocent, which he himself had been. Therefore, such a rich man, that is, one who is proud and wicked

19. Ps 37 (36):2   20. Si 24:23   21. 1 K 21:2-13   22. Ps 1:3
23. Lk 16:22

and places earthly ahead of heavenly joys, *will languish in his ways,* that is, he will perish in his evil actions because he has neglected to enter the Lord's straight way. But when he falls off like the hay under the sun's heat, the righteous on the contrary like a fruit-bearing tree endures the heat of the same sun, that is, the severity of the judge, unblemished, and in addition brings forth fruits for which he will be rewarded for ever. Properly there is added then:

1:12 Happy the man who endures temptation, for when he has been tested he will receive the crown of life which God has promised to those who love him. This is like the saying in the Apocalypse, *Be faithful even to death, and I will give you the crown of life,*[24] which *God has promised,* he says, *to those who love him,* clearly advising that one ought more to rejoice in temptations the more definitely evident it is that on those whom he loves God often places a heavier burden of temptations, that through the training of temptations they may be proven perfect in faith. When however they have been proven to be truly faithful, that is, *perfect and unblemished, lacking in nothing,*[25] justifiably may they receive the promised crown of eternal life.

1:13 Let no one, when he is tempted, say that he is tempted by God. Up to this point he has discussed temptations which we bear outwardly with the Lord's assent for the sake of being tested. Now he begins to treat of those which we sustain inwardly at the devil's instigation or even at the persuasive frailty of our nature. Here first he refutes the error of those who think that, just as it is clear to us that good thoughts are inspired by God, so also evil ones are produced in our mind at his instigation. *Let no one,* therefore, *when he is tempted, say that he is tempted by God,* with that temptation, namely, which *the rich man* falling into *will languish in*

24. Rv 2:10   25. Jm 1:4   26. Jm 1:11

his ways;[26] that is, let no one, when he has committed
robbery, theft, calumny, murder, rape, or other things of
this kind, say that he felt he had to perpetrate them because
of God's compulsion, and therefore that he was quite
unable to avoid doing them. **For God is not the intender**[2]
of evil—there is understood—temptations; **for he himself
tempts no one,** with that temptation, namely, which deceives
the unfortunate into sinning. For there is a twofold kind of
temptation, one which deceives, the other which tests.
According to that which deceives, *God tempts no one;*
according to that which tests, *God tempted Abraham;*[27]
about that, too, the prophet begs, *Test me, Lord, and
tempt me.*[28]

1:14 **Each one, in fact, is tempted, drawn on and lured by
his own concupiscence,** and so on, *drawn on* from the right
way and *lured* into evil. About this verse Jerome writes
against Jovinian:[29]

> Just as in good works, (he says) the perfecter is
> God, *For it depends not on the will or striving but
> on God's having mercy,*[30] and helping us to be
> able to reach the goal, so in evils and sins the seeds
> are our own prompting, perfection the devil's.
> When he sees that on the foundation of Christ we
> have built hay, wood, straw, he adds fire; let us
> build gold, silver, precious stones,[31] and he will
> not dare to tempt. Although even in this let there
> not be definite and secure possession. In truth a lion
> *sits in ambush in hiding that he may kill the
> innocent.*[32] And, *The furnace tests the vessels of
> the potter, the temptation of tribulations, however,
> righteous men.*[33]

1:15 **Then concupiscence, when it has conceived, brings**

26. Jm 1:11   27. Gn 22:1   28. Ps 26 (25):2   29. Jer. *Adv. Iov.* 2.3;
PL 23:286D-7A   30. Rm 9:16   31. 1 Co 3:12   32. Ps 10:8 (9:29)
33. Si 27:6

forth in sin, but sin, when it has been carried out, produces death. 'Temptation is carried out in three ways, by suggestion, by delight, by consent,'[34] by the suggestion of the enemy, or by the delight, or even by the consent of our frailty. But if even at the enemy's suggestion we are unwilling to take delight in or to consent to sin, temptation itself carries us on to the victory by which we may deserve to receive the crown of life. If in fact at the enemy's suggestion we begin gradually to be drawn from the right intention and lured into vice, we offend by taking delight but we do not yet incur the death-penalty. But if bringing forth evil action also follows the delight in wickedness conceived in the heart, then the enemy departs victorious from us, already blameworthy of death. May we illustrate this by examples: Joseph was tempted by the words of his mistress, but because he did not have the concupiscence of lust, he was able to be tempted by suggestion alone and not also by delight or consent; therefore he escaped victorious.[35] David was tempted by the sight of another's wife, and because he had not yet conquered the desire of the flesh, he was *drawn on and lured by his own concupiscence,*[36] and when he carried out the crime he had conceived he incurred, even by his own admission,[37] the sentence of guilt, which however he escaped by repenting. Judas was tempted by acquisitiveness, and because he was greedy,[38] being *drawn on and lured by his* very *own concupiscence,*[39] he tumbled to destruction by consenting. Job was tempted in many ways, but because he put neither possessions nor health of body above divine love, he was able to be tempted indeed by the enemy's suggestion but was quite unable to consent or even delight in sin.[40] What is said, therefore, that *sin, when it has been carried out, produces death,* contrasts with what was said above about him *who endures temptation, for when he has been tested he will*

34. Greg., *Hom. ev.* 1. 16. 1; PL 76:1135C.
35. Gn 39:7-9   36. Jm 1:14   37. 2 S 11:2–12:13
38. Jn 12:6   39. Jm 1:14   40. Jb 1:22

receive the crown of life.[41] For just as someone who when tempted wins the rewards of life, so certainly someone who when lured by his own concupiscences is overcome by temptation rightly incurs the ruin of death.

1:16 Accordingly, do not make the mistake, my most beloved brothers, namely, of judging that the temptations to vices take their origin from God, although we should know that some, when the deserts of earlier wicked deeds demand, have fallen again into other crimes with the just permission of the strict judge. Hence there is that statement of the apostle, *And just as they did not prove to have God in mind, he handed them over, filled with all iniquity, to an unseemly realization, that they would do things that are not fitting.*[42]

1:17 Every best gift and every perfect gift is from above, coming down from the father of lights. After he has taught that the vices by which we are tempted are present in us not from God but from ourselves, he shows on the contrary that whatever good we do we have received as a gift from God. Hence he also calls him *the father of lights,* because he knows that he is the author of spiritual charisms. That statement of the apostle Paul, *For what do you have that you have not received?*[43] agrees with this. **With whom there is no change or shadow of alteration.** Because there is no changeableness in the nature of God nor does his light occur, as does the light of this world, with any shadow of alteration, it is certainly apparent that he sends us only the gifts of light and not also the darkness of errors.

1:18 For he begot us willingly by the word of truth. The Lord says also in the Gospel, *You have not chosen me, but I have chosen you;*[44] and in the prophet Hosea, *I shall love them voluntarily.*[45] Consequently he expands what he had

41. Jm 1:12   42. Rm 1:28-9   43. 1 Co 4:7   44. Jn 15:16
45. Ho 14:5

said, therefore, that *every best gift and every perfect gift* comes down from God by adding that he has changed us from sons of darkness into sons of light through the water of regeneration, not because of our merits but because of the generosity of his will. **That we may be some beginning of his creation.** Lest from his saying, *he begot,* we should think that we become what he himself is, he shows that a certain preeminence in creation has been granted us by this adoption. Someone has translated these verses: 'Willingly he begot us by the word of truth, that we may be the first-fruits of his creation', that is, that we may be better than the other created things we behold. For the law that commanded that the first-fruits of crops and living things be consecrated to the Lord[46] ordered that the first-fruits of gold and silver, that is, all the best metals, be brought for the work of the tabernacle[47] and the prophet Jeremiah said about the ancient people of God, *Israel is holy to the Lord, the first-fruits of his crops.*[48]

1:19 You know, my beloved brothers. It is well known to you, he says, that you had it in yourselves to slip into vices; it came about from the Lord, however, that you were enlightened, not by your own effort but by grace from on high anticipating you. **However, let every man be quick to listen, slow however to speak and slow to anger.** From this point on he has instructed the hearer by moral commands. And properly he first advises each to lend his ear rather quickly to someone teaching, but only later to open his mouth to teach, because it is foolish for anyone to wish to preach to others what he himself had not learned. Let anyone who loves wisdom, therefore, first beg this from God, as he advised above,[49] then let the humble hearer seek out a teacher of truth, and all the while let him not only most carefully restrain his tongue from idle conversations

46. Ex 22:29-30 47. Ex 25:2-3   48. Jr 2:3   49. Jm 1:5

but also hold back from preaching the very truth which he has recently learned. Hence Solomon, writing about differences of times, says, *There is a time for keeping silence and a time for speaking.*[50] Hence the Pythagoreans, who were endowed with the capacity to teach natural knowledge, order their listeners to keep silence for five years and thus at last they allow them to preach.[51] The truth is more safely heard than preached, for when it is heard humility is safeguarded, but when it is preached it is difficult for [the preacher] to escape some minimal boasting. Hence Jeremiah, describing the life of a well-instructed young man, reckons the restraint of keeping silence among the first pursuits of the virtues. *It is good for a man,* he says, *when he has borne the yoke from his youth; he will sit in solitude and be silent.*[52] *And slow,* he says, *to anger,* because the maturity of wisdom is only acquired with a quiet mind. For it has been written, *Because anger abides in the bosom of a fool.*[53] He does not forbid the swiftness of anger in such a way that he approves its slowness, but he is rather advising that even at a time of agitation and quarreling we avoid letting anger creep in, or if by chance it does creep in that we restrain its violence behind the barrier of our mouth, and when the hour of crisis has passed, we more freely cleanse it entirely from our hearts gradually. Or at least he has commanded us to be slow to anger that we may not change the calmness of our countenance into harshness for just any reason except for a definite one. For example, if we perceive that those around us, particularly those who have been entrusted to us, are not otherwise able to be corrected, we may show towards them harshness of word or even of a more severe judgment, provided that the condition of our mind remain calm, as far as human nature allows. I believe that Phinehas,[54] Samuel,[55] Elijah,[56] and Peter[57] were slow to anger, and yet they destroyed sinners

50. Qo 3:7   51. Jer., *Comm. in Eccle.* 3. 7; CC 72:276, 116/8.
52. Lm 3:27-8   53. Qo 7:10
54. Nb 25:6-8   55. 1 S 13:7-14   56. 2 K 1:3-4   57. Jn 18:10

by the sword or by a word. But even Moses, though he was a very mild man, *went forth from Pharaoh*, whom he saw was incorrigible, *exceedingly angry*,[58] after having threatened him with a punishment that he also eventually brought down on him.

1:20 For the anger of man does not bring about the righteousness of God. The meaning is easy, that he who heedlessly gives in to the vice of anger, although he may appear righteous to people, in the divine judgment he is not yet perfectly righteous. But this can be understood more deeply, because it has been said to the Lord, *But you, O Lord of virtues, judge with serenity*.[59] Any sort of human judge judges someone failing in his duty with serenity of mind, even if he judges justly; but he is not able to imitate the justice of divine judgment, into which emotion does not know how to enter.

1:21 Wherefore, casting aside all uncleanness and profusion of wickedness, in meekness accept the implanted word. First he orders that they cleanse both body and mind from vices, that they may be able to be worthy to receive the word of salvation. For anyone who does not first turn aside from evil is not able to do good.[60] Indeed, he speaks of *all uncleanness,* both of body and of soul; *wickedness,* however, belongs particularly to the perversity of the inward man. *Accept,* he says, *the implanted word* of God, that is, accept by learning the word we place in your hearts by preaching. Or at least it should be interpreted thus, 'The word which was implanted in you on the day of your redemption, when God *willingly begot*[61] you, accept even now more perfectly by carrying out in deeds what you already hold in mystery'. **Which is able to save your souls,** even if you suffer temptations in your body or are destroyed

58. Ex 11:8   59. Ws 12:18
60. Ps 37 (36):27   61. Jm 1:18

by the wicked in death.

**1:22 However, be doers of the word and not hearers only,
and so on.** So also Paul says about the adherents of the law,
*Hearers of the law are not righteous before God, but doers of
the law will be made righteous;*[62] and in the Apocalypse
when John had said, *Happy is he who reads and those who
hear the words of the prophecy of this book,* he immediately
added, *and keep the things which have been written
in it.*[63]

**1:25 But he who has looked at the perfect law of liberty
and remained in it.** He calls the grace of the Gospel the perfect law of liberty. *For the law brought nothing to perfection;*[64] and elsewhere, *For you have not received the
spirit of slavery again in fear, but you have received the
spirit of adoption of sons;*[65] and again, *For where the spirit
of the Lord is, there is liberty;*[66] and the Lord himself says,
If the Son has liberated you, you will be truly at liberty.[67]
**Having become not a forgetful hearer but a doer of the
work, this man will be happy in his action.** Happiness is prepared not by an empty hearing of the word but by carrying it out in deed, just as the Lord, speaking to his disciples,
says, *If you know these things, you will be happy if
you do them.*[68]

**1:26 If anyone, however, considers himself religious, not
bridling his tongue but deceiving his heart, his religion is
worthless.** He had advised them above not only to hear the
word of God but also to do it. Now he adds that even if
someone appears to carry out in actions the commandments
of God which he has learned, if he has not also bridled his
tongue from slanders, lies, blasphemies, foolish conversations,
even from the very act of speaking too much, and from the

---

62. Rm 2:13   63. Rv 1:3   64. Heb 7:19   65. Rm 8:15
66. 2 Co 3:17   67. Jn 8:36   68. Jn 13:17

other things in which he is accustomed to sin, in vain does he boast of the righteousness of his works, as Paul, showing his approval of the thought of a pagan poet, says, *Evil conversations corrupt good morals.*[69]

1:27 For religion pure and stainless before God and the Father is this. Admirably he added, *before God and the Father,* because there are those who appear religious to other people, when they are held by God to be idolaters. Hence Solomon also says, *There is a way which appears righteous to people, but in the end leads down to death.*[70] **To visit orphans and widows in their tribulation and to keep oneself stainless from this world.** Because he had said that the doer of the work would be happy in his action,[71] now he says what actions are particularly pleasing to God, namely, mercy and innocence. For when he orders us *to visit orphans and widows in their tribulation* he implies all the things we ought mercifully to do for our neighbor. How much this avails at the very time of judgment will be manifested when the judge comes to say, *As long as you did it for one of the least of these my brothers, you did it for me.*[72] In turn, when he commands us to keep ourselves stainless from this world he shows in detail all things in which it behooves us to keep ourselves spotless. Among these are also those things that he had advised us above to observe, that we be slow to speak and slow to anger.[73]

2:1 My brothers, do not have the faith of our Lord Jesus Christ, the Lord of glory, while showing favoritism toward individuals. He shows that those, to whom he was writing, were indeed imbued with the Gospel faith but devoid of works. And because he had taught that the commandments of the Lord must be carried out in giving offerings for the poor but saw on the contrary that they had instead done for

69. 1 Co 15:33   70. Pr 14:12   71. Jm 1:25   72. Mt 25:40
73. Jm 1:19

the rich for the sake of earthly advantages what ought to be
done for the poor for the sake of eternal rewards, therefore
he rebuked them as they deserved. And aptly at the beginning of this statement he calls our Lord Jesus Christ the
Lord of glory, that we may remember that his orders are
rather to be obeyed, *who when he is the brightness of
glory*[74] rewards with everlasting glory whatever is given to
the poor for love of him, rather than any honors accorded
persons of consequence, concerning whom it has generally
been said that *all flesh is hay, and all its glory like the blossom of hay,*[75] and so on.

**2:2–3   And indeed if there has entered into your gathering
a man having a golden ring, in clean clothes, yet there has
also entered a poor man in dirty clothes, and you pay attention to him who is wearing excellent clothing and say, 'You
sit here,' but to the poor man you say, 'You stand there,' or,
'Sit below my footstool.'** In the explanation of this thought
let us use the words of blessed Augustine:[76]

> If we apply, (he says of this) a distinction between
> sitting and standing to church honors, it must not
> be considered a light sin to have the faith of our
> Lord Jesus Christ, the Lord of glory, while show-
> ing favoritism to individuals. For who would put
> up with having a rich man chosen to a place of
> honor in the Church when a poor man, more
> learned and holier, is rejected? If, however, it is a
> question of everyday seatings, who does not sin
> here, if indeed he sins, whenever he so judges
> within himself that that man appears to him better
> the richer he is.

He appears to have indicated this by appending:

2:4   Do you not judge among yourselves and have become

74. Heb 1:3   75. Is 40:6, 1 P 1:24
76. Aug., *Ep.* 167.18; CSEL 44:605, 10-606, 3

judges of wicked thoughts? There follows:

2:5 Hear, my most beloved brothers. Observe more carefully, he says, that those are richer in the eyes of the world are not better in the divine judgment. **Has not God chosen the poor in this world to be rich in faith and heirs of the kingdom which he has promised to those who love him?** By the poor he means the humble and those who because of their disregard for visible things but because of their faith in invisible riches appear contemptible to this world. For *God, our Lord Jesus Christ, has chosen* such as these by saying, *Do not fear, little flock, because it has been pleasing to your Father to give you the kingdom.*[77] He chose such as these when he created poor parents for himself, by whose devotion he might be brought up on coming into the world, but nevertheless he made them famous and noble because of their anticipation of the future kingdom.

2:6 You, however, have dishonored the poor, namely on account of him to whom it was said, *'You stand there,'* when to the one having a golden ring it was said, *'You sit up here.'* **Do not the rich oppress you by their power and drag you to courts?**

2:7 Do they not blaspheme the good name that has been called down upon you? Here he shows more clearly who are the rich, whose humiliation and destruction he had discussed above,[78] those undoubtedly who prefer their riches to Christ, and further, separated from faith in him, also oppress with their power those who believe, dragging them to judgments of the more powerful and blaspheming the *name* of Christ which is *above every name.*[79] That quite a few of the leading men both of the gentiles and particularly of the Jews did this in the apostles' time is sufficiently clearly shown both in the

77. Lk 12:32   78. Jm 1:10-11   79. Ph 2:9

Acts of the same apostles and in the Letters of the apostle
Paul.

**2:8–9   If, nevertheless, you carry out the royal law accord-
ing to the scriptures, 'You shall love your neighbor as yourself,' you do well; but if you show favoritism to individuals
you commit sin, being refuted by the law as transgressors.**
    See how he calls transgressors those who say to a
    rich man, '*You sit here*', and to a poor man, '*You
    stand there*'. And lest they should consider it a
    slight sin to transgress the law in this one matter,
    he went on and added:

**2:10–11   For anyone who has observed the whole law and
offends in one thing has become guilty of all. For he who
said, 'You shall not commit adultery', also said, 'You shall
not kill'. But if you do not commit adultery, and yet you
kill, you have become a transgressor of the law,**
    on account of what he had said, '*being refuted by
    the law as transgressors*'. Since this is so, the
    consequence, it appears, unless it may be shown to
    be understood in another way, is that someone
    who has said to a rich man, '*You sit here*', and to a
    poor man, '*You stand there*', paying greater honor
    to one than to the other, is both an idolater and a
    blasphemer and an adulterer and a murderer, and,
    lest I rake up everything, which is long, he must
    be judged guilty of all crimes, for by offending in
    one he has become guilty of all.
It must be asked, therefore,
    If someone who has observed the whole law
    offends in one thing, how does he become guilty
    of all? Is it perhaps because *the fullness of the
    law is charity*[80] —by which God is loved and our

80. Rm 13:10

neighbor, and on these commands of charity *'depend the whole law and the prophets,'*[81] —that quite rightly he becomes guilty of all who acts against that on which all depend? No one, however, sins except by acting contrary to [the law], because, *'You shall not commit adultery, you shall not commit murder, you shall not steal, you shall not covet, and if there is any other commandment, it is summed up in this sentence, "You shall love your neighbor as yourself.' Love of neighbor does not bring about evil; the fullness of the law, however, is charity.'*[82] Accordingly, he becomes guilty of all by acting against that on which all depend. Why, therefore, may sins not be said to be equal? Is it perhaps because he who sins more seriously acts more flagrantly against charity, less who sins more lightly? Nevertheless, even if he has offended in one thing, he is guilty of all, because he acts contrary to that on which all depend.

2:12 So speak and so act as if you were beginning to be judged by the law of liberty.

The law of liberty is the law of charity, about which he says,[83] *'If, nevertheless, you carry out the royal law according to the scriptures, "You shall love your neighbor as yourself", you do well'.*[84]

By stating this, therefore, he says, by acting in this way, you see to it that by loving your neighbor you deserve to be loved by God; by showing mercy to your neighbor you become worthy of mercy in the divine judgment.

Alternatively: Just as *the law* of slavery is what *was given by Moses,* so the law of liberty is *the grace* of the Gospel

81. Mt 22:40   82. Rm 13:9-10   83. Jm 2:8
84. Aug, *Ep* 167. 3. 16-19; CSEL 44:590, 16-91, 10; 603, 13-4; 604, 9/13, 17/18; 606, 4/7

which *came through Jesus Christ*,[85] and the apostle bears witness who says, *For you have not received the spirit of slavery again in fear but you have received the adoption of sons by which we cry, 'Abba, Father'*;[86] and again, *For where the spirit of the Lord is, there is liberty.*[87] Therefore he says, *So speak and so act as if* about to be *judged by the law of liberty*, for this is when you *begin to be judged*. For anyone who despises the law of Moses will be judged more seriously than someone who despises the natural law; likewise will he be judged more seriously who disregards the recognized grace of the Gospel than he who disregards the commands of the law of Moses. For, *Everyone to whom much has been given, much is asked from him, and to whom they have entrusted much, they will seek more.*[88] Hence the apostle also says, *For if any word spoken by angels has been made steadfast, and every transgression and disobedience has received the just retribution of its wages, how shall we escape if we have neglected such great salvation? when it had first been told by the Lord, it was confirmed for us by those who heard;*[89] and again, *Anyone making void the law of Moses dies without mercy on [the word] of two or three witnesses; how much worse punishments do you consider are deserved [by him] who has despised the son of God and held the blood of the covenant, (in which he has been made holy) profane, and outraged the spirit of grace?*[90] Each sense, however, leads to one conclusion, that responding to divine grace by righteous works, we should be *kind to one another, merciful, forgiving one another, just as God in Christ has forgiven us.*[91]

2:13 For there will be judgment without mercy on him who has not acted mercifully. He will be judged without mercy who, when he was able to do so, did not act mercifully

---

85. Jn 1:17   86. Rm 8:15   87. 2 Co 3:17   88. Lk 12:48
89. Heb 2:2-3   90. Heb 10:28-9 91. Eph 4:32

before he could be judged. Since this may be properly felt about all who are without mercy, it is clear in every way that the greater the mercy each one has obtained from the Lord, the more unjust he is in denying mercy to a neighbor needing it and the more justly has he paid the penalty for his wickedness. Hence the Lord advises prudently, *Do not judge that you may not be judged, do not condemn and you will not be condemned; forgive and it will be forgiven you, give and it will be given to you.*[92] *There will be judgment, therefore, without mercy to anyone who has not acted mercifully.* **But mercy triumphs over judgment,** because just as the one who has not acted mercifully will be sorrowful when he is condemned by God's judgment, so the one who has acted mercifully will exult and rejoice.

Alternatively: *Mercy triumphs over judgment.*[93]

> It was not said, 'Mercy conquers judgment', for it is not opposed to judgment, but, '*triumphs over*', because more persons are joined by mercy, but those who have shown mercy. For, *Happy are the merciful, since God will have mercy upon them.*[94]

Also, *Mercy triumphs over judgment,* mercy is placed ahead of judgment. In someone in whom there has been found a work of mercy, although he may by chance have something for which he may be punished at the judgment, the fire of sin is extinguished as if by the water of mercy.

2:14 **What advantage will it be, my brothers, if anyone says that he has faith, but he does not have works?** and so on. From here on he discusses more thoroughly

> the works of mercy, that he may console those whom in the preceding thought he had greatly terrified, by advising how even daily sins, without

---

92. Lk 6:37-8   93. Aug., *Ep.* 167. 19; CSEL 44:607 1/5
94. Mt 5:7

which there is no living here, may be atoned for
by daily remedies. [He has done this] lest the person who when he has *offended in one thing becomes guilty of all*[95] by offending in many things,
because *we all offend in many things,*[96] may bring
before the judgment seat of so great a judge a
great load of his guilt that has been gradually collected and may not find that mercy which he has
not done, but rather by forgiving and giving he
may deserve to have his debts forgiven him and
the promised things given.[97]

**2:15–17 If, however, a brother or sister be naked and in
need of daily sustenance, one of you may, however, say to
them, 'Go in peace, be warmed and fed,' but not give them
the things which are necessary for the body; what advantage
will that be? So also faith, if it does not have works, is dead
in itself.** It is evident that just as words of concern alone do
not help a naked or hungry person if food or clothing is not
provided, so faith observed in name only does not save, for it
is dead in itself if it is not made alive by works of charity, by
which it may be made to come to life. Nor is that contrary
to this statement which the Lord uttered, *He who believes
and is baptized will be saved,*[98] for it must be understood
there that only he truly believes who carries out in deed what
he believes. And because faith and charity cannot be separated from one another—as Paul bears witness by saying,
and *faith which works through love*[99]—appropriately the
apostle John brings forward a statement about charity akin
to James' about faith, saying, *Anyone who has the world's
substance and sees his brother in need and closes his heart
against him, how does the charity of God remain in him?*[100]

95. Jm 2:10   96. Jm 3:2
97. Aug., *Ep* 167. 20; CSEL 44; 608, 4/13
98. Mk 16:16   99. Ga 5:6
100. 1 Jn 3:17

2:19 **You believe that God is one, you do well; the demons also believe and they tremble.** You should not think you are doing something great by believing that God is one, for the demons also do this, nor do they believe only in God the Father but also in God the Son. So it is Luke says, *The demons also went out from many shouting and saying, 'That you are the Son of God;' and rebuking them, he did not allow them to speak, because they knew that he was the Christ.*[101] And they do not only believe, they also tremble. So the legion, who were besieging the man, cried out to him in a beseeching voice, *'What is there between me and you, Jesus, Son of the most high God? I earnestly entreat you by God, do not torment me.'*[102] Therefore, those who do not believe that there is a God, or believe and do not fear, must be judged slower-witted and more shameless than the demons. But it is no great thing to believe there is a God and tremble if one does not also believe in him, that is, if love for him be not held in the heart. For it is one thing to believe him, another to believe that he exists, another to believe in him.[103] To believe him is to believe that the things he speaks are true; to believe that he exists is to believe that he is God; to believe in him is to love him. Many, even the wicked, are able to believe that the things he speaks are true; they believe that they are true and do not wish to make them their own because they are too lazy to do anything about them. Even the demons were able to believe, however, that he is God. But they alone know how to believe in God who love God, who are Christians not only in name but also in action and [way of] life, because without love faith is empty; with love it is the faith of a Christian, without love the faith of a demon. Therefore, anyone who does not wish to believe that Christ is God still does not imitate the demons. He believes that Christ [is] but hates Christ, he makes a confession of

101. Lk 4:41   102. Mk 5:7
103. *credere illi ... credere illum ... credere in illum.*

faith out of fear of punishment not out of love of a crown. For they too were afraid of being punished. Accordingly, when blessed Peter, confessing the Lord, said, *You are the Christ, the Son of the living God,*[104] he appears to utter by his mouth almost the same words as the demons; but their confession, because it was uttered with hatred for Christ, was rightly condemned, his, because it came forth from inward love, was rewarded.

2:20–21 Do you wish, however, O foolish man, to know that faith without works is worthless? Was not our father Abraham made righteous by works? and so on. Since the apostle Paul, preaching that *man is made righteous by faith without works,*[105] was not well understood by those who took this saying to mean that when they had once believed in Christ, even though they might commit evils and live wickedly and basely, they could be saved by faith, [James] explains how the passage of the apostle of Paul ought to be understood to have the same meaning as this letter. And all the more therefore he uses the example of Abraham about faith being useless if it does not issue in good works, because the apostle Paul also used the example of Abraham[106] to demonstrate that man is made righteous without deeds. For when he recalls Abraham's good deeds which accompanied his faith, he shows well enough that the apostle Paul does not teach by Abraham that man is made righteous without works to the extent that anyone who believes it has no responsibility to perform good works, but for this reason instead, that no one should think he has come to the gift of righteousness which is in faith by the merits of his former good deeds. In this matter the Jews wished to set themselves above the gentiles who believed in Christ, because, they said, they had come to the grace of the Gospel by the merits of the good works which are in the law, and therefore many of those

104. Mt 16:16   105. Rm 3:28   106. Rm 4:1-25

who believed were scandalized that the grace of Christ was being given to uncircumcised gentiles. Hence the apostle Paul says that a man can be made righteous by faith without works, but [he means] previous works. For how is the person made righteous by faith able to act, if not righteously? When, therefore, James says, *Was not our father Abraham made righteous from works, offering his son Isaac upon the altar?*, he intentionally advised that an example of good work was to be learned from the patriarch himself, challenging those among the Jews who had believed they like good offspring, were following the actions of their first and most outstanding ancestor. And since he was advising them not to fall away in temptations and to prove their faith through works, he chose an example from the patriarch, by which he might be able to instruct them in each virtue. For what greater temptation, except for those which concern injuries to one's own body, can happen than that someone, an old man, should be compelled to slay his only and most beloved son? Would he delay giving a tunic or his own food to the poor for the sake of divine love when he did not delay giving over to death immediately at the order of the Lord the son whom he had received as his heir when he was an old man? Accordingly, this statement of blessed James agrees with what Paul says, *By faith Abraham, when he was tempted, offered Isaac, and he was offering his only-begotten son who had received the promises, to whom it was said, 'That in Isaac will your seed be called,' thinking that God is able to raise even the dead.*[107] Indeed, in one and the same action of blessed Abraham James has praised the outstanding quality of his works, Paul the constancy of his faith; and nevertheless Paul has brought forward a statement not dissimilar and different from James. For they both knew that Abraham was perfect both in faith and in works, and therefore each of them has emphasized in preaching on him the virtue which

107. Heb 11:17-19

he perceived his hearers needed more. For because James was writing to those who held that faith without works was wasted, fittingly he brought forward that example in which the superior faith of Abraham which was also previously praised by the witness of scripture[108] showed itself, because it had not become listless and useless in his heart but had flamed up and was now ready to obey the divine commands. But because Paul was instructing those who were boasting of their works without the grace of faith, he showed that *without faith it is impossible to please God,*[109] and in order to refute and correct their rashness, having gathered together the examples of all the patriarchs, he clearly taught that *all were approved by the witness of faith.*[110] So too, he referred especially to the faith with which Abraham offered Isaac, *reckoning,* he said, *that God is able to raise even the dead.*[111] He added, therefore, the work of faith of him who thereupon chose to offer his son because he believed that God would immediately raise him up; for he believed that he would be raised up by God after death because he believed what he had heard was true, *'That in Isaac will your seed be called.'*[112] Blessed James also afterwards explains this connection between each virtue, saying:

2:22–23 You see that faith worked together with his works, and by his works his faith was preserved? And the scripture was fulfilled which said, Abraham believed God, and it was accounted to him for righteousness, and he was called a friend of God. Paul treated of this witness most emphatically to the Romans, clearly teaching that so great is the virtue of faith that as soon as its mysteries are perceived it can make a righteous person out of an irreverent one.[113] For because Abraham believed God with so great and lively a faith that he was ready in his mind[114] to do everything God

108. Gn 15:6   109. Heb 11:6   110. Heb 11:39   111. Heb 11:19
112. Heb 11:18   113. Rm 4:5   114. *animo*

ordered, deservedly was his faith accounted for righteousness by God, who knew his heart. And that we also might
know his faith by which he was made righteous, God
tempted him, ordering him to offer his son, *and by his
works his faith was fulfilled*, that is, how perfect it was in his
heart was tested by the performance of works. Nowadays,
too, if anyone coming recently to the faith receives baptism
and then, intending with his whole heart to observe God's
commandments, shortly goes home from this light, then
surely he has gone home made righteous by faith without
works, because, by the determination of God himself, in
whom he believed he did not have time to test his faith; but
those who, having received the sacraments of faith, live on
for a long time and do not take care to follow up with good
works, must have it impressed upon them what blessed
James, after bringing forward the example of the faith
together with the works of Abraham, at once appended,
saying:

**2:24 You see that a person is made righteous from works
and not from faith only.** What he says, *from works,* means
from the works of faith, because no one can have perfect
works without faith but many faith without works if they
lack the time for works. Of them it has been said, *He was
taken away lest wickedness change his understanding or
craftiness deceive his mind.*[115]

**2:25 In the same way, however, was not the harlot Rahab
made righteous from works, receiving the messengers and
sending them out by another way?** Lest they plead that they
are not strong enough to imitate the works of such a great
ancestor, Abraham, especially when no one now would
compel them to offer their sons to God to be killed but God
himself through the scriptures prohibited this to be done,

115. Ws 4:11

he adds also the example of a woman, an iniquitous woman, a foreign woman. Yet she, by works of mercy, by showing hospitality to the servants of God even at risk to her life, deserved to be made righteous from sins, to be enrolled as a member of the people of Israel, to be counted on the list of their royal lineage, to mingle with the families of our Lord and saviour himself[116] which have descended from the patriarchs, to be plucked from the devastation of the vanishing fatherland, whose perfidy she rejected. By these examples, therefore, of a woman turned towards better things, he persuades his listeners to avoid the ruin of a vanishing fatherland and to remember to sever themselves as well by fruitful works from this land from whose heinous deeds they had withdrawn by believing, since they deserve to be joined to the ranks of the saints and to belong to the community of their Redeemer. And he urges them, therefore, to receive the messengers of Jesus, that is, to listen gladly to the preachers of the word of the Gospel, and although they know that they were rejected by their fellow countrymen or hounded to death—as their Acts teach frequently happened—they themselves, on the contrary, having received from them the plan of salvation, may send them back in peace to the Lord Jesus. The aforementioned book of the Acts of the Apostles tells how Gamaliel, the teacher of the blessed apostle Paul,[117] a man respected at one time by the entire Jewish people[118] and now still more respected by the whole church of Christ because of the revelation of the relics of the blessed protomartyr Stephen,[3] did this: when the council of the Jews was determined to kill the apostles, he counteracted their proposals by a wiser plan and, having rescued the apostles from their plot, sent them back unharmed to preach the Gospel of Jesus.[119]

116. Mt 1:5   117. Ac 22:3   118. Ac 5:34   119. Ac 5:33-40

3:1 Do not a number of you, my brothers, become teachers, knowing that you are taking on a greater judgment. The Acts of the Apostles teach that there was in their day great eagerness among believers to spread the word more widely, so much so that Apollo, a man very learned in the scriptures, knowing only the baptism of John, preached Christ faithfully; nevertheless, because he was wise, as soon as a teacher was present, he very easily filled in what he was missing and then returned perfect to the task of preaching.[120] Others with greater ineptitude, coming down from Judea to Antioch, were teaching that unless believers from among the gentiles were circumcised according to the law of Moses they could not be saved, and brought no small labor of investigation to sound preachers.[121] Blessed James, therefore, removed them and teachers of their kind from the responsibility of [preaching] the word lest they be an obstacle to those able to carry it out properly. *Knowing,* he says, *that you are taking on a greater judgment.* For just as someone who performs his ministry well wins for himself a good station,[122] so he who tries to grab the responsibility of teaching for himself without being taught, who proclaims Christ from mixed motives,[123] deserves judgment of condemnation more than if he should perish alone in his wicked deed.

3:2 For we all offend in many things. He did not say, 'you offend', when he was accusing those whom he saw to be less perfect both in knowledge and in action, and it was these he was removing from the chair of authoritative teaching, fearing that either by preaching error they might do harm to the little ones and by being heard first might turn aside their ears from hearing the more learned or they might at least taint by the disrepute of improper conduct those things which they were preaching properly and in this way obscure the life of gospel perfection by their unsavory reputation. No,

120. Ac 18:24-8 121. Ac 15:1-2 122. 1 Tm 3:13 123. Ph 1:17

he said, *we offend,* although a very great apostle of Christ was speaking, and he appended, *in many things,* and added, [we] *all,* that all might more carefully acknowledge themselves imperfect in acting or speaking the more they know most definitely that not even the perfectly good and those who proceed under the guidance of the grace of the Holy Spirit are able to pass along the way of this life without committing some offense, according to what has been written elsewhere, *The heavens are not clean in his sight,*[124] and as Solomon says, that *there is not a righteous person on earth who does not sin.*[125] **If anyone does not offend in word, this is a perfect man.** How can he say that the man is perfect who does not offend in word, when he has just said, *We all offend in many things?* Is it because the elect are able to offend even in many things and yet remain perfect? Yes, it must be understood in this way. For there are different kinds of offenses. The elect offend in one way, the condemned in another; Solomon is a witness who says, *For the righteous falls seven times and rises again, but the wicked will sink down into evil.*[126] For although the righteous may offend perhaps through the frailty of the flesh or through ignorance, nevertheless he does not cease to be righteous, because just as there is daily and unavoidable offense of this kind, so also there is the daily remedy of prayers and good works that quickly raises up the righteous offender, so that he may not tumble to the ground and befoul with the dust of vices the marriage dress of charity and faith. *If anyone,* therefore, *does not offend in word, this is a perfect man*—a word, namely, whose utterance human weakness is not able to avoid, as a word of deceit, slander, cursing, pride, boasting, making excuses in sins,[127] jealousy, argument, heresy, lying, perjury, but even of worthless and also of unnecessary speaking in these things that appear necessary—certainly everyone keeping himself from offense in this kind of word, *this is a perfect*

124. Jb 15:15   125. Qo 7:21   126. Pr 24:16 127. Ps 141 (140):4

man. For, *He who guards his mouth and his tongue guards his soul from difficulty.*[128] **He can also lead his whole body around with a bridle.** This verse is connected with the previous one. *If anyone,* he says, *does not offend in word, this is a perfect man,* and he *can also lead his whole body around with a bridle.* This is to say clearly, 'If anyone avoids a slip of the tongue, which is almost unavoidable, this person by fixed habit of the same restraint also learns how to keep guard over the other members of his body, which are more easily restrained, to keep them from turning aside from the right way'.

3:3 For if we put bits into the mouths of horses to make them obey us, we also control their entire body, you understand, 'how much more fitting is it that we put a bit of restraint in our mouths to make them obey our creator, since through guarding the tongue we may also be able to maintain uprightness of works?' But if we read, as certain manuscripts have it, 'For just as we put bits into the mouths of horses', there will be no difficulty, because it is joined to what is said in what follows, *so also the tongue indeed is a small member,*[129] and so on.

3:4 Look at ships also; though they are large and are threatened by strong winds, they are brought around by a small rudder to where the action of the helmsman wishes. The large ships on the sea are the minds of men, whether good or bad, in this life; the strong winds by which they are threatened are the very appetites of the minds by which they are naturally driven to do something as a result of which they may reach a good or a bad end; the rudder by which the ships of this world are brought around where the inclination of the helmsman wishes is the very intention of the heart by which the elect, after having passed through the waves of this

128. Pr 21:23   129. Jm 3:5

world, arrive at the happy harbor of the heavenly fatherland; the condemned, however, killed by the stormy errors of this life, as it were by Scylla and Charybdis, which they did not know how to escape, perish. And because *from the abundance of the heart the mouth speaks,*[130] properly he adds:

3:5   So also the tongue is indeed a small member and exalts great things. Certainly it exalts great rewards if the action of the mind at the helm directs it well, according to that saying of Solomon that, *The understanding person shall take the rudder;*[131] but if [the mind directs the tongue] badly on the other hand, it exalts great evils of destruction for itself and its connections. So Solomon also says, *Death and life are in the hands of the tongue.*[132] It exalts life, therefore, if it teaches the church well, death on the contrary if it behaves perversely, for it is opposed to those who, destitute of both life and knowledge, presumed to teach and thereby did greater harm to the church. But if, as is found in certain manuscripts, it be read, 'it boasts[4] of great things', that boasting certainly ought here to be understood concerning which in what follows, after he had listed very many vices of the tongue, he added, *But now you boast in your proud deeds; all such boasting is evil.*[133] From this, too, the mother of blessed Samuel restrains us by a devout admonition, saying, *Do not continue to speak of lofty matters, boasting.*[134] The tongue, therefore, boasts of great things; looking down on the interpretations and words of others, it holds itself up as extraordinarily wise and eloquent. **Look at how great a fire ignites so huge a forest.** *How great,* he says, rather than 'how small'. Accordingly, certain other manuscripts have it as, 'Look at how small a fire.' For just as from a small spark a spreading fire often ignites a great forest, so an unrestrained tongue, feeding on its own trivialities, destroys

130. Lk 6:45   131. Pr 1:5   132. Pr 18:21   133. Jm 4:16
134. 1 S 2:3

the great stuff of good works, many fruits of the spiritual life, after it has spoiled them, but it also often devours countless leaves of speech which appeared excellent.

3:6 The tongue also is a fire, a world of wickedness. The tongue is a fire, because by speaking evilly it consumes the forest of the virtues. Hence the wise man says about the foolish, *And the opening of his mouth is a setting on fire.*[135] That saving fire which, devouring wood, hay, straw,[136] enlightens the secrets of the heart is contrary, namely, to this destructive fire. Holy teachers are set on fire by it both that they themselves may burn with loving and that by preaching they may set others on fire with fiery tongues, as it were. About them it has been well written that, *There appeared to them separate tongues of fire, as it were, and it settled upon each one of them, and all were filled with the Holy Spirit.*[137] It is rightly said of the uncontrolled tongue, however, that it is *a world of wickedness,* because almost all villainous deeds are either planned by it (as robberies, rapes), or carried out by it (as perjuries, false witnesses), or defended by it (as when some sinner by making excuses denies the evil he has committed and by boasting feigns a good that he has not done). **And having been set on fire by hell, it sets on fire the wheel of our life.** By *hell,* he says, 'by the devil and his angels', for whom hell was made[138] and who always everywhere take with them the torments of flames, whether they fly in the air or wander on the earth or beneath the earth or are kept [there. They are] like a person with a fever who, even if he is placed on ivory beds or in sunny places, still cannot avoid the heat and the chill of the illness within him. So therefore the demons, even if they are worshipped in golden temples or move around through the air, always burn with hellish fire and, being reminded from their own punishment, they also suggest through envy to

135. Si 20:15   136. 1 Co 3:12   137. Ac 2:3-4   138. Mt 25:41

gullible men, the fuel of vices from which they too may
perish. As the opposite of this, the holy city of God, the new
Jerusalem, is said to come down from heaven from God,[139]
because undoubtedly whatever heavenly we do on earth,
we have surely received help from heaven to do it. He says,
however, *the wheel of our life,* the ceaseless advance of our
earthly life by which we are continuously moved from the
day of our birth right up to death as if by the always turning
wheel of a carriage. Hence Solomon, when he said well,
*Remember your creator in the days of your youth before the
time of affliction comes,*[140] a little further on added, *And
the wheel above the cistern is broken, and the dust returns
to the earth it came from.*[141] The tongue, therefore, sets on
fire the wheel of our life when by speaking evil things it
spoils the whole condition of our way of life. Likewise he
says *the wheel of our life,* because having lost our inner
stability as a result of the first sin we are carried away this
way and that by an unsettled mind and in running hither and
thither in our uncertain examination of all things do not
know where salvation is, where danger is. This wheel of our
life is, however, set on fire by the fire of the tongue which
does harm when the vice of inborn disorder is increased by
foolish and even harmful discourses.

3:7 **For every kind of beasts and birds and serpents, even of
other things, is tamed and has been tamed by mankind.**
We read in Pliny that the most dreaded of serpents, the
asp, was tamed in Egypt by the head of a family and
emerged daily from its cave to get its allotted portion of
food from his table. We read likewise in the writings of Marcellinus the Companion that a domesticated tiger was sent
from India to the ruler Anastasius.[5] He wishes it to be
understood, therefore, that the tongue of the depraved sur-
passes beasts in cruelty, birds in fickleness and exaltation,

139. Rv 21:2   140. Qo 12:1   141. Qo 12:6-7

serpents in deadliness. For there are people like beasts who *have sharpened their tongues like a sword*,[142] there are people like birds who *have placed their mouth into the sky*,[143] and *whose mouth has spoken lies*,[144] there are people like serpents about whom it has been said, *The poison of asps is under their lips*.[145]

3:8 No one, however, is able to tame the tongue. This thought can be understood properly in two ways: both that no learned good man can tame the tongue of those who neglect to restrain themselves from foolish outbursts; and that there is no one who speaks who does not occasionally lapse by his tongue. Accordingly, it has been truthfully said about a perfect man when he was at the critical point of a very great temptation, *In all these things Job did not sin with his lips*.[146] And yet after he heard the words of God he chided himself for the inappropriateness of his silly speech, saying, *One thing I spoke which I wish that I had not said, and another, to which I shall not add further*.[147] **A restless evil, full of deadly poison.** He adds, *a restless evil* to what he had said to the effect that it could not be tamed when beasts and birds are tamed, *full*, in fact, he says, *of deadly poison*, that he might explain why he said it was untameable when it is clear that even serpents can be tamed. After this he adds more about the harshness of the poison:

3:10–11 And from the same mouth proceeds blessing and cursing. It is not fitting, my brothers, that these things be thus. Does a fountain pour forth sweet and bitter water from same opening? Just as sweet and bitter water are not able to bubble forth at the same time from one opening of a fountain but even if they be combined in a vessel or well the sweet indeed becomes bitter from the bitter, the bitter, however, is unable to be changed into sweet after being mixed with the

---

142. Ps 64:3 (65:4)
143. Ps 73 (72):9
144. Ps 144 (143):8
145. Ps 140 (139):3
146. Jb 2:10
147. Jb 39:35

sweet, so blessing and cursing are in no wise able to come together in one mouth; but [in] anyone who is accustomed to bless God in praying or in preaching his word without avoiding also cursing people, it is clear that the bitterness of cursing destroys the sweetness of his blessing. For, *A small amount of yeast leavens the whole dough,*[148] and, *Praise is not admirable in the mouth of a sinner.*[149] Accordingly, if you make a pipe with a double mouth by which the water may come in, a single one from which it may go out, and in one you let in bitter water, in the other sweet, without any doubt when they come together at the one opening of the way out each will appear thoroughly combined and bitter, because certainly when something sweet and bitter are mixed the sweet is much more easily turned into bitter than the bitter into sweet. From this example it is inferred that just as *evil conversations corrupt good morals,*[150] as the apostle bears witness, so also they corrupt good words.

3:12 My brothers, can a fig tree yield olives or a grapevine figs? It is obvious that just as a tree is unable to lose its natural ability to produce its own fruit yet produce the fruit of another tree, so the person who curses can in no way have the fruit of blessing, even though he appears at the time to speak some good. But if anyone wishes these things to be analyzed at a deeper level, there can be understood in the fig tree, with whose leaves our first parents covered their private parts after recognizing their sin,[151] the covering of making excuses, by which they attempted then both to turn aside the reproof of the creator from themselves and to lay it on the creator himself,[152] and now very many foolish persons turn aside their heart into an evil word *to make excuses in sins;*[153] there can be recognized in the olives the fruits of mercy, in the grapevine the warmth of love. *For I, like a*

---

148. 1 Co 5:6   149. Si 15:9   150. 1 Co 15:33 151. Gn 3:7
152. Gn 3:12-13 153. Ps 141 (140):4

fruitful olive tree in the house of the Lord, have hoped in the mercy of my God,[154] that is, just as he who produces the fruit of mercy has himself hoped for mercy from the Lord, and he likewise says, *And your cup which inebriates, how excellent it is,*[155] which, it is clear, has been said about the charity of God that *has been poured in our hearts by the Holy Spirit who has been given to us.*[156] Therefore, the fig tree cannot produce olives, because anyone who tries to make excuses for himself in sins rather than accuse himself by no means bestows the works of devotion which are done in propitiation for sin on his neighbors with a perfect heart but rather with a proud one, nor [is] the grapevine [able to produce] olives, because anyone who perfectly inebriates himself with divine love no longer accuses anyone except himself for his sins.

3:13 Let him who is wise and learned among you show from his good way of life the result in the meekness of wisdom. Because he had imposed silence on wicked teachers and had forbidden to hold the rank of teacher those whom he beheld having neither perfection of life nor restraint of tongue, subsequently he advises that if anyone among them may be, or may appear to himself to be, wise or learned, let him show his learning more by living wisely and according to learning than by teaching others. For he who brings about the good which he can with a meek heart and a well-controlled mouth certainly gives plain evidence of a wise mind. For, *The beginning of wisdom is fear of the Lord.*[157] But someone who is more prone to preaching the word than to doing it very often through love of boasting, through eagerness for strife, through skillfulness of eloquence, through envy of other teachers, through ignorance of the catholic truth, incurs guilt for his foolishness. To him is well

---

154. Ps 52:8 (51:10)   155. Ps 23 (22): 5
156. Rm 5:5   157. Pr 9:10

suited that saying of Solomon that *Where there are many words, there is often need.*[158] Hence even here there is also properly added:

3:14 But if you have bitter zeal and strife in your hearts, do not glory. He says *bitter zeal,* because there is also a sweet zeal by which even the apostle Simon deservedly received the name of a perfect heart,[159] which Elijah also had when he said, *I have been greatly zealous for the Lord God of hosts, because the sons of Israel have forsaken your covenant,*[160] as did the apostle Paul; *For I am jealous of you,* he says, *with the jealousy of God.*[161] There is also a good kind of strife which the Lord orders us to have, saying, *Strive to enter through the narrow gate.*[162] **Do not glory,** he says, **and be liars against the truth,** because truth itself proves that they are not worthy of glory who, bringing forth words of wisdom from their mouth, bear bitter zeal and eagerness for unfruitful strife in their heart.

3:15 That is not the wisdom coming down from above but [wisdom which is] earthly, animal,[163] diabolical. Paul also says that *Animal man does not perceive the things which are of the spirit of God.*[164] It must be noted, however, that animal man or animal wisdom is not derived from [the word] *animal* but from *anima* [meaning soul, life-giving principle];[⁶] the apostle bears witness that *The first man, Adam, was made into a living soul,*[165] *the last Adam into a life-giving spirit;*[166] *but it is not the spiritual which is first but the animal.*[167] The evidence of the Greek language shows that this [word *animal*] is derived from *anima* [meaning 'life-giving principle'], for in this language, ψυχή, 'life-giving principle', is the origin of ψυχικόν, 'physical'. In

158. Pr 14:23   159. Lk 6:15   160. 1 K 19:10
161. 2 Co 11:2   162. Lk 13:24   163. *animalis:* physical
164. 1 Co 2:14   165. *in animam viventem*
166. *in spiritum vivificantem*   167. 1 Co 15:45-6

turn, although animals may appear to have received their name in Latin from *anima* [meaning life-giving principle], in Greek they have a diverse and different etymology, for they get their name from the fact that they are alive, since among the Greeks ζωή means 'life', ζῶα 'animals'. When, therefore, the apostle in his Letters speaks very often of carnal man, he calls him animal, he calls him spiritual. He says that the Lord himself who, in body and soul was filled with the Holy Spirit, was spiritual, as is every one of the elect who, naturally being made up of body and soul, also receives the grace of the Holy Spirit *according to the measure of the gift of Christ,*[168] by which he is enlightened. But he calls carnal or animal the person who, having no spiritual grace, knows only how to think about or do those things which are naturally implanted in the senses of the flesh and soul. Deservedly, therefore, contentious and proud wisdom is mentioned as being earthly, animal, and diabolical, because as long as the soul seeks earthly glory, so long as it, remaining alone, bereft of spiritual grace after the sentence of the first sin, thinks only of those things which are naturally implanted in it and, being justifiably deceived by the evil spirit turns to doing those things which are frenzied and harmful.

3:16 For where there is zeal and strife, there also is instability and every perverse work. *With all care,* he says, *keep your heart, for from it life proceeds.*[169] For all the fruit of action is in the sight of the internal arbiter of the same sort as the root of the heart, and every work of the person who has concealed the wickedness of envy or strife in his heart is warped, however straight he may appear to men to be, on account of the instability of his mind wavering this way and that because it has neglected to attach itself to the one anchor of the heavenly vision.

168. Eph 4:7   169. Pr 4:23

3:17 But the wisdom from above is, first of all modest, then peaceful, restrained, docile, in agreement with what is good. This is the *meekness of wisdom*[170] which he instructed above that we should have, opposed certainly to the zeal of bitterness and foolish strife; by it the virtue and teaching of holy preachers are in turn joined together in the peace of charity and concord. *First,* he says, *it is modest, then peaceful,* modest because it understands modestly, yet peaceful because through pride it separates itself very little from the company of its neighbors. *Restrained,* indeed, *docile, in agreement with what is good,* because surely it behooves a wise man to give assent to the persuasion of the good—as Peter, though agitated, bowed to Paul's rebuke—[171] but to reject with one's entire effort, either by teaching or living, the teaching of the wicked. **Full of mercy and good fruits.** This is also the good way of life which above[172] he advised the wise and learned to show, namely, by being merciful in mind[173] manifesting outwardly the fruits of that same mercy through works of devotion. **Judging without pretense.** The more modest wisdom personally makes use of this virtue, the more it utterly lacks a blasphemous and contentious wisdom. For it is very necessary for anyone who wants to appear more learned and more perfect than others to work at being able to correct his neighbor artfully, as if he were less keen-witted [than himself], and also that he may sometimes deceitfully pretend to have done or said those things to which he is a stranger.

3:18 But the fruit of righteousness is sown in peace for those who make peace. Everything we do in this life is the seed of future reward, yet the reward itself is the fruit of present works, as the apostle bears witness who says, *For whatever a man sows, this also shall he reap, and anyone*

---

170. Jm 3:13   171. Ac 15:1-30, Ga 2:11-14
172. Jm 3:12   173. *animo*

*who sows in the flesh from the flesh will reap corruption, but
anyone who sows in the spirit from the spirit shall reap
eternal life.*[173] And therefore it is said properly that *The fruit
of righteousness is sown in peace for those who make peace.*
For the fruit of righteousness is eternal life which is a reward
for righteous works, because those who seek peace and follow
after it[174] cover the ground of their heart with the very
peace for which they are eager, as it were with the best sow-
ing, so that through the daily increase of good action they
may be able to reach the fruit of heavenly life about which it
has been written elsewhere, *Those who sow in tears will
reap in joy,*[175] and so on to the end of the psalm. The condemned also sow and reap, however, because in the judgment
they will receive what they deserve. But they are said to reap
not fruit but corruption, because they do not enjoy[176] eternal goods—fruit indeed is called so after fruition—but in
return for the corruption in which they lived they will pay
the penalty of eternal punishment.

**4:1 Why are there wars and quarrels among you? Are they
not from this?**, that is, from zeal and contentiousness which
he had forbidden above?[177] So also here in explaining the
same thing more extensively, he goes on, saying, **From your
lusts that war in your members.** Lusts war in our members
when the hand or the tongue or a combination of the other
members immoderately obeys those things which a base
mind perversely suggests; concerning this he says in the
earlier part of this Letter, *Each one, in fact, is tempted,
drawn on and lured by his own lust,*[178] and so on. Lusts,
however, can be understood in this place as also referring to
earthly goods, that is, desires for a kingdom, for riches,
honors, dignities. For it is on account of these things and
and countless other things of this sort that quarrels and

173. Ga 6:7-8   174. ᴰs 34:14 (35:15)   175. Ps 126 (125):5
176. *fruuntur*   177. Jm 3:14   178. Jm 1:14

wars are frequently carried on among the evil.

4:2 You quarrel and make war, and you do not have, because you do not ask. He says, *You quarrel and make war* for the sake of temporal glory and you are not able to procure it, surely for the reason that you have not taken care to ask the Lord to bestow upon you all those things that lead to salvation. For if you would ask him with devout intention, he would grant you necessary earthly things to use now and good things from above to enjoy forever.

4:3 You request and you will not receive, because you request wickedly that you may indulge in your concupiscences. He had just said that they did not ask and now he says that they request wickedly, because in the sight of the inward witness he who requests wickedly already appears to request nothing. He, however, requests wickedly who, despising the commands of the Lord, desires benefits from above from the Lord; he also requests wickedly who, having lost the love of things above, seeks only to obtain the lowest goods, and these not for the support of human frailty but for the superfluity of unnecessary pleasure. For this is what he [means when he] says, *that you may indulge in your concupiscences.*

4:4 Adulterers, do you not know that the friendship of this world is an enemy of God? He properly calls adulterers those whom he rebukes for having abandoned the love of heavenly wisdom and turned instead to the clutches of worldly friendship, whom he saw despising the Creator to serve mammon. Indeed he had said above concerning the open enemies of God, *Do not the rich oppress you by their power and drag you to judgments? Do they not blaspheme the good name that has been called down upon you?*[179]

179. Jm 2:6-7

But that you might not consider enemies of God only those who openly blaspheme him, who persecute the saints for their faith in him, and condemn them by unjust judgments, he shows that they are also enemies of God who after faith and confession of his name become slaves to the delights and love of the world, who are faithful in name only and prefer earthly to heavenly things. He also insists more urgently upon this in the following verse, appending, **Whoever, therefore, wishes to be a friend of this world is an enemy of God.** Therefore, all lovers of the world, all seekers after trifles, are enemies of God; all belong to those of whom it is said, *Look, how your enemies, O Lord, will perish.*[180] They may enter the churches, they may not enter the churches, they are enemies of God. For a time they are able to flourish as grass, but when the heat of judgment appears they will perish and the loveliness of their countenance will vanish.[181]

4:5 **Or do you think that the scripture says idly,** namely, that scripture which, forbidding the faithful fellowship with the wicked, speaks thus through Moses, *You shall not enter into a covenant with them or with their gods, they shall not dwell in your land, lest by chance they make you sin against me if you serve their gods, which will definitely be a stumbling-block to you,*[182] and again, *You shall not do their works but you shall destroy them and break their images,*[183] **'Does the spirit that dwells in you have a desire for envy?'** This must be read as a question of rebuke, as if it said, 'Does the spirit of grace with which you were signed on the day of your redemption desire this, that you envy one another? Certainly it is not the good, but the wicked spirit that brings about in you the vice of envy.' This is similar to the manner of speaking in the psalm, *A brother will not redeem, will a man redeem?*[184] For it is understood thus, 'If Christ,

180. Ps 92:9 (91:10)   181. Jm 1:10-11   182. Ex 23:32-3
183. Ex 23:24   184. Ps 49:7 (48:8)

who deigned to become a brother to us through his humanity, did not redeem us, is some mere man in a position to
redeem us?' Certain people have explained this thought,
'Does the spirit that dwells in you have a desire for envy?'
thus: 'He has a desire against envy, that is, he desires that the
disease of envy be overcome and rooted out of your minds'.
Others understand it as said of the spirit of man, so that the
sense would be, 'Do not have desires, do not cling to the
friendships of this world, because while the spirit of your
mind desires earthly things it certainly desires to envy, while
you envy others having those things which you yourselves
desire to possess.'

4:6 **But he gives greater grace.** The Lord gives greater grace
than does the friendship of the world, because this grants
earthly goods for a time and things that are to be lost with
sorrow; he bestows the eternal joy of life. On what sort he
bestows this grace, however, he explains in succession:
**Wherefore he says, 'God resists the proud but gives grace to
the humble.'** God indeed punishes thieves, perjurers, dissolute persons, and other sinners, as despisers of his commandments, but he is said particularly to resist the proud, because
they certainly are punished with a greater penalty who trust
in their own strength, who neglect to be made subject to
divine power by repenting, who refuse to seek the help of
grace from above, as if they are sufficient by themselves to
achieve salvation. *But,* on the other hand, he *gives grace to
the humble,* because they who in the midst of the wounds of
their vices humbly put themselves in the hands of the true
physician rightly receive the gift of the hoped-for cure. It
must be noted, however, that blessed James has set this
thought about the proud and humble from the parables of
Solomon[185] according to the ancient translation,[7] just as
Peter also did in his Letter.[186] In its place in our edition,

185. Pr 3:34 (*LXX*)   186. 1 P 5:5

that comes from the original Hebrew, there is the reading, *He himself will deceive mockers and will give grace to the meek.*[187] For the Lord will deceive mockers according to what Paul says about those who, refusing to receive him who comes in the name of his Father, will accept the antichrist coming in his own name.[188] *Because they did not receive the love of truth that they might be saved,* he says, *therefore God sends them the working of error that they may believe a lie.*[189] He deceived mockers when, while the Jews were saying, *If he is the king of Israel, let him come down now from the cross, and we believe him,*[190] he patiently endured until, dead and buried, he might overcome both their insults and death itself by his swift resurrection. He will give grace, however, to the meek, because he bestows both the perfection of their good work and the gifts of a blessed everlasting life on those who humbly follow him.

4:8 Draw near to the Lord, and he will draw near to you. Draw near to the Lord by following his footsteps through humility, and he will draw near to you by freeing you from your difficulties through his mercy. For not everyone is far from God by distances, but by dispositions.[191] For though both he who is inclined to virtues and he who falls away in the filth of vices dwell in one place on the earth, the one is far from God, the other has God near. Hence the psalmist also says, *The Lord is near to all who call upon him in truth,*[192] and again, *Salvation is far from sinners,*[193] that salvation is certainly of which we sing, *The Lord is my light and my salvation.*[194] And the Lord himself, when he was urging us to draw near to him, saying, *Come to me all you who labor and are burdened, and I will refresh you,*[195] immediately pointed out that this was to be fulfilled not by

---

187. Pr 3:34 (Vulg.)   188. Jn 5:43   189. 2 Th 2:10-11
190. Mt 27:42   191. *affectibus*   192. Ps 145 (144):18
193. Ps 119 (118):155   194. Ps 27 (26):1   195. Mt 11:28

the feet but by actions when he appended, *Take my yoke upon you and learn of me, because I am meek and humble of heart.*[196] **Cleanse your hands, sinners, and purify your hearts, you double-minded.** This is truly [the way] for us to draw near to the Lord, namely, by having cleanness of work and simplicity of heart. *The innocent in hands,* he says, *and the person with a clean heart, he will receive a blessing and mercy from the Lord.*[197] And this is truly how the Lord draws near us, by giving to us, who seek in simplicity, the gifts of his devotion. *For the Holy Spirit of discipline will flee deceit and will remove himself from thoughts that are without understanding.*[198]

4:9–10   Be wretched and grieve and weep; let your laughter be turned into grief and your joy into sorrow. Be humbled in the sight of the Lord, and he will exalt you. Do not love to be made rich, he says, and to rejoice in this world, but mindful of the heinous deeds you have done see instead to this, that through the short-lived miseries and poverty and passing lamentation of this life you may reach the eternal joys of the heavenly kingdom rather than beg, grieve, pay the penalty of torments everlastingly in return for temporal joy and wealth which you have amassed through wicked labor.

4:11   Do not slander one another, my brothers. This vice of slander also refers to the deadly poison of the tongue about which he says, *You quarrel and make war.*[199] **He who slanders his brother or judges his brother, slanders the law and judges the law.** He who slanders his brother slanders the law as if it did not decree properly when it forbade slander, saying though the prophet, *I pursued the one who slanders his neighbor in secret,*[200] and in Leviticus, *You shall not be an accuser and whisperer among the people.*[201] It can also be

---

196. Mt 11:29   197. Ps 24 (23):4-5   198. Ws 1:5
199. Jm 4:2   200. Ps 101 (100):5   201. Lv 19:16

understood thus, *He who slanders his brother* who carries out
the commands of the law *slanders the law and judges the law*
for giving such commands. For example, the law commanded, *You shall not be mindful of the injury of your
fellow-citizens.*[202] Therefore he who slanders his brother and
judges his brother whom he sees gladly sustaining injuries for
the love of God, certainly slanders the law and judges the law
which commanded us to forget injuries.

4:12 But who are you who judge your neighbor? He exposes
the rashness of the one who takes delight in judging his
neighbor and does not take care to examine the uncertain
condition of his own frailty and temporal life. And sometimes because through a flick of the right hand of the most
High these who were judging their neighbor are made subject
to the power of him whom they are judging, sometimes he
survives while they are taken out of the world, he goes on to
expose the rashness of those also who, having no certainty
about their own life, project their mind into the future over
the income from a much longer time, for there follows:

**4:13 Look, you who now say, 'Today or tomorrow we
shall go to that city and shall indeed spend a year there and
shall carry on business and shall make a profit.'** He notes the
many aspects of the foolishness present in an arrangement
of this sort, because, namely, they both make a plan about
the increase of profits and think that they will live a long
time and assert that where they will spend a year is within
their power, and in all these things they reject calling to
mind the investigation of the judge on high.

**4:14 For what is your life? It is a mist appearing for a little
while and after that it will be driven away.** He does not say,
'What is our life?' but he says, *What is your life?* because the

202. Lv 19:18

righteous then begin to live more truly when they reach the
end of this life. *For the enemies of the Lord, as soon as they
are honored and exalted, will vanish utterly like smoke.*[203]
But it must not be imputed that this is the same opinion that
the wicked are described as having said to each other in the
book of Wisdom, *Because we have been born from nothing
and after these things we shall be as if we have not been,
since the breath in our nostrils is smoke and speech [is]
sparks to make our heart beat, because the body will be
extinguished ash and the spirit is scattered like a gentle
breeze.*[204] For they reached these conclusions who believed
that there was no life except this one, saying with Epicurus,
'After death there is nothing, and death itself is nothing'.
Blessed James, however, brought it up to teach that the life
of the wicked is short for the present, yet eternal death will
follow it in the future, according to that saying of blessed
Job, *They spend their days in good things and in a moment
they go down to the lower world.*[205]

**4:17 For some, one who knows the good and does not do
it, this is a sin, therefore.** Throughout the whole text of this
Letter blessed James has shown that they to whom he wrote
had the knowledge to do good things and at the same time
they had so learned a right faith that they presumed to be
able to become teachers even for others; but still they had
not yet attained perfection of works or humility of mind or
restraint of speech. Hence it terrifies them now to no small
degree that he says amidst other words of rebuke and
encouragement that someone who knows how to do good
and does not do what he knows has a greater sin than the
one who fails through ignorance, although neither the one,
who has sinned unwittingly, can be entirely free from guilt,
for the ignorance of good is itself no small evil. Truly the

203. Ps 37 (36):20   204. Ws 2:2-3   205. Jb 21:13

Lord says, then, *The servant who knows the will of his master and has not made preparations and acted according to his will shall be beaten much; but the one who does not know and has done things worthy of blows shall be beaten lightly.*[206]

5:1 Come now, you rich, weep, bewailing the miseries that will come upon you. *Now,* while it is *the acceptable time,* while it is *the day of salvation,*[207] avoid, he says, the future miseries of punishments by weeping and giving alms.

5:3 Your gold and silver have corroded, and their corrosion will be a witness for you and will eat up your flesh like fire. Not only does the visible fire of hell torture the wicked and unmerciful rich in torments but also the very memory of decayed and worthless riches by which they might have been able to redeem their nefarious deeds will very easily burn up their souls no less before the judgment and after the resurrection their flesh as well, when they begin to be seriously angry with themselves for having been unwilling to cleanse their wicked deeds by alms. Accordingly, the corrosion of riches had been turned into a witness of wickedness and into an increase of punishment for that rich man clothed in purple when he heard through the rebuke of Abraham, *Son, remember that you received good things during your life, and Lazarus in like manner evil things.*[208] By the word 'flesh' can also be understood those fleshly delights which the corrosion of riches eats up like fire while the raging flame tortures the dissolute soul outwardly and the piercing sorrow of its obstinacy accuses it no less inwardly. It also happens rather often in this life that some persons lose the riches which they were putting to evil use and, having lost their resources, they begin too late to regret that they held them without fruit and lament that they have not given their possessions to the poor when, because poverty is impending,

206. Lk 12:47-8   207. 2 Co 6:2   208. Lk 16:25

they themselves are forced to beg. **You have heaped up as treasure wrath in the last days,** when having neglected the nakedness and hunger of the poor you rejoiced in accumulating treasures of money for yourselves, not foreseeing that you were yourselves heaping up wrath of the internal judge for yourselves. Although this has not yet appeared, it remains already most certain in the last days, that is, when the end of the days of time will be at hand.

5:4 Look, the pay of the workers who have harvested your land [and of him] who has been defrauded by you cries out. How great is the wickedness of the proud who, when they have sufficient riches, disdain not only to receive and help the poor who come occasionally, but are also unwilling to give to their very tired hands and household servants the due reward of their labor. Blessed Job implies that he is careful to avoid this vice of ungodliness when he says, *If my land cries out against me and its furrows with it weep tears, if I have eaten its fruit without payment and have afflicted the soul of its farmers, may thorns spring up for me instead of grain and weeds instead of barley.*[209] **And their cry has reached the ears of the Lord of sabaoth.** He calls him the Lord of sabaoth, that is, the Lord of hosts, to terrify those who think the poor have no protector. With this place agrees that of the psalmist, *For the poor man is committed to you, you will be the helper of the orphan;*[210] and does what has been written in the book of blessed Job, *For God will not listen in vain, and the Almighty will have regard for the pleas of individuals.*[211]

5:5 You have feasted upon earth. Having neglected heavenly joys to which you were able to come through afflictions and fasts, you like only carnal feasts, which such great hunger and thirst will follow in future that not even one

209. Jb 31:38-40   210. Ps 10:14 (9:35)   211. Jb 35:13

drop of water can then somewhere be acquired by which your burning tongue may be cooled for a little while.[212] **And you have nourished your hearts in self-indulgence.** They nourish their hearts in self-indulgence who, according to the word of Ecclesiastes, do not prevent their heart from enjoying every wish and from delighting itself in the things which they have prepared, and they count it their due if they themselves make use of their own labors,[213] having no care for the support and solace of the poor.

5:5–6 **On the day of slaughter you have denounced and slain the righteous man; he did not resist you.** He calls the Lord [our] Saviour the righteous man; about him the blessed first martyr Stephen speaks, *Which of the prophets have your ancestors not persecuted? And they slew those who brought the message about the coming of the righteous man, of whom you have now been the betrayers and murderers.*[214] From that place where he says, *Come now, you rich, weep, wailing,*[215] it is clear therefore that blessed James is addressing those rich men who had conspired to kill the Lord and who had not yet received the faith in his name by which they might be saved; about them he also speaks above to believers, *Do not the rich oppress you by their power and drag you to the courts? Do they not blaspheme the good name that has been called down upon you?*[216] And because he is writing to the twelve tribes which are in dispersion,[217] he thus advises the faithful to do the works of faith that he may also urge those who had not yet believed to be converted to faith in the Lord and at the same time to the works of faith, recalling to their memory that they slew the son of God and, as if they had done nothing wicked, they gave themselves in addition to self-indulgence and avarice and did not take care to expiate such great wickedness by repentance and alms.

212. Lk 16:24   213. Qo 2:10   214. Ac 7:52   215. Jm 5:1
216. Jm 2:6-7   217. Jm 1:1

What he says about avarice eating up their flesh like fire and how they have stored up wrath for themselves at the last days[218] is especially fitting for them. For it becomes evident that this was fulfilled in their case after the slaying of James himself, when the city of Jerusalem and likewise the whole province of Judea was taken and destroyed by the Romans in punishment, manifestly, for the blood of the Lord and for the other heinous deeds that they had committed.

5:7 Therefore be patient, brothers, until the coming of the Lord. After he had rebuked the proud and unbelieving, he again turns to those who had been oppressed by their wickedness, encouraging them to be patient and implying that the end of these tribulations is close at hand, namely, either when they are taken away to the Lord and receive the fruit of their patience or when their persecutors are deprived of their power to persecute. **Look, the farmer waits for the prized fruit of the land, bearing [it] patiently until he receives the early and the late,** and so on. If he labors so patiently for the fruit of the land which he waits for and hopes in time will come forth, how much more ought you to hold up under all adversities now for the fruit of the heavenly reward which you can possess for ever? For indeed you will receive the fruit in time, the life, namely, of the soul after death; you will also receive later on at the judgment the incorruption of your flesh, or at least the early in the works of righteousness, the late in the reward of your labors according to the saying of the apostle, *You have your fruit in sanctification, the end, in fact, eternal life.*[219]

5:9 Do not complain, brothers, against one another, as if you suffer greater adversities than you deserve, and your persecutors, when they have committed very great abominations, appear to bear no adversity, **that you may not be**

218. Jm 5:3   219. Rm 6:22

judged, with that judgment, namely, of condemnation from the fact that you blame the just judge as if he judges wickedly. **Look, the judge stands before the door,** who will render both to you the rewards of patience and to your adversaries the punishment they deserve. He stands before the door, however, either because he stands ready to know all things that you do or he will come quickly to pay both to you and to your persecutors what each of you has deserved.

5:10 **Accept, brothers, from the prophets who spoke in the Lord's name, the example of the issue of wickedness and long-suffering, of labor and patience.** See, he says, that the prophets who were so holy, so free from sin that the Spirit of God spoke his mysteries to men through them, had a bad issue by suffering death from the faithless, as Zechariah, Uriah, and the Maccabees, martyrs, and in the New Testament John, Stephen, James the son of Zebedee, and very many others, and yet they chose not to complain about this sort of issue but rather to bear it with long-suffering. Others sustained long labors but bore them patiently and without murmuring, as Noah in building the ark through a hundred years, Moses in saving and leading the people through forty years, David in having suffered exile without fault, Joseph in enduring slavery by his brothers' deceit. To each of these, however, he added an outstanding example and one that could be imitated, saying,

5:11 **You have heard of the endurance of Job and you have seen the end of the Lord.** You have known by reading, he says, the labor and patience of Job, and how by the Lord's compassion he received twice as much of all he lost through the wickedness of the enemy.[220] You yourselves, standing by, have also seen the fate of the Lord on the cross which he bore with long-suffering and have also learned through the

220. Jb 42:10

preaching of the Gospel the glory of the resurrection and his ascension into heaven. **Because the Lord is merciful and compassionate,** that either in the present he may free his own from temptations and glorify them even before men while they are alive for the firmness of their faith or crown them in secret after death and not even thus take away from men the memory of praise which they have deserved.

5:12 Above all things, however, my brothers, do not swear, and so on. Because he wishes to draw out the deadly poison of the tongue entirely in his hearers, having forbidden them from slandering one another, having prohibited them from judging their neighbor, having restrained them from complaining against one another in adversities, which are obvious sins, he adds also what to some people appears slight, that he may remove the custom of swearing at all. For this also is clearly evident that it must not at all be taken lightly by those who carefully weigh that thought of the Lord in which he says, *Every careless word which men have spoken they will render an account of on the day of judgment.*[221] **That you may not fall under judgment.** I restrain you from the fault of swearing, he says, for the reason that in swearing often to the truth you may also sometimes fall into perjury, and also that you may be further from the vice of perjury the more you do not wish to swear solemnly to the truth except under pressing necessity. But he also falls under the judgment of guilt who, although he never commits perjury, nevertheless swears solemnly to the truth more frequently than is necessary, because certainly he sins by the very carelessness of overmuch speaking and offends the judge who has forbidden both a useless word and every oath.

5:13 Is anyone of you sad? Let him pray with a quiet mind and sing psalms. He who above restrained the brethren from

221. Mt 12:36

complaining against one another in difficulties now himself shows what must on the contrary be done. If any oppressive sorrow, he says, has come upon any of you either by an injury brought on perhaps by other people or by a besetting fault or by an overwhelming, domestic loss or if you have been made sad for any reason at all, you should by no means gather at that hour to murmur against one another and place the blame on God's judgments but rather come together at the church and on bended knee pray to the Lord that he may send the grace of his consolation, lest the sadness of the world which brings death swallow you up.[222] You yourselves also drive away the harmful disease of sadness from your heart by the frequent sweetness of psalm-singing.

5:14—15 Is anyone sick among you? Let him bring in the presbyters of the Church, and let them pray over him. Just as he had given advice to the one who was sad, so he gives advice also to the one who is sick, how he should be on his guard against the foolishness of murmuring, and according to the measure of the wound he assigns as well the measure of the cure. He admonishes the one who is sad to pray for himself and sing psalms, but commands the person who is sick either in body or faith that as the blow he has suffered is greater he should remember to cure himself with the help of more persons, and this of the presbyters; and let him not report the reason for his weakness to the younger and less learned, lest by chance he receive from them some harmful advice or counsel. **And let them pray over him,** he says, **anointing him with oil in the name of the Lord, and the prayer of faith will save the sick person.** We read in the Gospel that the apostles also did this.[223] And now the custom of the Church holds that those who are sick be anointed with consecrated oil by the presbyters, with the prayer that goes with this, that they may be cured.

222. 2 Co 2:7, 7:10   223. Mk 6:13

62   *Commentary on James 5:15—5:17*

Not only for the presbyters, but, as Pope Innocent writes,[224] even for all Christians is it lawful to use the same oil for anointing at their own necessity or that of their [relatives], but the oil may be consecrated only by bishops. For what he says, *with oil in the name of the Lord,* means with oil consecrated in the name of the Lord or at least that when they anoint the sick person they ought also to invoke the name of the Lord over him at the same time. **And if he [has committed] sins, they will be forgiven him.** Many persons on account of sins committed in the soul are struck with sickness or even death of the body. Hence the apostle says to the Corinthians, because they had been accustomed to receive the body of the Lord unworthily, *Therefore, many among you are sick and weak and many have fallen asleep.*[225] If, therefore, the sick [have committed] sins and have confessed them to the presbyters of the Church and have sincerely tried to leave them behind and to amend, these will be forgiven them. But sins cannot be forgiven without a firm promise of amendment. Hence properly there is added:

5:16—17 Therefore, confess your sins to one another and pray for each other, that you may be saved. However, in this statement there ought to be this distinction, that we confess our daily and minor sins to one another as peers and believe that we are saved by their daily prayer; in turn, according to the law,[226] let us make known the uncleanness of more serious leprosy to the priest and take care to be purified in the manner and for the length of time his judgment has decreed. **For the continuous prayer of the righteous person can accomplish much. Elijah was a man like us, subject to suffering, and he prayed assiduously that it would not rain upon the earth, and it did not rain for three years and six months.** He illustrates by an appropriate example how

224. *Ep. ad Decentium* (PL 20:554B-5A) Cf. Bede, *Act. Ap.* (CC 121: 39-40, 22/27)
225. 1 Co 11:30   226. Lv 13:49, 14:2-3

much the unremitting prayer of the righteous person can accomplish, when Elijah by praying only once closed up the heavens for such a long time,[227] kept showers away from the earth, denied fruits to mortals, and again, when he wished, when he ascertained that it was time, when he saw that the heart of the proud king of an idolatrous people was inclined to repentance because of the prolonged ill results of famine, he prayed only once[228] and restored the fruits of water which he had denied to the earth. For it continues thus:

5:18 And again he prayed, and the heaven gave forth rain, and the earth gave forth its fruit. He prayed once, therefore, both before and afterwards, and yet the one man Elijah obtained as much as the constant prayer of very many righteous persons can accomplish. But lest our frailty take fright, thinking itself unable to do things like so great a prophet who was worthy of being taken up to heaven in a fiery chariot,[229] blessed James when he was about to speak of his prayer, advisedly began thus, *Elijah was a man like us, subject to suffering.* For he *was a man,* and yet second to no man in virtue, *like us* of fleshly origin, *subject to suffering* as we are because of the frailty of both mind and body. For he showed that he was frail in body by asking for food from the widow of Zarephath;[230] he made it clear that he was also subject to suffering in mind when, after he had restored water to the earth and killed the prophets and priests of idols, being terrified at the threats of one unimportant woman, he fled into the desert.[231] How much it is worth with the Lord to pray for the sick and to call those who confess their sins back to their lost salvation he makes clear by appending:

5:19—20 My brothers, if anyone of you has strayed from

227. 1 K 17:1   228. 1 K 18:41-5   229. 2 K 2:11
230. 1 K 17:8-11   231. 1 K 19:1-4

the truth and someone has brought him back, he ought to
know that whoever has brought a sinner back from the error
of his way will save his soul from death. Because in the
earlier parts of this Letter our tongue is restrained from evil
or useless speaking, fittingly is it made clear at the end what
particularly we ought to be speaking. We are ordered, therefore, to pray and sing psalms to the Lord as often as we are
struck by any adversities, likewise to confess our sins to one
another and to pray for each other, that we may be saved;
to provide care, as far as we can, not only for the temporal
health of our neighbors but much more for their eternal wel-
fare. For if it is a matter for great reward to snatch the body,
which is going to die in the end, from death, how worthwhile is it to set free from death the soul which will live for
ever in the heavenly homeland? It must be noted surely that
certain manuscripts have, 'he will save his own soul from
death', and from the ambiguity of the Greek it can also
correctly be interpreted this way. And in truth the one who
corrects someone who strays through this gains for himself
the higher rewards of heavenly life. He will save his soul from
death, he says, and covers a multitude of sins. Anyone who
turns a sinner back from straying, through this act of turning
him back both hides his sins from the sight of the inward
judge by the superimposition of a better life and by curing
his neighbor conceals as well his own misdeeds, however he
offends, from the gaze of him who sees all things, according
to the saying of the psalmist, *Blessed are they whose wicked
deeds have been forgiven and whose sins have been concealed.*[232] In urging this, blessed James is not forgetting what
he says earlier on, *Do not a number of you, my brothers,
become teachers.*[233] For there he is removing those who were
imperfect in their own lives from the office of teaching,
which they were seeking through vainglory; but here he is
teaching those who are instructed in every way they ought

232. Ps 32 (31):1   233. Jm 3:1

to do concerning the salvation of their neighbors out of love for the brotherhood. For what he proposes here for a teacher to do, in another place is mentioned as what charity does; as when blessed Peter says, *Because charity covers a multitude of sins.*[234] And it must not be overlooked that this turning back of someone who strays is accomplished not only by speaking but very often also by acting well. For if anyone shows his neighbors the examples of good action and turns them back to imitating the works of almsgiving or hospitality or of the other virtues which they had neglected, even though his tongue be silent, he actually executes the office of teacher and obtains from the devoted judge a sure reward in return for the salvation of his brother whom he has corrected.

234. 1 P 4:8

NOTES TO COMMENTARY ON JAMES

1. Latin *omne*. Normally, *omnis* means 'all'. But that it may also mean 'complete' is shown by Horace, C 3. 30. 6: *'non omnis moriar'*; *Ep* 1. 1. 11; *'et omnis in hoc sum'*.

2. Latin *intemptator*. A. Souter, *A Glossary of Later Latin to 600 A.D.* (Oxford: Clarendon Press, 1949), s. v., suggests that the Latin word is an unintelligent translation of the Greek word meaning 'inexperienced in, unacquainted with'.

3. The sources of the story of the revelation of the burial place of the body of St Stephen by Gamaliel are given by M. L. W. Laistner, *Retractatio in Actus Apostolorum* (Cambridge, Mass.: The Mediaeval Academy of America, 1939) 115,22-116,5; 121, 13-122,3.

4. Latin *exultat*. Bede first adopts the Latin reading, *exaltat*, meaning 'exalt'. Here he gives an alternate explanation of the verse if the reading *exultat*, 'boast', is used instead of *exaltat*.

5. See M. L. W. Laistner, 'Bede As a Classical and a Patristic Scholar,' *Transactions of the Royal Historical Society* 16 (1933) 77-8. Laistner suggests the possibility that Bede, either through a lapse of memory or an inability to check his sources, confused a story related by Pliny (*Nat. Hist.* 8. 25. 65) about a tame tiger exhibited at the dedication of the theater of Marcellus with a story told by Marcellinus (*MGH auct. ant.* 11, 72) about an elephant and two giraffes sent to the emperor Anastasius from India. No one seems to have located the source of the tale about the tame asp in Egypt.

6. Bede's derivation and interpretation here of Latin and Greek words is almost impossible to convey in English. He derives the Latin adjective *animalis* from the Latin noun *anima* and not from the noun *animal*, which normally would be translated 'animal'. The problem is further complicated when Bede brings in the Greek equivalents, *psyche*, 'life-giving principle', and *psychicon*, 'physical', since the English word 'psychic', which comes from these Greek words, has quite a different connotation. Bede also equates the Latin word *animalia*, 'animals', with the Greek word *zoa*, 'living things', having as its base the Greek noun *zoe*, 'life'.

7. One cannot always be sure exactly what Bede means by the

expression, 'ancient translation'. It could refer to the old Latin translations, made before Jerome's Latin Vulgate, or to the Septuagint Greek,
which was frequently the basis for the old Latin translations. Bede
possibly had in mind here the Septuagint Greek, since he continues by
contrasting the version given by James and Peter in their Letters with
the Latin Vulgate translation made by Jerome from the original Hebrew
text of the book of Proverbs.

COMMENTARY ON 1 PETER

1:1 **P**ETER, **an apostle of Jesus Christ, to the elect newcomers of the dispersion in Pontus, Galatia, Cappadocia, Asia and Bithynia.** Newcomers in Latin are called converts in Greek. The Jews called by this name those who, having been born as gentiles, wished to believe in God and, after having received circumcision according to the Jewish custom, to lead a life in compliance with the law of God. There were certain from among their number who on the holy day of Pentecost, when the apostles received the Holy Spirit under the appearance of fire, believed in Christ because of their preaching, for scripture says that *Jews also and converts*[1] were present. He calls them *elect newcomers,* therefore, who were worthy to progress from paganism to the recognition and undertaking of the divine law, and, having received the sacraments of the old law, to the acceptance of the grace of faith. Hence the holy priest Jerome, speaking of them, says that[2]

> Peter, after being bishop of the church of Antioch
> and preaching to the believers of the circumcision
> who were dispersed throughout Pontus, Galatia,
> Cappadocia, Asia and Bithynia, in the second year
> of Claudius came to Rome to refute Simon Magus.[3]

But we also, if we can truly say to God with the prophet that in your sight we are dwellers on earth and travelers like all our fathers,[4] ought to believe that the Letters of blessed Peter were written to us as well and to read them as having

---

1. Ac 2:11   2. Jer., *Vir. ill.* 1; TU 6, 22/27
3. Ac 8:9-24   4. Ps 39:12 (38:13)

69

been sent to us. Accordingly, in these Letters he advises us as if we have a fatherland elsewhere, saying, *Dearly beloved, I entreat you as newcomers and strangers to keep yourselves from bodily desires.*[5] But what is added, *of the dispersion,* means that they were dispersed from Jerusalem in the persecution that followed the death of Stephen[6] or at least ill-treated for their faith and often driven from their homes either by the Jews or by the gentiles, as we read in the Acts of the Apostles. But Paul also says to the Galatians, *Did you suffer so greatly without a reason? Yes, it was without a reason.*[7] *Of the dispersion,* he says, *in Pontus, Galatia, Cappadocia, Asia, and Bithynia.* These are all Greek provinces in Asia [Minor]. But there is also another Bithynia in Europe, from which the Bithynians who are in Asia [Minor] are alleged to trace their origin. That Bithynia which is in Asia [Minor], however, is also called greater Phrygia, and the river Hiera forms the boundary between it and Galatia.[8]

1:2 According to the foreknowledge of God the Father for the sanctification of the Spirit for obedience and the sprinkling of the blood of Jesus Christ. These verses belong with what he had said, *to the elect newcomers.* For they had been elected according to the foreknowledge of God the Father. Hence Paul also says, *Those whom he foreknew he also predestined to be conformed to the image of his son;*[9] and elsewhere, *As he elected us in him before the creation of the world.*[10] They had been elected, however, for this, that they might be sanctified through the giving of the Spirit and, having been cleansed from all sins,[11] they who through the disobedience of the first man, Adam, had perished might begin to obey the Lord Jesus Christ, that sprinkled by his blood they might avoid the power of satan. It was in this way, through the blood of the lamb, that Israel escaped the

5. 1 P 2:11   6. Ac 8:1   7. Ga 3:4
8. Isid., *Etymol.* 14. 3. 39; Plin., *Nat. hist.* 5. 41. 145, 5. 43. 149
9. Rm 8:29   10. Eph 1:4   11. 1 Jn 1:7

sway of the Egyptians.[12] He says 'sprinkling', however, according to the manner of the Old Testament, where things that were to be sanctified were accustomed to be sprinkled with the blood of the sacrificial victims.[13] Moreover, he says clearly about himself, *Unless you eat of the body of the son of man and drink his blood, you will not have life in you.*[14] **May grace and peace be multiplied in you,** that you may carry through to perfection what you have begun well. It is well that he speaks first about grace and then about peace, because without the grace of Christ we cannot reach the peace of his reconciliation, indeed we can have nothing peaceful except through his grace.

1:3 Blessed be God and the Father of our Lord Jesus Christ. He relates the praises of blessing to God the Father this way that he may show the Lord our saviour to be both God and man. For when he says, *God and the Father of our Lord Jesus Christ,* he is calling [him] the God indeed of our Lord Jesus Christ, because he recalls that the very Lord Christ was made man; he calls [him] the Father, however, of our Lord Jesus Christ, because he does not doubt that the same Lord of ours always existed as the Son of God. **Who according to his great mercy has granted us a new birth to living hope through the resurrection of Jesus Christ from the dead.** God is justifiably[15] blessed by us to whom, when because of our deserts we had been born for death, in his mercy he granted a new birth for life. And this [was accomplished] through the resurrection of his son, since he loved our life to such an extent that he saw to it that he died for it and, when the same death was destroyed through his resurrection, he showed us the hope and example of rising again. For he died that we should not be afraid of dying; he rose from the dead that we also may hope to rise again through him.

12. Ex 12:7-23   13. Ex 29:20-21, Lv 8:30
14. Jn 6:53   15. *iure*

1:4 For an imperishable and undefiled and unfading inheritance, *imperishable* because the heavenly life is untouched by old age or disease or any sorrow, *undefiled* because no unclean person can enter into it, *unfading* because the heavenly way of life cannot at last become worthless in the minds of the blessed from long use, as the luxuries and delights of the present time sometimes become a cause for revulsion through daily habit and use. **Reserved in the heavens in you.** He says, *reserved in you,* instead of saying, 'reserved for you', that is, reserved now for this reason that it may be given to you at the appointed time in the heavens. Or at least [he means] *reserved in the heavens in you,* because he who *gave* to believers *the power of becoming sons of God*[16] is he who gave the same persons the power of receiving an inheritance in heaven by persevering to the very end that they may be saved. And therefore he says that the inheritance is reserved in those by whose merits—with the Lord's help—he knows that inheritance must be attained, because those who have not observed the Father's discipline do not deserve to receive their inheritance from him.

1:5 We who are kept by the power of God through faith for the salvation prepared to be revealed at the end of time. And the Lord says in the Gospel, *In my Father's house there are many dwelling places;*[17] and again, *It is not mine to give, but to those for whom it has been prepared by my Father.*[18] Seats have been prepared therefore, in the kingdom of God, dwelling places have been prepared in the Father's house, salvation has been prepared in the heavens; only let anyone who wishes to receive these make himself worthy. But because no one by his own effort alone can become worthy of achieving eternal salvation by his own strength, this is quite properly prefaced, *We who are kept by the power of God through faith.* For no one by dint of his own freedom

16. Jn 1:12   17. Jn 14:2   18. Mt 20:23, Mk 10:40

can manage to be kept in good, but in everything we must seek the help of him from whom we have received the beginning of the good action if we are to bring it to completion.

1:6 **In this you will rejoice, even if it is fitting that you be saddened for a little while now in different kinds of temptations.** What he says, *in this,* means in the fact that at the end of time the prepared salvation will be revealed and given to those who are worthy. The Lord also says about this, *Yet again shall I see you, and your heart will rejoice, and your joy no one shall take from you.*[19] *If now it is fitting that you be saddened for a little while. It is fitting,* he says, *that you be saddened,* because it is only through the sadness of the passing world and afflictions that one can reach eternal joys. He says, *for a little while,* however, because when the eternal reward is given, everything that appeared hard and harsh in the midst of the tribulations of the world will appear brief and light.

1:7 **So that the testing of your faith may be much more precious than gold, which is tested by fire.** The Book of Wisdom also compares the sufferings of the saints to gold which is purified by fire, saying about the Lord, *He tested them like gold in the furnace and received them as if they were a sacrificial victim, whole burnt offerings,*[20] because undoubtedly in the joy of making the reward he takes as a sacrificial victim pleasing to himself those whom he has tested and proven faithful in the fire of tribulation. And the endurance[21] of the saints is well likened to gold, because just as there is no metal more precious than gold, so this [endurance] is most worthy of all praise in the sight of the Lord. For indeed from this it has been written, *Precious in the sight of the Lord is the death of his saints.*[22] For just as gold shut up in the furnace is purified by the flames but

19. Jn 16:22   20. Ws 3:6   21. *patientia*   22. Ps 116 (115):15

gleams when it is brought out, so the perseverance of the faithful appears contemptible and foolish indeed during the persecutions of the faithless, but when the struggle with tribulations is over and the time of retribution is at hand, then it is clear how worthwhile their glory is, how much their virtue has produced in the flames of their sufferings. Hence appropriately there is added: **It may be found for praise and glory and honor in the revelation of Jesus Christ.** The testing of faith is found, however, for praise when the judge praises it and says, *I was hungry, and you gave me to eat,*[23] and so on. It is found for glory when he glorifies the same [testing] by prefacing, *Come, you blessed of my Father, take possession of the kingdom prepared for you from the creation of the world.*[24] It is found for honor when as the wicked fall into eternal punishment the righteous will go into eternal life. He himself says about this [kind of person], *If anyone serves me, my Father will honor him.*[25]

1:8   When you see him, you will be glad with unspeakable and glorified happiness. Paul also says, *The eye has not seen nor the ear heard nor has it entered into the heart of man what things God has prepared for those who love him.*[26]

1:10   The prophets who prophesied about the grace to come in you searched and scrutinized over this salvation. Over the grace of the Gospel to come from the Lord and his angels they searched and scrutinized in secret as to the time and manner that eternal salvation would come to the world. This is found in their books. Hence also one of them, because of his great love of knowledge of salvation, deserved to be called by the angel *a man of desires.*[27] They prophesied, however, by speaking openly to mankind and explaining what they themselves had come to know in the secrecy of inward contemplation.

23. Mt 25:35   24. Mt 25:34   25. Jn 12:26   26. 1 Co 2:9
27. Dn 9:23

1:11 They examined the time and conditions the spirit of Christ was pointing out to them when he foretold the sufferings and future glories which are in Christ. The evangelist pointed out these glories when he said, *For the Spirit had not yet been given, because Jesus had not yet been glorified.*[28] There are two glorifications of the Lord, however, according to the human form which he took on: one when he rose from the dead, and the other when he ascended into heaven before his disciples' eyes. There is yet a third, and that in the sight of men, when he shall come in his majesty and that of his Father and of his holy angels to reward everyone according to his work.[29]

1:12 It was revealed to them that they were serving not themselves but you in those things which have now been proclaimed to you. Among the many hidden things that were revealed to the prophets when they were carefully searching and scrutinizing over the salvation to come, even this was revealed to them, that the same salvation would come not in their days but rather in yours, who are born at the end of the ages. He says these things to warn them to take care of the salvation offered [them], which the prophets and earlier righteous persons loved all along, longing to live in the world at that time when it would be immediately possible for those taken away from the world to mount up to the heavenly kingdom. **By those who preached the Gospel to you by the Holy Spirit sent from heaven.** He had said previously that the spirit of Christ had foretold his sufferings and subsequent glories to the prophets, and now he says that the apostles are proclaiming the same things to them by the Holy Spirit sent from heaven. Hence it is evident that the same spirit of Christ was formerly in the prophets as was afterwards in the apostles, and therefore each was preaching the same faith in the suffering and subsequent glory of

28. Jn 7:39   29. Mt 16:27

Christ to the peoples, the [prophets] that it was still to come,
the [apostles] that it had already come; and because of this
[they preached] that there is one Church, part of which preceded the bodily coming of the Lord, part of which followed
[it]. **On whom the angels long to gaze.** It is clear that so
great a glory of the man Jesus Christ who suffered for us
followed that even the angelic powers in heaven, though they
are perfect in their eternal happiness, rejoice always to behold
not only the immortal splendor of the Godhead but also the
honor of the humanity he took on. [Surely] we ought to look
more carefully at what he says about the angels longing to
gaze on him, since 'long' is not usually said of something we
have but of something we wish to have, for no one longs for
what he has. How, therefore, do they long to gaze on Christ,
whose face they never cease to behold, unless the contemplation of the divine presence makes the citizens of the
heavenly home so happy that in an ordering to us ineffable
they are both satisfied at seeing his glory always and always
insatiably hunger after his sweetness as if it were new? For,
as blessed Pope Gregory admirably distinguishes between the
pleasures of the heart and body and says:

> When bodily pleasures are not possessed, they
> enkindle a serious desire for them [in us], but
> when they are possessed and consumed, right
> away through being satisfied they produce a loath-
> ing in the one who enjoys them. But on the other
> hand, when spiritual pleasures are not possessed,
> they are loathed; on being possessed, however,
> they are desired, and the more hungrily they are
> sought after by the one who enjoys them, the
> more also are they enjoyed by the one who hun-
> gers for them. In the former, appetite brings about
> satiety and satiety loathing; in the latter, however,
> appetite causes satiety and satiety appetite. For
> spiritual pleasures increase desire in the mind while
> they satisfy, because the more greatly their flavor

is apprehended, the more is it perceived that there is something greater to be loved.'[30]

What he says, *On whom the angels long to gaze,* can also correctly be understood of the Holy Spirit, about whom he had prefaced, *Those who preached the Gospel to you by the Holy Spirit sent from heaven.* For blessed Peter relates to the grace of divine condescension the fact that [God], for the sake of human salvation, sent to the earth his spirit, who has such great majesty and glory that the sight of him—just as that of the Father himself and of the Son, which is undoubtedly the same—is longed for by the angels in heaven, and poured him forth to enlighten the minds of the faithful.

1:13 Wherefore, having girt up the loins of your mind and being sober, perfectly hope for that grace which is being offered you in the revelation of Jesus Christ. Because this has been promised you, he says, that after this life you may see the revelation of Jesus Christ which the angels now see, the greater is the grace promised you, the more greatly take care that you are worthy to receive it. For he girds up the loins of his body who curbs dissoluteness in his disposition,[31] he girds up the loins of his mind who checks it as well in his thoughts. And rightly does he say, **Hope for that grace which is being offered you in the revelation of Jesus Christ,** for someone who, having girt up the loins of his mind, that is, being chaste both in mind and body, awaits the Lord's coming, rightly looks forward to the time of his revelation. Yet someone who knows that he has not pleased the Lord, lacking the hope of those who are good, deservedly fears that he will come too quickly.

1:14 As obedient children. Rightly does he wish those to be completely obedient whom at the outset he had said were

---

30. Greg., *Hom. ev.* 2. 36. 1; PL 76: 1266AB   31. *ab affectu*

elected for obedience and the sprinkling of the blood of Jesus Christ.[32]

1:15 But according to the holy one who called you, be yourselves also holy in your whole way of life. This is like the saying in the Gospel, *Therefore, you also be perfect, just as your heavenly Father also is perfect.*[33]

1:17 And if you call upon him as Father, by saying in prayer, *Our Father who are in heaven,*[34] **who judges according to each one's work without showing favoritism,** not like a physical father who is accustomed to spare his own sons when they sin more forbearingly than [he does] his servants. But God is such a just and devoted father that he both changes humble and obedient servants, indeed even enemies offering him their hand, by the adoption of sons, and again those who seem worthy of honor by their designation as sons he utterly disinherits forever for the fault of disobedience. **Live out the time of your life here in fear,** lest namely through sloth and carelessness you become unworthy of so great a father, and, while you may live out the time of your life here safely, you may not be able to reach the promised happiness of the fatherland.

1:18–19 Knowing that you have been redeemed from the useless way of life of your ancestral tradition not by perishable gold or silver but by the precious blood of, as it were a spotless and stainless lamb, Jesus Christ. The greater the price of your redemption from the corruption of your bodily life, the more greatly ought you to fear lest, by returning perchance to the corruption of vices, you offend the sensibilities[35] of your Redeemer.

1:23 Having been reborn not from perishable but from

32. 1 P 1:1-2   33. Mt 5:48   34. Mt 6:9   35. *animus*

imperishable seed through the word of God who lives and abides forever. There is a similar verse in the Gospel of John, *To these who believe in his name, who were born not of blood nor of the will of the body nor of the will of man but of God.*[36] Just as the price of the Lord's passion, by which we were redeemed, is therefore imperishable, so also is the sacrament of the sacred font by which we were reborn imperishable. These are so interrelated to each other that the one without the other cannot confer salvation, because, namely, the Lord at the time of his incarnation so redeemed us all at the same time by his sacred blood that we also in our own time through the rebirth of baptism ought individually to attain a share in the same rebirth. It has been well said about this rebirth that it has been brought about *not from perishable seed but through the word of God who lives and abides for ever,* so that from this it may be gathered that just as the body which decays is born from perishable seed, so life which knows no end is granted us through water consecrated by the word of God. He appropriately also illustrates this by the witness of the prophet[37] when he adds:

1:24–25 Because all flesh is hay, and all its glory like the blossom of hay; the hay has dried up, and its blossom has fallen off, but the word of the Lord remains for ever. Just as a perishable body, therefore, begets a perishable body, so also the word of the Lord which remains for ever gives eternal life in the body and soul at the same time to those whom it creates anew from water. Saint Cyprian thus recalls this witness in his book on the dress of virgins:[38]

> 'Cry,' says God to Isaiah, '*All flesh is like hay, and all its honor like the blossom of hay; the hay has dried up, and its blossom has fallen off, but the word of the Lord remains for ever.*' It does not

36. Jn 1:12-13   37. Is 40:6-8
38. Cypr., *Hab. virg.* 6; CSEL 3,1:192, 2/11

become a Christian, and it particularly does not become a virgin, to count any honor or distinction of the body but only to seek the word of God, to embrace good things which will remain for ever; or, if she must glory in her body, then clearly let it be when she is tortured in confessing the Name, when (though but a woman) she is found braver than the men who are tormenting her, when she suffers fire or the cross or the sword or the beasts, that she may be crowned. These are the precious jewels of the body, these are the better adornments for her person.

It should not disturb the reader, however, that in this statement from the prophet he has used the word 'honor' while ours uses the word 'glory', for both are usually translated into Latin[1] from the single Greek word, which is δόξα.

2:1–2 So, putting aside all malice and all deceit and hypocrisy and envy and all slander, now like newborn children desire milk that is reasonable and without deceit. Because you have been recently reborn, he says, and made sons of God through baptism, now through attention to a good way of life be like children just issued from the womb, by nature of their blameless age, namely, unacquainted with malice and deceit, inexperienced in every way with pretence, envy, slander and other vices of this kind. Just as they naturally desire their mother's milk so that they can grow up healthily and acquire the ability to eat bread, so do you also seek first the simple basic elements of faith from the breasts of your mother, the Church, that is, from the teachers of the Old and New Testaments, who have either written or also preach to you orally the divine words, that by learning well you may reach the nourishment of the living bread which came down from heaven,[39] that is, through the sacraments of the Lord's

39. Jn 6:51

incarnation by which you have been reborn, and nourished by which you may attain the contemplation of the divine majesty. **Desire milk that is reasonable and without deceit,** he says, **that in it you may grow up to salvation.** By his admonition about desiring the milk of the word he touches those who come unwillingly and with contempt to listening to sacred readings, unacquainted with that thirst and hunger of which the Lord says, *Blessed are they who hunger and thirst after righteousness.*[40] And therefore they attain rather slowly the perfect growth of salvation at which they can be fed with the solid food of the word, that is, perceive the divine secrets and accomplish greater good.

2:3 **Yes, you taste that the Lord is sweet.** By this stipulation, he says, by getting rid and cleansing your heart of malice and evil, desire the life-giving food of Christ and so taste the fullness of the divine sweetness. For it is no wonder that the person does not avoid degrading his mind by earthly attractions who tastes nothing in it of the sweetness from on high. For the psalmist does well to advise us to taste how sweet the Lord is,[41] because there are some persons who sense not how sweetly God may taste within but how he may sound when struck from without. Although they perceive certain secrets by their understanding, they cannot experience their sweetness, and if they know of their existence, they do not know, as I have said, how they taste. And since in that psalm from which he took this verse there was prefaced, *Draw near to him and be enlightened,*[42] rightly blessed Peter appended, saying:

2:4 **Drawing near to this living stone, rejected by men, indeed, but chosen and honored by God.** He also takes the witness about this stone from the psalm in which it has been written, *The stone which the builders rejected has become*

---

40. Mt 5:6   41. Ps 34:8 (33:9)   42. Ps 34:5 (33:6)

the chief cornerstone.[43] But that no one might consider in
the Jewish sense that this had been sung by the prophet about
a physical stone which was being put by divine judgment in
the building of some earthly house contrary to human
arrangement, he advisedly added, *living,* saying, *Drawing near
to this living stone,* that he might indicate that it was said
about Christ. He is rightly called a stone, because coming in
the flesh he deigned to insert himself into the building of his
holy Church that he might strengthen it, a living one, however, because he was able to say, *I am the way, the truth and
the life.*[44] He was rejected by men when they said, *We have
no king but Caesar,*[45] chosen however by God when he himself said, *But I have been established king by him,*[46] and so
on, and adorned when, after the death on the cross, *God
exalted him and gave him a Name which is above every
Name,*[47] and so on.

**2:5 And you yourselves like living stones are to be built
into the edifice, spiritual houses.** He says that they are being
added to the building, because without the Lord Jesus Christ,
namely the living stone, no spiritual building is able to stand.
For no one can lay another foundation except[48] him. By
being joined with him, the faithful are made into living
stones, who because of their unfaithfulness had been dead
stones, namely, hard and unfeeling. To them it was rightly
said, *I shall take away from you your heart of stone and give
you a heart of flesh.*[49] But they are fitted like living stones
into the spiritual building when at the discrimination of a
learned teacher they have their undesirable actions and
thoughts cut off and are squared off by the blow of a ham-
mer, as it were. And just as some rows of stones in a wall are
held up by others, so all the faithful in the Church are held
up by the righteous who preceded them, they themselves

43. Ps 118 (117):22   44. Jn 14:6   45. Jn 19:15   46. Ps 2:6
47. Ph 2:9   48. 1 Co 3:11   49. Ezk 36:26

by their teaching and support hold up those who come after even to the last righteous person. He, though he is held up by those who went before, will have no one coming after him whom he ought to hold up; but he who holds up the entire building and is himself held up by no one is the Lord Christ—hence he is also called by the prophet a precious stone laid in the foundation.[50] He likewise calls the elect living stones that he may indicate the struggle of good intent or action in which they ought always to be engaged with the grace of God preceding and accompanying them. For when dead, that is, material, stones are being prepared or laid up on a building, they cannot help the builder's work in any way and can do nothing but fall; but however and wherever they are laid by the builder, they stay there in the same place without any feeling or they even slip down and fall. But blessed Peter does not wish us to imitate the hardness and lack of feeling of such stones but to be built into the building as living stones on the foundation of Christ that, with the help of his grace, namely, by living soberly and righteously and godly,[51] we may work together [with him] after the example of him who said, *And his grace was not without effect in me, but I labored more than all those.*[52] For a living stone in the building of holy Church was he who strove to labor diligently lest he have received the grace of God in vain; and lest he appear to have attributed anything of the same devoted labor to himself, he added carefully, *It was not I, however, but the grace of God with me.*[53] Therefore, anyone who with his gift and help takes care to press on untiringly in his good works is being built by Christ as a living stone into his house. But anyone who, after being incorporated into holy Church through the grace of rebirth, has striven to do no further work towards his salvation is, like a dead stone, unworthy of the heavenly building, in a word, and therefore to be rejected by the divine judgment; and another who is

50. Is 28:16   51. Tt 2:12   52. 1 Co 15:10   53. Ibid.

worthy is to be substituted in his place—according to the
command of Leviticus by which the leprous stones of houses
are commanded to be inspected by a priest, and if they
cannot be made clean, to be then counted as unclean and
removed from the course of clean stones.[54] *You are to be
built into the edifice,* he says, *spiritual houses.* Thus he says
that they ought to become spiritual houses, although there is
one house of Christ made up of all the elect angels and
human beings, in the same way as although there is one
catholic Church spread throughout the whole world they are
frequently called 'churches' in the plural, namely, on
account of the gatherings of the faithful in many places
spread over many tribes, tongues, and peoples. Hence he himself says, *I, Jesus, have sent my angel to you to give witness
about these things in the churches.*[55] Nor must the fact be
overlooked that certain manuscripts have in the singular,
'You are to be built a spiritual house', and others have, 'You
are to be built into a spiritual house', in which the unity itself,
namely, of the entire holy Church is more clearly referred to.
Yet when he had said, *You are to be built into the edifice,* or,
'a spiritual house', he added, **A holy priesthood,** in order that
he may very clearly urge us, being ourselves a holy priesthood,
to be built upon the foundation of Christ. Therefore, he calls
the entire Church *a holy priesthood,* a name and office that
the house of Aaron alone had under the law, because
namely we are all members of the high priest, we all are
signed with the oil of gladness;[56] there applies to all what he
appends: **To offer spiritual sacrificial victims acceptable to
God through Jesus Christ.** Yet he calls our works of almsgiving and prayers *spiritual sacrificial victims* to distinguish
them from the bodily victims under the law. But what he
says in conclusion, *through Jesus Christ,* applies to everything that he had said previously, because through his grace
we are both added to the building in him by wise architects,

54. Lv 14:33-45   55. Rv 22:16   56. Ps 45:7 (44:8)

that is, the ministers of the New Testament, and we are made into spiritual houses, strengthened against rains, winds, floods of temptations by his spirit, and we are able both to share in his holy priesthood and to do something good and acceptable to God only through him. For *just as the branch cannot produce fruit by itself unless it remains on the vine, so neither can you,* he says, *unless you remain in me.*[57]

2:6 Wherefore, there is found in scripture, 'Look, in Zion I lay a cornerstone, chosen, precious'. He gives this witness from Isaiah[58] to strengthen what he had said previously, *Drawing near to this living stone,*[59] expanding and asserting that the Lord saviour is called a stone by the prophets on account of his firmness. And when he adds, **And everyone who believes in him will not be disturbed,** he gives on account of what he had said, *And you like living stones to be built into the edifice.*[60] This word of the prophet and the apostle in which it is said that those who draw near the the living stone and believe in him will not be disturbed are admirably fitting to the verse of that psalm in which, when it had been said, *Draw near to him and be enlightened,* at once there was added, *and your faces will not be ashamed.*[61] Like this is what John says, *And now, little children, remain in him so that when he appears we may have confidence and not be confounded by him at his coming.*[62]

2:7 For you, therefore, who believe, an honor, that honor undoubtedly that we be not thrown into confusion by him at his coming, but as he himself says, *If anyone serves me, my Father will honor him.*[63] **But for those who do not believe the stone which the builders rejected,** that just as they rejected him when they were building their actions by being

57. Jn 15:4   58. Is 28:16   59. 1 P 2:4   60. 1 P 2:5
61. Ps 34:5 (33:6)   62. 1 Jn 2:28   63. Jn 12:26

unwilling to lay him in the foundation of their heart, so also will they be rejected by him at his coming when he will be unwilling to accept those who rejected him into the building of his house which is in heaven. And this distinction between honor for those who believe but rejection for those who do not believe extends up to this point [of the verse]. From here on he adds likewise about those who believe, **This has become the cornerstone,** because namely just as a cornerstone joins two walls, so the Lord has united to himself the people of the Jews and gentiles in one company of faith.[64] And at once he adds about unbelievers:

2:8 And a stone of offence and a rock of stumbling. Hence Paul also says, *We preach Christ crucified, to the Jews indeed a stumbling block but foolishness to the gentiles.*[65] **For those who stumble at the word and do not believe in that to which they have also been appointed.** They stumble at the word who from the very fact that it behooves them to hear the word of God, stumble in their mind by being unwilling to believe what they hear. He has exaggerated their foolishness and added, *They do not believe in that to which they have also been appointed,* because they have been appointed to this, that is, to this made human beings by nature, that they may believe God and obey his will, as Solomon attests when he says, *Fear God and obey his commandments, for this is [the duty of] every human being,*[66] that is, every human being has been naturally made for this purpose, that he may fear God and obey his commandments. Certain manuscripts have, 'in which they have also been appointed', which is understood according to what Paul says in speaking about God: *For in him we live and move and are.*[67]

2:9 But you are a chosen race, a royal priesthood, a holy

64. Eph 2:14-16   65. 1 Co 1:23
66. Qo 12:13   67. Ac 17:28

nation, a people whom he has gained. The apostle Peter now rightly gives to the gentiles this attestation of praise which formerly was given by Moses to the ancient people of God,[68] because namely they believed in Christ who like a cornerstone brought the gentiles into that salvation which Israel had had for itself. He calls them *a chosen race* on account of their faith, that he may distinguish them from those who by rejecting the living stone have themselves become rejected, *a royal priesthood,* however, because they have been joined to his body who is their real king and true priest, who as king grants to his own a kingdom and as their high priest cleanses them of their sins by the sacrificial victim of his own blood. He names them *a royal priesthood* that they may remember both to hope for an eternal kingdom and always to offer to God the sacrificial victims of a stainless way of life. They are also called *a holy nation* and *a people whom he has gained* according to what Paul says, explaining the thought of the prophet[69] saying, *Yet my righteous one lives by faith, but if he withdraws he will not be pleasing to my soul: We are not those who withdraw to our destruction but [people] of faith to the gain of our soul;*[70] and in the Acts of the Apostles, *The Holy Spirit has placed the bishops to rule the church of the Lord, which he has gained by his blood.*[71] Therefore, we have become the people whom he has gained in the blood of our Redeemer, because there was once the people of Israel redeemed from Egypt by the blood of a lamb. Hence in the following [part of the] verse also he both mystically recalls the ancient history and teaches spiritually that his also is to be fulfilled in the new people of God, saying, **that you may make known his mighty deeds who has called you out of darkness into his own wonderful light.** For just as those who were freed by Moses from slavery in Egypt sang to the Lord a triumphant song after the crossing of the Red Sea and the

68. Ex 19:6   69. Hab 2:4
70. Heb 10:38-9   71. Ac 20:28

drowning of Pharoah's army,[72] so it is fitting also for us to render worthy thanks for heavenly benefits after receiving the forgiveness of sins in baptism. For the Egyptians who ill-treated the people of God—reasonably, too, because they are interpreted to mean 'darkness' or 'tribulations'[²]—appropriately signify sins washed away in baptism but still troubling us. The freeing of the children of Israel and their being brought out into the fatherland once promised them is also linked with the mystery of our redemption. By means of it we make our way to the light of the dwelling place on high with the grace of Christ lighting our way and guiding us. That cloud and column of fire that both protected them through-out the whole of their journey from the darkness of the nights[73] and led them by a sure path to the promised homes of the fatherland also prefigured the light of this grace.

2:10 You who were once not a people but now are the people of God, who did not seek after mercy but now have received mercy. By these verses he indicates clearly that he has written this Letter to those who had come from the gentiles to the faith, who were once separated from the way of life of the people of God but then through the grace of faith were joined to his people[74] and obtained the mercy which they did not know how to hope for. He takes them, however, from the prophet Hosea who predicted the calling of the gentiles and said, *I shall call [those who were] not my people my people and [those who did] not receive mercy [a people] having received mercy, and it will be in the place where it was said, 'You are not my people,' there they will be called the sons of the living God.*[75]

2:11 Dearly beloved, I entreat you as newcomers and strangers to keep yourselves from bodily desires that fight

72. Ex 15:1-18   73. Ex 13:21-2
74. Eph 2:12-13   75. Ho 1:9 (10), 2:24, Rm 9:25-6

against the soul. Up to this point blessed Peter has been instructing the Church in general, enlarging on either the benefits by which the divine condescension deigned to call us to salvation or on the gifts with which he deigned once to honor the Jews but now us. From this point on he skillfully urges the various classes of the faithful not to show themselves unworthy of so great a grace of the spirit by living according to their bodily desires, lest any of those marked with the royal and priestly name, driven on by the wickedness of their vices, fall away from the glory of the nobility granted or promised them. Therefore, he particularly addresses first those who are free and slaves, then women and men, and then after a passage of general exhortation he points out to the old and young also how they ought to conduct themselves. Appropriately, however, he teaches those who are free to keep themselves *from bodily desires,* because the freedom of a more relaxed life is accustomed to be exposed to the greater dangers of enticing allurements *that fight against the soul,* because while the body weakly gives in to pleasant concupiscences, the army of the vices is being strongly armed against the soul. He suitably calls them *newcomers and strangers* that they may the less subject their mind to earthly affairs the more they remember that they have a fatherland in heaven. For there is accustomed to be this difference in this life between the elect and the condemned: that the elect as strangers and exiles now look for a fatherland in the future and are less pleased with the passing joys of the present the more they hope to receive future joys without end and to reign with Christ for ever; but the condemned on the other hand have their fatherland here and know how to yearn after the pleasures of this life alone, and therefore after this life they are banished into everlasting exile where, deprived of all pleasures, they suffer only adversity in torments.

2:12 That although they may slander you as evildoers,

serving you from your good works, they may glorify God on the day of his visitation. It often happens that pagans who censure the faith of Christians for having abandoned their gods afterwards, observing their chaste way of life and their insuperable belief in Christ, cease slandering them and begin more to glorify and praise God who because of the goodness and righteousness of his worshippers is proved to be good and righteous. *They glorify God,* he says, *on the day of his visitation,* that is, even now unbelievers recognize how great is the glory to be given you by God at the time of retribution, once they have seen you earnestly following him amid the dangers that stand in your way.

2:13–14 Be subject to every human institution for the sake of God. *To every human institution,* he says, to everyone of rank, to every personage, to every governor to which divine providence wishes you to be subject. For this is what he says, *for God's sake,* because *there is no power except from God,*[76] and, *He who resists the [civil] power resists the disposition of God.*[77] What institution he subsequently explains, adding, **whether it be to the king as having supremacy or to the representatives sent by him.** He speaks only of the king and his representatives but not of masters, because, as we have said, here he is instructing those particularly who are masters of servants; subsequently, however, he advises servants also how they should serve their masters. Therefore, he teaches the faithful subjects of the eternal king namely to be subject even to the powers of the world lest even in this the faith and the christian religion may be able to be slandered, because through [such slander] the rights of the human condition are disturbed. For what has been said, *to every human institution,* can even thus be properly understood as denoting both believing and unbelieving lords of things. **For the punishment of evildoers, but the praise of the**

76. Rm 13:1   77. Rm 13:2

good, not that all [rulers] because they are kings or his representatives know how either to punish evildoers or praise the good, but he is simply telling what ought to be the action of a good governor, that is, that he ought to restrain evildoers and reward those who behave properly. Even if he acts unjustly, if he condemns the good, nevertheless his actions redound to their praise if they bear patiently with his wickedness and wisely resist his foolishness. Hence Paul also says, If *you wish not to fear power, do good, and you will receive praise from it.*[78] He does not say, 'You will be praised for it', but, *You will receive praise from it,* because even though the worldly power does not praise you, indeed even if it persecutes you, if it slays you with the sword, as it did Paul, if it crucifies you, as it did Peter, you will receive praise for it from the fact that while it is acting wickedly against you who are righteous and innocent the virtue of your patience deserves the crown of praise.[79] For that blessed Peter also had this in mind in this context the following words show when it is said:

2:15 Because this is the will of God, that by doing what is right you put to silence the ignorance of foolish people. Therefore, this is the praise of the good for which he says that representatives are sent by the king, when the good use the ignorance of foolish governors for their own everlasting praise by doing what is right.

2:16–17 As free men and not as using your freedom as a cloak for maliciousness. They do what is right as free men who, the more they make use of greater freedom in the sight of men, the more narrowly, indeed the more freely, are they made subject to divine service. But then they also do well as free men who, following the example of the patriarch Joseph, although they are held captive in the service of men,

78. Rm 13:3   79. Aug., *Serm.* 302.13; PL 38:1389-90

are in no way forced to be servants of the vices.[80] But on the other hand they use their freedom as a cloak for maliciousness who, the less they are restrained by the yoke of human service, are the more widely set free for the oppression of sins, and when they become servants of vices with impunity, they call this freedom and cover up their fault under this name. This verse can be understood in a general way, however, according to the thought of the apostle Paul, *You have been called into freedom, brothers, only do not employ your freedom for an opportunity of the flesh.*[81] For we are rightly called free because we have been set free from the bonds of sin through baptism, because we have been redeemed from the slavery of the devil, because we have been made sons of God. Yet we do not receive with the gift of freedom a better opportunity and licence to sin. Indeed if we sin we soon lose our freedom and become slaves of sin, and whoever considers that he was set free by the Lord for this reason, that he might sin more freely, changes his freedom into a cloak for maliciousness. Blessed Peter, however, wishes us to be free from the slavery to our faults so that we can remain faithful servants of our good creator. Hence he subsequently adds, **But as servants of God honor all men, love the brotherhood, fear God, respect the king.** He advises us, therefore, to pay fitting honor to all and according to the Lord's command to render to Caesar what is Caesar's and to God what is God's.[82] And well among other things he orders free men to love the brotherhood, that they may recall that those who by their temporal condition are subject to them have also been made their brothers in Christ, calling upon him together with them as the *Father who judges without showing favoritism.*[83]

2:18 Slaves, be subject to your masters in all fear, not only to the good and restrained but also to the unrestrained. *To the unrestrained,* he says, to the unlearned.[3] This word

---

80. Gn 39:1-20   81. Ga 5:13   82. Mt 22:21   83. 1 P 1:17

has been derived from the Greek, because in Greek a school is called a place in which young people are accustomed to apply themselves to liberal studies and to have leisure for listening to teachers. Hence a school is interpreted as [a place of] leisure. Accordingly, in the psalm where we sing, *Be at leisure and see that I am God,*[84] where we say, *be at leisure,* there is found in Greek σχολάσατε. Therefore, scholars are learned, those who are unrestrained are unlearned and rough. But he wishes those who are servants to obey both kinds, explaining more openly how he has ordered us to be subject to every human institution. Another reading has 'difficult' for *unrestrained,* and the holy bishop Fulgentius in his writings has this, 'Serving with fear not only the good and restrained but also the more difficult'.[⁴]

2:20–21 But if in doing what is right and suffering you hold up, this is a grace from God. For you have been called for this, because Christ also suffered for us, leaving you an example, and so on. It must be noted most carefully how highly he glorifies the condition of servants who, in doing what is right and being beaten by cruel and wicked masters when they are blameless, he asserts are imitators of the Lord's passion. You hear, however, *Christ suffered for us,* and you rejoice, because Christ died for you. Pay attention to what follows, *leaving you an example that you may follow in his footsteps,* an example of tribulations, not of gratifications, of insults, scourgings, sorrows, taunts, thorns, the cross, wounds, death. It has been written in the psalm, *On account of the words of your lips I have kept hard ways.*[85] On account of what words of the lips of God, except those in which he promises eternal life?

2:24 He himself bore our sins in his body upon the wood. Although, above, he was addressing servants in particular,

84. Ps 46:10 (45:11)   85. Ps 17 (16):4

he now gives general advice that he may recall even to their masters' memory what the Lord God underwent for them. Indeed he instructs the entire Church on what its founder bore for its freedom. For he does not say, 'your sins', but including himself as well he says, *He himself bore our sins in his body upon the wood.*

2:25 For you were like wandering sheep. How does he call them *sheep* and *wandering* ones, when those who lead their life in error are reckoned goats rather than sheep,[86] except because *the Lord knows those who are his.*[87] He bears for a long time even with many who lead bad lives whom nonetheless he foresees are to be saved in the number of his sheep. **But you have been converted now to the shepherd and searcher[88] of your souls.** This resembles the Gospel parable where the devoted shepherd left the ninety-nine sheep in the desert and came to search for the one which had wandered off.[89] For what was said there, that after having found it he placed it joyfully on his shoulders,[90] blessed Peter anticipated by saying, *He himself bore our sins in his body upon the wood,* because surely he wished so much to redeem us that he would place on his shoulders the wood on which he took away our sins.[91] Therefore he says, *to the shepherd and searcher of your souls,* the shepherd, namely, because he gives us the pastures of eternal life, he provides pastures of temporal graces in the present; the searcher for our souls, however, because *the daystar from on high has searched us out, to enlighten those who sit in darkness and in the shadow of death.*[92] He searches daily by preserving that very light which he has given us that it may not fail, indeed by helping that it may increase. Certain manuscripts have the literal Greek, 'to the shepherd and overseer[5] of your souls'. For the Latin word 'overseer' means 'one who

---

86. Mt 25:33   87. 2 Tm 2:19   88. *visitator*   89. Lk 15:4
90. Lk 15:5   91. Jn 19:17   92. Lk 1:78-9

watches over',[6] because undoubtedly *the eyes of the Lord
are over the righteous and his ears [are open] to their
prayers,*[93] that *he* may *free them from all their tribulations.*[94]

**3:1 Likewise let wives also be subject to their husbands,
that if any do not believe the word they may be won over
without a word through the women's way of life,** and so on.
It must be noted that blessed Peter desires good and upright
women to be subject to unbelieving husbands with this condition, that not only do they do nothing evil at their command but also remain invincibly constant in so chaste a way
of life that they may be able to be an example of chastity
and faith even to these men.

**3:3 Let not their external adornment be their tresses or the
wearing of gold or the clothing of dresses,** because, as
Cyprian says, women clothed in silk or purple are not able to
put on Christ, those adorned with gold and pearls[95] and
jewels have lost the ornaments of their heart and breast.
He says:[96]

> 'But if', Peter says, 'women who are accustomed
> to excuse their adornments because of their hus-
> bands ought to be restrained and directed to church
> discipline by religious observance, how much more
> proper is it for a virgin to be careful to observe it;
> for her there is no excuse for adorning herself
> nor can the blame for her fault be placed on an-
> other but she alone is guilty?'

**3:4 But the person of a hidden life is one who is so in the
imperishableness of a quiet and restrained spirit, which is
wealth in God's sight.** He is preaching chastity and the

---

93. Ps 34:15 (33:16)   94. Ps 34:17 (33:18)   95. 1 Tm 2:9
96. Cypr., *Hab. virg.* 8; CSEL 3, 1: 193,26–194, 4

adornment of the inner man in the imperishability of a quiet
and restrained spirit, saying, so to speak, 'Since your outward
man has perished and you have ceased to have the happiness
of being inviolate, which is the characteristic of virgins, imitate the imperishability of the spirit through a continence
late in coming, and show in your mind what you have not
been able to show in your body; for Christ seeks these riches
and these adornments of your relationship'. It is astonishing
that even in [the philosophy of] Pythagoras, with only the
law of natural knowledge as guide, this thought is found, that
the real adornments of ladies are modesty, not clothing.

**3:7 Likewise husbands living together [with their wives]
according to knowledge, bestowing honor as on the weaker
womanly vessel.** He says, *Likewise,* urging husbands to imitation, because he had above admonished them already,
saying, Let husbands *regard your chaste way of life;*[97] *according to knowledge,* however, that they may know what God
desires and accord honor to the weaker womanly vessel. If
we abstain from sexual relations, we accord honor; if we do
not abstain, it is evident that sleeping together is contrary to
honor. **So that your prayers may not be hindered.** Paul also
says, *Do not refuse one another except perhaps by agreement
for a time, that you may have leisure for prayer.*[98] He mentions, therefore, that prayers are hindered by the conjugal
duty, because as often as I perform what is due my wife I am
not able to pray. But if according to another statement of
the apostle we must pray without ceasing,[99] I must therefore
never gratify my conjugal duty, lest I be hindered at any hour
from prayer, in which I am ordered always to persevere.

**3:8 All of you, however, be of one mind in faith, com-
passionate,** and so on. Because he was previously teaching
different persons, conditions, sexes, with the distinction

97. 1 P 3:2   98. 1 Co 7:5   99. 1 Th 5:17

befitting each, he now advises all to have one heart and mind[100] in the cause of their faith in the Lord.

3:9 Because for this you have been called, that you may possess a blessing as an inheritance, because namely the judge says, *Come, you blessed of my Father, receive the kingdom.*[101] The blessing of an inheritance can also be understood as that by which the Church blesses the Lord in the future life for ever. Hence even now in the hope of things to come it sings jubilantly, *I will exalt you, God, my king, and I will bless your name for ever and ever.*[102] Everyone, therefore, tries to meditate on and do in the present what he desires to find in the future, namely, both to bless his Creator and his neighbor with a sincere voice and to make himself also worthy of divine and fraternal blessing alike.

3:12 Because the eyes of the Lord are upon the righteous and his ears [are open] to their prayers; the face of the Lord, however, is against those who do evil. Because blessed Peter had forbidden us to render evil for evil—indeed he had ordered us to bless those who curse us[103] —he properly illustrates by the witness of the prophet[104] that both the good and the wicked are always seen by the observer from on high. He wants us to remember that both our patience, with which we put up with the evil [and], our good will, by which we desire good for our persecutors, are to be rewarded with an eternal reward and our persecutors are to be visited with a worthy punishment if they are unwilling to repent; but if they repent we also will receive from the Lord a crown of due congratulation for their salvation for which we prayed.

3:13 And who is there who may harm you if you are zealous for the good? He is speaking of those things that

---

100. Ac 4:32   101. Mt 25:34   102. Ps 145 (144):1
103. 1 P 3:9   104. Ps 34:15-16 (33:16-17)

come our way through insulting words from our adversaries, through losses of our temporal goods, through bodily afflictions. For these and all such things, when they are brought on the faithful, at least on those who are zealous for the good and this full knowingly, are in no wise able to harm them but rather provide a palm of patience to those who bear them unruffled, and contrariwise they do very much harm to those who bring them on by heaping up eternal punishment. But if anyone is overcome by adversities of this kind and becomes disheartened, it is not he who caused the evil who has harmed him, but he has harmed himself by refusing to bear this patiently. For the house that the wise man built did not fall because it did not hold up under the violence of the storms but because it was built upon a rock, nor again did that which the foolish man foolishly erected fall because it was struck by the storms but because it had been set upon sand;[105] for adversity beat upon and tested each one equally, but the strength of the foundation gave the crown of perseverance to the one, the foolishness of the fragile structure destroyed the other. For no disaster brought on either by the devil or by a wicked person or by the general upheaval of passing things can harm someone perfectly zealous for the good. Moreover, it is clear that very many of those who are zealous for the good have been harmed by others when they are badly instructed in the knowledge of the truth which they love. For of those yearning to believe in God according to the Catholic belief and to live righteously in the Church, how many did the madness of Arius deceive, how many the extravagance of Sabellius or other heretics when they were unaware? Read the book of John Chrysostom which he wrote about this, *No one can be harmed except by himself.*[7]

3:14   But if you suffer anything for righteousness' sake, you

105. Mt 7:24-7

will be blessed. Not only does he do you no harm who brings evils upon you when you do what is right, he says, but also even when an enemy attacks you for the good he denounces he provides you with a reason for greater happiness by testing the strength of your patience, according to that saying of the Gospel, *Blessed are they who suffer persecution for righteous' sake.*[106]

3:15 Make holy our Lord Jesus Christ in your hearts. What is it, to make the Lord holy in our hearts, except to consider in the innermost disposition[107] of our heart how his holiness is of unimaginable glory? This is our greatest protection against the deceit and violence of a terrifying enemy, namely, to reflect always on how much courage to overcome he can give to those who hope in him whose indescribable holiness shines forth. **Always ready to give a satisfactory account to him who demands from you the reason for the hope and faith that is in you.** In two ways ought we to give a reason for our hope and faith to those who demand it: both by communicating the due motives for our hope and faith to all who ask, whether believers or unbelievers; and by always keeping the profession of our faith and hope unimpaired even amidst the pressures of our adversaries, showing by our patience how reasonably we have learned that they are to be kept, for whose love we fear neither to suffer adversities nor undergo death.

3:15–16 But having a good conscience with restraint and fear. He advises that in this knowledge of doctrine the trait of teaching be observed, namely, that humility 'which is the mistress and mother of all virtues'[108] be spoken of in preaching and demonstrated in living, **that insofar as they slander you as evildoers, they may be put to shame who**

---

106. Mt 5:10   107. *affectus*
108. Greg., *Moral.* 23. 12. 24; PL 76:265B

who calumniate your good way of life in Christ, that those
who mock in you the faith and hope in heavenly things
which they cannot see may see your good deeds and be
put to shame by these, which they cannot deny are overtly
good. Or at least it ought to be interpreted thus, 'Take care
by doing what is right that those who slander your good way
of life may be put to shame when the time of the future
judgment comes, seeing you crowned with Christ while they
with the devil are condemned'.

**3:17 For it is better to suffer for doing what is right, if that
is God's will, than for doing what is wrong.** This statement
intentionally censures the foolishness of those who, when
they are censured for their faults by their brothers or even
restrained by punishment, bear it entirely patiently; but if
they suffer without fault, either verbal insults or loss of possessions or any adversities from their neighbors they quickly
give way to anger, and those who appeared blameless up to
this point, by their impatience and murmuring make themselves blameworthy. However, that the far unequal gap in
misfortune may be seen in unequal deserts, let us observe
that Tobit,[109] Saul[110] and Elymas[111] were struck by one
and the same hardship of blindness: but Tobit for the reason
that the virtue of his patience might shine more widely for
all as an example; Saul for the reason that Saul the persecutor
might be changed into Paul the apostle; Elymas that paying
the due penalty for his treachery he might cease from his
attempt to confuse those who had also been on the point of
believing. And if the choice were given me, I should prefer
as a righteous man to be subjected to divine or human
scourging with so great a father than by the force of scourging to be dragged from unrighteousness to the pursuit of
righteousness, and again I should prefer to be dragged back
from faults by misfortune than to be forced to undergo

109. Tb 1:1 ff.   110. Ac 9:1 ff.   111. Ac 13:8-11

eternal punishment for the incurable weight of sins.

3:18 Because Christ also died once for our sins, the righteous for the unrighteous. Therefore, he who is righteous and suffers, imitates Christ; he who is corrected by misfortune imitates the thief who on the cross recognized Christ and after the cross entered paradise with Christ;[112] he who in the midst of misfortunes does not cease from his faults imitates the thief on the left who mounted the cross for his sins and after the cross went headlong to the lower world.[113] He recalls that Christ died once, however, to bring to our memory also that an eternal reward will be granted for our short-lived sufferings. **That he might offer us to God, having been put to death indeed in the body but made alive in the spirit.** About this being put to death in the body and made alive in the spirit which they have who labor for the Lord through patience, the apostle Paul also says, *Although our outward man is wasting away, yet he who is within is being renewed from day to day.*[114] Christ therefore offers us to God the Father when through being put to death in the body we rejoice at being sacrificed for him, that is, he shows that in the sight of the Father our life is praiseworthy. Or at least he offers us to God when he brings us, freed from the body, into the eternal kingdom. To be sure, Saint Athanasius, bishop of Alexandria, relates what is said, *but made alive in the spirit,* not to the spirit of man—which, when the body has been put to death, is quickened in a better way, since the prophet says of the Lord, *That he may quicken the spirit of the humble and quicken the heart of the contrite*[115] —but rather to the grace of the Holy Spirit who bestows eternal life on those who put their bodies to death. For he uses this as a witness also against the Arians who deny the equality of the Holy Trinity, explaining that by their undivided unity

112. Lk 23:33-43   113. Lk 23:33-9   114. 2 Co 4:16
115. Is 57:15

of divine operation the Father quickens, the Son quickens, the Holy Spirit quickens; the Father and Son, namely, because it has been written, For just as the Father raises up and makes the dead to live, so the Son also quickens those whom he will,[7] the Holy Spirit, however, as is made clear in this witness in which it is said of the Son, *That he might offer us to God, having been put to death indeed in the body but quickened in the spirit,* and therefore the substance or essence of those whose operation is one cannot be unequal.[9]

3:19–20 Coming at this time in the spirit, he preached also to those who had been shut up in the body, who had formerly been unbelievers. He who coming in the body in our times preached to the world the way of life, he also coming in the spirit before the flood preached to those who had then been unbelievers and had lived for the body. For through the Holy Spirit he was in Noah and the rest of the saints who lived then and through their good way of life he preached to the wicked men of that age, that they might be converted to better things. For he calls shut up in the body those who were fiercely weighed down by bodily desires. Hence Scripture says of them that *every body had corrupted its way.*[116] For what he says, *at this time,* applies to the time of which he had spoken previously, *That he might offer us to God,* because even then if any had wished to believe at the Lord's preaching, which he manifested through the life of the faithful, he rejoiced to offer them also to God the Father, if any, however, slandered the good as evildoers[117] these were put to shame at the coming of the flood. For what he says, *at this time,* that is, *Coming at this time in the spirit, he preached also to those who had been shut up in the body,* can also be understood of both [classes], that through his same preaching might arise both the crown of praise for those who believed and confusion for those who had persisted in

116. Gn 6:12   117. 1 P 2:12, 3:16

their unbelief. Certain manuscripts have, 'Coming at this time in the spirit, he preached also to those who were in prison'.[¹⁰] This applies to the same intent of the crooked and unbelievers who, since they have their apprehension obscured by darkness, are rightly said to have been shut up in prison even in this life. They are weighed down in this prison, namely, still in interior darkness, that is, in the blindness of their mind and in unrighteous works, until being freed from their body they are cast out into exterior darkness and into the prison of eternal damnation about which the Lord says in the Gospel, *And the judge shall hand you over to the guard and you shall be sent to prison.*[118] Although even the saints, when they thirst for the joy of the fatherland on high, may rightly cry out that they are placed in prison in this life, according to the saying of the psalmist, *Bring my soul out of prison, that I may confess your name.*[119] But indeed there is a great difference between each type of prison, for the condemned are in the prison of sins and ignorance, but the righteous, with their heart open to God, even though placed in the prison of tribulations, always enjoy the light of righteousness, which the apostles Paul and Barnabas showed when, although bound in the middle of the night in the innermost terror of a prison and scourged, they sang a hymn of praise to God with a very happy voice.[120] A certain person has interpreted this passage as follows, that the saints resting in the lower world longed for that consolation about which the Lord says to his apostles, *Many prophets and righteous persons have longed to see what you see and did not see it and to hear what you hear and did not hear it,*[121] about which the psalmist also says, *My eyes have failed at your message, saying, 'When will you comfort me,'*[122] and that this consolation and encouragement was preached by the Lord when he went down into the lower world even to those

118. Mt 5:25   119. Ps 142:7 (141:8)   120. Ac 16:25
121. Mt 13:17   122. Ps 119 (118):82

who were in prison and were once in the days of Noah
unbelievers. He may have said this. But the Catholic faith
holds that when the Lord went down into the lower world
and brought his own out from there, it was the faithful alone
and not unbelievers whom he took with him to the heavenly
kingdom; and to the souls that had put off their bodies and
were condemned in the prison of the lower world he did not
preach the salvation which they had neglected before their
death but daily either through himself or through the
example of his followers or through the words of the faithful
shows the path of life to those who are shut up in the prison
of their crimes in this life. It is well said about these:

**3:20 Who had formerly been unbelievers, when the pa-
tience of God was waiting in the days of Noah, when the ark
was being constructed.** For that very patience of God was
also his preaching, when Noah, pressing on with the work on
the ark for a hundred years,[11] showed by the daily performance of the work what was to happen to the world.
Hence Paul says, *Do you not know that the patience of God
is leading you to repentance?* and so on.[123] Another translation has this passage as follows: 'Christ died once for our
sins, the righteous for the unrighteous, that he might
lead[12] us to God, being put to death in the body but made
alive[13] in spirit; this spirit[14] he preached also to those who
had formerly been unbelievers, when the patience of God was
waiting in the days of Noah', and so on.

**3:20–21 In which a few, that is, eight souls were saved
through water. Baptism, of which this was the type, now
saves you also.** He calls the type of baptism similar to the ark
and the waters of the flood, and quite properly, because the
very construction of the ark from smooth planks[124] signifies
also the building of the Church which comes about by the

123. Rm 2:4   124. Gn 6:14

collection of the souls of the faithful by the architects of the word. And that a few, that is, eight souls were saved through water when the entire world was perishing, indicates that the number of the elect, compared with that of the perishing gentiles, Jews, heretics and false faithful, is much smaller. Hence of the narrow gate and difficult way *that leads to life* it is said, *And few are they who find it;*[125] and again, *Do not fear, little flock, because it has been pleasing to your Father to give you the kingdom.*[126] Here also about this little flock there has appropriately been added, **Not the removal of the body's dirt but as the examination of a good conscience for God.** For where is a good conscience except where there is sincere faith? For the apostle Paul teaches that *the purpose of the commandment is charity from a pure heart and a good conscience and unfeigned faith.*[127] The fact, therefore, that the water of the flood did not save those outside the ark but slew them without doubt prefigured every heretic who, although having the sacrament of baptism, is to be plunged into the lower world not by other waters but by those very waters by which the ark is raised up to the heavens. The number eight itself of the souls which were saved through water also signifies that the holy Church receives the washing of baptism through the mystery of the Lord's resurrection, that just as he rose *from the dead through the glory of the Father, so we also,* cleansed from sins through the water of rebirth, *may walk in newness of life.*[128] For when the Lord rose from the dead on the eighth day,[15] that is, after the seventh day, the sabbath, he showed us both an example of the future resurrection and the mystery of the new way of life by which we, though still situated on earth, might live a heavenly life. Peter also, by way of explaining this, himself adds, saying:

3:21–22 Through the resurrection of Jesus Christ who,

125. Mt 7:14   126. Lk 12:32   127. 1 Tm 1:5   128. Rm 6:4

having gone into heaven, is at the right hand of God, swallowing up death, that we might become sharers of eternal life. For just as he rose from the dead and ascended into heaven and sits at the right hand of God, so also he signified that through baptism the way to salvation and the entrance to the heavenly kingdom was open to us. He does well, however, to say, *swallowing up death,* for what we swallow we cause by the action of our body to be assimilated that it may never perish. And the Lord swallowed up death which, rising from the dead, he so completely consumed that it would have no further power over him through the touch of any corruption; and while the outward appearance of his real body remained, all trace, in a word, of former frailty would be absent. It is promised that this will happen also to us in the end when the apostle says, speaking of our resurrection, *Then will come to pass the saying which has been written, 'Death is absorbed in victory.'*[129] [He does] well [to say] *absorbed,* because when we also have been made sharers in eternal life, the power* of our immortal body undoubtedly removes all taint of past corruption in the same way as a flame by the power of its heat is accustomed to consume a drop of water that is put in it. **Having gone into heaven,** he says, **with the angels and authorities and powers and made subject to him.** No one can doubt that the angels and all the authorities and powers of the heavenly fatherland were always subject to the Son of God, whom with the Father and the Holy Spirit they praise as the one God without beginning, tremble before, and adore. But blessed Peter judged it necessary to caution that his assumed humanity in rising was lifted up to such height of glory that by an inestimable eminence it is set above all rank of angelic dignity, according to what the psalmist also, when he was speaking about the Father, *You have made him a little less than the angels,* immediately added, *You have crowned him with glory and honor and you*

129. 1 Co 15:54   *virtus

have established him above the works of your hands, you have placed all things under his feet.[130]

4:1 Since Christ, therefore, suffered in his body, you also be armed with the same thought. After he had explained the example of the Lord's resurrection and our cleansing which comes about in baptism from the mystery of the ark and the flood, he returns to what he had started to say, that imitating the work of our Redeemer in the midst of the good that we should patiently put up with the wickedness of evildoers. It must be noted, however, how definite he is when he says, *Since Christ, therefore, suffered in his body,* because as Saint Ambrose says,[131]

> His body suffered but his divinity was free from death; his body yielded to suffering by the law of human nature. Can the divinity, then, die, when the soul cannot? *Do not fear those,* he says, *who slay the body but cannot slay the soul.*[132] If, therefore, the soul cannot be slain, how can the divinity?

4:1–2 Because he who has suffered in the body has ceased from sins, that he may live now for the remaining time in the body not by human desires but by the will of God. Any of the saints who has subjected his body to the violence of the persecutors for martyrdom has without doubt kept from sinning to the end of his life, as far as this is humanly possible. For how could anyone who was affixed to wood or surrounded by the blows from stones or exposed to the nibbling of beasts or set on flames of fires or flayed by the excruciating lash or weakened by any other kind of punishment think about committing sin, about bodily desires; what could he turn over in his mind except the will of God? He

130. Ps 8:5-6 (8:6-8)   131. Ambr., *De fide* 2. 7. 57; PL 16:571B
132. Mt 10:28

was compelled to desire this alone, when with the contest over he would receive the crown of life. Blessed Peter, therefore, wants us always to imitate the mind of such persons when, after bringing forward the example of the Lord's passion, he admonishes us to be armed with the same thought against the wickedness of evil and against the allurements of the vices. He wants it to be understood that if we put on the garb of patience even while we are at rest [in times] when the Church is at peace, with the Lord's help we easily avoid the faults of sins and subdue all human desires to the commands of the divine will. Accordingly, the psalmist also entreats the Lord, saying, *Pierce my body with fear of you, for I have been afraid of your judgments;*[133] and the apostle says, *Those, therefore, who are Christ's, have crucified their body with its vices and concupiscences.*[134] The one, therefore, who because of fear of the heavenly judgment has rid himself of bodily concupiscences in his mind, being now like the person crucified and suffering for Christ and, as it were, dead to sins, lives only for the service of God.

4:4 In this they wonder that you do not join them in the same shame of self-indulgence, blaspheming. Because you have crucified your body with its vices and concupiscences, he says, it comes about truly that, although in their perfidy they blaspheme you as separated from their companionship, yet they always see in your way of life the works of righteousness and devotion which they rightly wonder at and for which they justifiably praise and venerate the christian faith.

4:5 They will render an account to him who is ready to judge the living and the dead. Therefore, he says, be less concerned, be less sorrowful, if when you do what is right you are blasphemed by the condemned, because although

133. Ps 119 (118):120   134. Ga 5:24

you are silent, *God,* who is certainly *a righteous judge,*[135] nonetheless will not be silent and hold his peace.[136] He will bestow worthy rewards both on them for their blasphemy and on you for your patience.

4:6 For this is why the Gospel was preached even to the dead, that they might be judged indeed like human beings in the body but might live according to God's [ordinances] in the spirit. God has such great concern, such great love, such great desire that we be put to death in the body but quickened in the spirit, that he has commanded [us] to preach the Gospel, the word of faith, to those also who are implicated in greater crimes and justifiably must be accounted among the dead, namely, because of their *self-indulgence, desires, insobriety, gluttony, drunkenness and unlawful worship of idols,*[137] since even they, when they have passed judgment on, that is, rejected and put aside, their bodily desires, may be alive spiritually and may look for eternal life together with those whom the grace of the Gospel finds living innocently.

4:7 For the end of all things will approach. So that no one might deceive himself in thinking that the future judgement, in which he had said that the living and the dead are to be judged, is far off, he advisedly warns that, although the time of the arrival of the final judgment is indefinite, yet it is definitely clear to all that they are unable to continue for long in this mortal life. **Accordingly, be prudent and watchful in prayers.** In the Gospel, in view of the indefinite time of the end, the Lord has also admonished us to pray always and to be watchful. For he says, speaking of the day of judgment, *Accordingly, be watchful at all times, praying that you may be held worthy of escaping all those things which are to come and*

135. Ps 7:11 (7:12)   136. Ps 83:1 (82:2)
137. 1 P 4:3

standing before the Son of Man.[138] It is well that we are
ordered to be watchful in prayers, that when we stand for
prayer all bodily and worldly thought may depart and the
mind may then think of nothing else than that alone for
which it is praying. For frequently the enemy creeps in and,
cunningly deceiving us, draws our prayers away from God, so
that we may have one thing in our heart and express another
with our voice, when it is not the sound of the voice but the
awareness of the mind which ought to pray to God with sincere intention.

**4:8   Above all, however, having a mutual and lasting love for
one another.** He does well to add, *lasting,* because we are always able to love but we are not always able to be watchful
in prayers, because the frailty of our body stands in the way.
We are scarcely able constantly to perform those virtuous
actions, that is, hospitality, teaching, providing ordinary or
spiritual graces for our neighbors, and other things of this
sort, because it is surely necessary that the doing of these
things undoubtedly depends both upon the capacity of the
body and timely opportunities. But charity itself, at whose
prompting these things are carried out exteriorly, because it
rules over the inner man, can always be held in the same
place, although it cannot always be manifested in public.
Because charity covers a multitude of sins, particularly insofar
as a person says truthfully to God, *And forgive us our debts
as we forgive our debtors.*[139] And indeed all the good works
we perform wipe away and cover the faults which we commit,
but this is said particularly about charity by which we grant
to our neighbors those things which are due us, because it is
most righteous in the sight of God that it be measured out to
us according to the measure of devotion with which we have
measured,[140] just as, on the other hand, the wise man censures
the hard-hearted, saying, *Does a person harbor anger for*

138. Lk 21:36   139. Mt 6:12   140. Mk 4:25

another and seek healing from God?[141] And we must not doubt that in the case of the person who also acts through charity, as far as he can, for the correction of his neighbor by advising, rebuking, chastising, charity itself covers a multitude of sins according to the witness of James who says, *Whoever has brought a sinner back from the error of his way will save his soul from death and covers a multitude of sins.*[142]

4:11 If anyone speaks, [let it be] like the words of God, fearing, namely, lest he say or command anything contrary to the will of God or to what is clearly ordered in the holy scriptures and be found as a false witness of God or sacrilegious or bringing in anything foreign to the teaching of the Lord or at least abandoning or passing over any of the things pleasing to God, when he very clearly orders the preachers of the truth concerning those whom they were instructing, *Teaching them to observe everything that I have commanded you.*[143] For he orders them to pass on to their listeners to be observed both the things which he himself commanded, not other things, and these things not in part but in their entirety. **If anyone serves, [let it be] as it were from the power that God provides.** Let everyone be more humble in offering his neighbor the good he can, the more clearly he knows that he cannot have of himself what he is offering. **That in all things God may be honored through Jesus Christ,** according to the commandment of Jesus Christ himself where he says, *Let them see your good works and glorify your Father who is in heaven.*[144] God is honored in our actions, therefore, when everything we do that is right and according to his will we attribute not to our own deserts but to his grace, but on the contrary we ascribe the evils that we commit only to our own malice or sloth or ignorance.

4:12 Dearly beloved, do not wonder at the fiery ordeal that

141. Si 28:3   142. Jm 5:20   143. Mt 28:20   144. Mt 5:16

comes to you for a temptation. Certain manuscripts have, 'Do not go astray in your fiery ordeal'. The meaning of both, however, is clear: that none of the faithful ought to wonder why he suffers the fiery ordeal of temptations in this life when he is now being tempted by tribulations for a definite reason so that after he has been tested he may be held worthy of receiving the crown of the future life;[145] nor ought anyone think that he is a straggler and stranger to the members of Christ because he is beset by the adversities of the present time, when *both to the Lord belongs escape from death,*[146] and in his Church persecution at the hands of unbelievers has never ceased from the first martyr, 'Abel, to the last one of the elect who is going to be born at the end of time'.[147] Hence, when he had said, **Do not wonder at the fiery ordeal,** he did well to add, **as if something new were happening to you,** because it is very ancient and constant for the elect of God to bear the adversities of the present life for eternal salvation.

4:15 **For let none of you suffer as a murderer or a thief or a reviler.** For he suffers as a reviler who at the time of his suffering is unrestrained even while undergoing wrong from his persecutor.

4:17 **For it is time for judgment to begin from the house of God.** There are two judgments of God recorded by the scriptures, one hidden, the other manifest. The hidden judgment is the punishment by which every human being is either now being tried that he may be chastened, or cautioned, that he may be converted, or if he despises the call and discipline of God, blinded for condemnation. The manifest judgment, however, is when the Lord will come to judge the living and the dead. But it is said that now is the time for judgment to begin

145. Jm 1:12   146. Ps 68:20 (67:21)
147. Greg., *Hom. ev.* 1. 19. 1; PL 76: 1154B

from the Lord's house, that is, from the Church, which is being prepared for future joys by being faced with present afflictions. Yet the condemned are leading their transition life now much more securely and without any infliction of chastisement as is proportionate to the chastisement that awaits them in the future, according to the saying of blessed Job, *They spend their days in good things and in a moment they go down to the lower world.*[148] **But if [it begins] first with us, what [will be] the end of those who do not believe the Gospel of God?** From this is gathered with what severity the strict Judge will deal with those whom he condemns, if here he so torments those whom he loves. For if the sons are scourged, what ought the very wicked servants to hope for?

4:18 And if the righteous person is saved with difficulty, where will the wicked and sinner appear? The Pelagians are unwilling to believe that the whole mass of the human race was corrupted and condemned in one man. It is the grace of Christ alone that cures and frees from this corruption and condemnation. For why will the righteous be saved with difficulty? Is it a labor for God to set free the righteous? Far from it. But to show that [our] nature was rightly condemned the Omnipotent himself does not wish to set [us] free easily from so great an evil, because sins are easy to slip into and righteousness is strenuous, except for those who love; but charity, which makes them lovers, is of God. It must be noted, however, that blessed Peter has taken this statement from the Proverbs of Solomon according to the ancient edition at least, in place of which in our edition, that has come from the original Hebrew source, it is written, *If the righteous receives [retribution] on earth, how much more the wicked and sinner?*[149] This is to say clearly, 'If the frailty of mortal life is so great that not even the righteous who are to be crowned in heaven pass through this life

148. Jb 21:13   149. Pr 11:31

without tribulations on account of the countless slips of [our] flawed nature, how much more do those who are cut off from heavenly grace await the certain outcome of their everlasting damnation?'

5:1 Therefore I, a fellow elder and witness of the sufferings of Christ, entreat the elders among you, a witness, namely, insofar as he was present and stood near while He was suffering and saw everything as it was occurring, or at least because he himself also suffered prison, chains, and scourging for the name of Christ, as we read in the Acts of the Apostles.[150] **Who am also a sharer in his glory that is to be revealed in the future,** then, undoubtedly, when he saw the heavenly glory of His countenance on the holy mountain with James and John,[151] or when he saw the power of His resurrection and ascension with the other disciples who were present.[152]

5:2 Feed the flock of God that is among you. Just as the Lord ordered blessed Peter to take care of his entire flock,[153] that is, the Church, so Peter himself justifiably commands the succeeding pastors of the Church to protect with careful government that flock that each has with him. **Looking out for them not by constraint but willingly, according to God.** He feeds the flock of God and looks out for it by constraint who, on account of his lack of temporal means, does not have the wherewithal to live and for that reason preaches the Gospel that he may be able to live from the Gospel;[154] but he [does so] willingly and according to God who preaches the word of God with an eye to no earthly consideration but only to reward from on high. The apostle Paul distinguishes each of these from the other when he says, *For if I do this voluntarily, I have my reward, but if unwillingly, a commission has been entrusted to me.*[155] A commission, in truth,

150. Ac 5:40, 12:3-4   151. Mt 17:12
152. Mt 28:16-20, Mk 16:14-19, Lk 24:12-51, Jn 20:19-23
153. Jn 21:15-17   154. 1 Co 9:14   155. 1 Co 9:17

is said to have been entrusted to him who is commanded to have care of an external matter for a time, for example, the person who is ordered to distribute his master's grain to his fellow servants on time.[156] Anyone who preaches the Gospel not willingly but unwillingly is likened to him. **Not for the sake of base gain but from choice.** He looks out for the flock of God for the sake of base gain who preaches for profit and earthly advantages, when the works of religion ought all to be done willingly, in accord with that example of the building of the tabernacle which foreshadowed the present building of the Church. There, both *all the multitude of the sons of Israel with resolute and faithful mind offered the first fruits for the Lord for carrying out the work of the tabernacle,*[157] providing *everything of their own free will,*[158] and the *workmen offered themselves freely for the carrying out of the work.*[159]

5:3 Not as lording it over the [lesser] clerics but having become a pattern for the flock in your mind, that namely you yourselves may first both show in your action and preserve in your blameless mind the humility that you desire those subject to you to have both towards you and towards each other, according to that saying of the Lord, *You know that those who appear to rule over the gentiles lord it over them and their rulers have power over them; it is not so, however, with you, but whoever wishes to become greater will be your minister, and whoever among you wishes to be first will be the servant of all.*[160] Paul, carefully exercising this kind of authority, says, *For we preach not ourselves but Jesus Christ our Lord, us, however, as your servants through Jesus.*[161]

5:5 Likewise young men be subject to the elders. After he

---

156. Lk 12:42   157. Ex 35:20-21   158. Ex 35:26
159. Ex 36:2   160. Mk 10:42-4   161. 2 Co 4:5

taught the elders how to be in charge, it was fitting that he
also instruct the younger in obeying their paternal guidance.
There was no need, however, to speak to them at length but
only to give the command of submission, because surely,
once he had commanded the elders to become a pattern for
their subjects it was enough for the younger ones to pay
attention to the example of the well-behaved elders and
imitate it faithfully. But lest on hearing this those in charge
might consider that the practice of due humility was
to be observed only towards their subjects and not also
towards their peers, he immediately added by way of
general admonition: **All, however, manifest humility
towards one another.** And indeed he says *all,* both
elders and young men, who are both ordered to manifest the virtue of humility towards each other, the
former, namely, by ruling and the latter by obeying humbly.
We read that this was done for Peter himself and by him
when, as he was entering Caesarea, Cornelius came to meet
him and prostrated himself humbly at his feet, and he more
humbly *raised him up, saying, 'Arise, for indeed I am a man
just like yourself';*[162] and indeed Cornelius was not yet
reborn in Christ nor yet incorporated into the Church. He
teaches all, therefore, to manifest humility towards one
another either by example or also by word; because
undoubtedly he knew that the vice of pride which cast the
angels out of heaven must be avoided by all, he wholesomely
frightens and heartens all by adding a statement of Solomon
and saying, **Because God resists the proud but gives grace to
the humble.**[163] And he explains what is this grace which God
bestows on the humble when he subsequently adds and
advises:

**5:6 Be humbled, therefore, beneath the mighty hand of
God, that he may exalt you at the time of his visitation.** He

162. Ac 10:26   163. Pr 3:34 (LXX), Jm 4:6

grants this grace, therefore, to the humble, that the more they have been humbled for his sake at the time of the contest, the more gloriously they may be exalted by him at the time of reward. Humiliation, however, can be understood in this place in several ways, that is, both as that by which everyone beginning the way of the virtues is wholesomely cleansed for the washing away of the sins he has committed, and as that which is shown with a glad affirmation of mind by those more advanced for God's and our neighbor's sake during the peace of current circumstances, and as that with which the mind is armed and made invincible by the virtue of patience when the whirlwinds of persecution are blowing. That reward, however, follows every kind of humility faithful to God, that those who humble themselves during the time they are travelers are exalted at the time of his visitation.

5:8 Be sober, watchful, because your adversary, the devil, goes around like a roaring lion, seeking whom he may devour. In explaining this thought let us use not our own but the words of blessed Cyprian:[164]

> He goes around us individually, and like an enemy besieging those shut up, he examines the walls and explores whether there may be some part of our members less firm and less trustworthy, by entrance through which a way inside may be effected. He offers to the eyes unlawful appearances and seductive pleasures, that he may destroy purity through sight; he tempts the ears by harmonious music, that he may get rid of and weaken christian strength by the hearing of a pleasant sound; he arouses the tongue to reviling, he urges the hand to capricious murder when it is excited by injuries; he provides unjust gains, that he may make a cheat; he piles up dangerous profits, that he may ensnare the

164. Cypr., *De Zelo* 10.2-3; CC 3A: 75,20-76, 37

soul by money; he promises earthly honors, that
he take away heavenly ones; he manifests false
values, that he may steal away the true. And when
he is not able to deceive secretly, he threatens
clearly and openly, bringing forward the fear of
a violent persecution in order to overcome the
servants of God; always restless and always hostile;
[he is] cunning in peace, violent in persecution.
Wherefore, the mind ought to stand drawn up and
armed against either the deceitful traps or open
threats of the devil, always as ready to resist as the
enemy is always ready to attack.

**5:9 Stand up against him, strong in faith, knowing that the
same suffering happens to those of your brotherhood who
are in the world.** Be so much stronger in faith, he says, have
that much more confidence in your ability to overcome the
wiles of the devil, the more it is clear that it is not you alone
who are being tempted, but that the very suffering which
wearies you is shared also by the Church of Christ which is
throughout the entire world, your brotherhood, namely.
And let it be a matter of shame that you, above all, are not
able to bear with what the righteous have always suffered
from the creation of the world.

**5:12 I have written to you briefly by Silvanus, a faithful
brother, as I think, entreating and calling to witness that this
is the true grace.** What he says, *entreating,* can be both
related to what has preceded, because namely he wrote to
them briefly not commanding but entreating them to remain
strong in their faith, and properly joined to what follows,
that he may be understood as not only calling them to witness that this is their true grace which he preaches by
writing, because undoubtedly *there is salvation in no one else
in which it is fitting for us to be saved,*[165] but also as

165. Ac 4:12

entreating them to make their own this true grace in which they have been initiated in Christ. For the grace of Christ becomes the grace of those who accept it with a pure heart; for the person who rejects the grace of Christ does not lessen this grace but causes it not to be his, that is, he causes it to be of no advantage to him.

5:13 The church which is in Babylon, also elected, and my son Mark greet you. He speaks of Rome typologically as Babylon,[166] namely on account of the confusion[167] of her many different kinds of idolatry. Holy Church shone in her midst, then now unlettered and very small, according to the example of the people of Israel which once, being small in number and a captive, sat beside the rivers of Babylon and wept for the absence of the holy land and was not able to sing the Lord's canticle in a foreign land.[168] Blessed Peter, while he is encouraging his hearers to put up with present adversities, does well to speak also of the church which is established with him in Babylon, that is, in the confusion of tribulations, and yet he affirms that it is also chosen, that he may show that the holy city of God cannot be immune in this life from association with and persecution from the city of the devil, which Babylon signifies. He says that Mark the Evangelist is his son, who is said to have been made his son in baptism. Hence it is evident that he wrote the Letter before sending Mark from Rome to Alexandria to preach the Gospel. Peter and Mark both came to Rome during the time of the emperor Claudius and Mark himself, having written his Gospel at Rome, was sent to Alexandria. Hence it is gathered that when it is asked where and when Peter wrote this Letter, the place was Rome, the time that of Claudius Caesar.

5:14 Greet one another in a holy kiss, *a holy kiss,* a true

166. Jer., *Vir. ill.* 8; TU 14:12, 10/19
167. Jer., *Nom. Hebr.;* CC 72: 62, 18   168. Ps 137 (136):1-4

kiss, a peaceful kiss, a dove's kiss, not with a hypocritical, treacherous, dishonorable one, such as Joab used to slay Amasa,[169] such as Judas used to betray the saviour,[170] such as they use *who speak peace with their neighbor, but there are evil things in their hearts.*[171] Therefore, they greet one another with a holy kiss who *love not in word or with the tongue but in deed and truth.*[172] **Grace to you all who are in Christ Jesus.** He began the Letter with grace, he finished it in grace, he scattered grace throughout the middle of it, that he might condemn the error of Pelagius with every part of his speech but teach that the Church of Christ cannot be saved except through His grace. And when he said, *Grace to you,* advisedly he added, *all [of you] who are in Christ Jesus,* that he might show that those things which he wrote to the small churches, that is, of Pontus, Galatia, Cappadocia, Asia [Minor] and Bithynia, he wrote to all the churches of Christ throughout the world. In the same way John, too, when in the Apocalypse he was warning the seven churches of Asia [Minor] individually, as was necessary, added to each in conclusion this, *He who has ears, let him hear what the spirit says to the churches.*[173] He was clearly implying that everything that he wrote to each individual church he wrote for all who had salvation-bearing hearing and that he was writing to all the churches of the faithful.

169. 2 S 20:9-10   170. Mt 26:49   171. Ps 28 (27):3
172. 1 Jn 3:18   173. Rv 2:7,11,17,29; 3:6,13,22

NOTES TO COMMENTARY ON 1 PETER

1. Latin *claritas* and *gloria.*

2. This allegorical use of the literal meaning of Hebrew proper names was adopted by Bede from a short treatise of Saint Jerome, *De nominibus Hebraicis* (*CC* 72: 143, 28/29). Jerome got the idea of Jewish proper names having a mystical or fuller meaning from the Bible itself, where names of persons or places frequently indicate some function or historical action.

3. In his attempt to explain the meaning of the word in Latin, *discolis,*—here translated 'unrestrained' to fit into the context and to contrast with the preceding Latin word *modestis,* 'restrained'—Bede has recourse to a Latin synonym *indisciplinatis,* 'unlearned'. He then tries to show that *discolis* has as its root the Greek word *scholē* (Latin *scola*) that literally means 'leisure' or 'school' as a place of leisure to learn. So, *discolis* ends up meaning 'unrestrained' in the sense of 'unlearned' or 'rough'.

4. This quotation from Fulgentius where *discolis* is rendered into Latin by *difficilioribus* ('more difficult') I have not been able to locate among his writings.

5. Greek *episkopon,* Latin *episcopum.* While both the Greek and Latin words are frequently translated 'bishop' and indeed have philologically given us the English word 'bishop', Bede uses the literal meaning of the Greek word, 'overseer'. This is apparent from the Latin he gives as a synonym for *episcopus.* See the following note.

6. Latin *superintendens*

7. The title of a short treatise by Saint John Chrysostom.

8. An unidentified quotation, presumably from sacred scripture.

9. I have not been able to find this rather lengthy quotation among the writings of Saint Athanasius. Obviously, Bede got it at second hand from some other Latin writer, since no known Latin translation of Athanasius' Greek works existed during Bede's lifetime.

10. Latin *carcere,* 'prison', an alternative reading in place of the previous Latin *carne,* 'body'.

11. Bede was always intensely interested in chronology. The book of Genesis does not say that it took Noah a hundred years to build the

ark, but Bede probably arrived at this number from Gn 5:32, where it says that Noah was five hundred years old when he begot Shem, Ham and Japheth, and Gn 7:6, where it states that Noah was six hundred years old when the flood came; the intervening section, Gn 6:1–7:5, deals with the actual building of the ark.

12. Latin *adducat*, 'lead', in place of the previous reading *offerret*, 'offer'.

13. The Latin here has *mortificatus*, 'put to death', and *vivificatus*, 'made alive', in the nominative case, modifying Christ, whereas the earlier Latin reading used by Bede had *mortificatos* and *vivificatos* in the accusative case plural, modifying *nos*, 'us'.

14. Latin *in quo spiritu*, in place of the previous Latin text, *in quo [tempore]*, 'at this time'. In the earlier Latin text adopted by Bede the word *spiritu*, 'in the spirit', occurred farther down the line, modifying the Latin participle *veniens*, which is omitted in this particular Latin version of the passage in question. The use of the word *spiritus*, 'spirit', here probably is as a synonym for 'soul', referring to the fact that the soul of Jesus, separated from his body after his death, went down to the lower world to proclaim the good news of salvation to the souls of the righteous who had lived and died before Jesus' time.

15. This idea of the eighth day, that is, the day following the sabbath or Saturday, the final day of creation when God rested, indicating the unending day of eternal happiness and repose in heaven, is very prevalent throughout patristic writing.

COMMENTARY ON 2 PETER

1:1 **S**IMON PETER, a servant and apostle of Jesus Christ, to those who have obtained a faith of equal standing to ours. It has been written in what follows of this Letter, *Look, dearly beloved, I am writing this second Letter to you.*[1] Hence it is clear that he wrote this Letter to the same ones to whom he had also sent the former Letter, to the elect newcomers of the dispersion in Pontus, Galatia, Cappadocia, Asia [Minor] and Bithynia,[2] whom he recognizes as of equal standing with himself, not because they had received circumcision according to the law, which he had, being by nature a Jew, but because they obtained the same faith as he himself had received from the enlightening grace of Jesus Christ. For it is not legal circumcision but gospel faith alone that joins the peoples of the gentiles to the ancient people of God. Yet, because the same faith without works is not able to save, there is properly appended: **In the righteousness of our Lord and saviour, Jesus Christ.** Therefore, the apostle Peter writes a Letter to, he greets, those who have obtained a faith that is of equal standing with his and practise it through the works of righteousness, that righteousness, namely, which human prudence does not discover or legal custom teach but which our Lord and Saviour shows when, speaking through the Gospel, he says, *Unless your righteousness exceeds that of the scribes and Pharisees, you shall not enter into the kingdom of heaven;*[3] and again, *You have heard that it has been said to the ancients,*[4] *but I say to you.*[5]

1. 2 P 3:1   2. 1 P 1:1   3. Mt 5:20   4. Mt 5:21   5. Mt 5:22

1:2 **May grace and peace be fulfilled for you in the knowledge of our Lord Jesus Christ.** In the first Letter he wrote,
May grace and peace be multiplied for you,[6] but in this one,
May grace and peace be fulfilled for you, because undoubtedly
he wrote that Letter for beginners, this one for the more perfect. For peace and grace are multiplied for those who are
advancing well in this life through faith, but they will be fulfilled through sight in the other life for those who arrive.
Hence when he said, *May grace and peace be fulfilled for you,*
he did well to add, *in the knowledge of our Lord, Jesus Christ,*
because *this is eternal life,* he says, *that they may know you,
the one true God, and Jesus Christ whom you have sent;*[7]
and again, *If the Son has set you free, you will be truly free,*[8]
and you will know the truth, and the truth will set you free.[9]

1:3 **In the manner in which all things of his divine power
that [belong] to life and devotion have been given to us.**
This statement belongs with what precedes. For the meaning
is, 'May grace and peace be fulfilled for you in this, that you
may know our Lord Jesus Christ perfectly, and that you
may know this also through him, in what manner all things of
his divine power that are sufficient for maintaining and preserving life and devotion have been given to us through his
grace.' Hence he says, *Because all things, whatever I have
heard from my Father, I have made known to you;*[10] and
elsewhere, *I have given them the honor which you have given
me.*[11] But if there be read, as certain manuscripts have, [In
the manner in which all things of his divine power] 'that has
been given us for life and devotion', the meaning will be this:
'That you may know in what manner our Lord has provided
for us all the gifts of his divine power according to the measure of our ability to receive them, and that this power,
namely, has been given to us that we may attain life and

6. 1 P 1:2   7. Jn 17:3   8. Jn 8:36
9. Jn 8:32   10. Jn 15:15   11. Jn 17:22

devotion'. For indeed this manner of speaking is quite customary in the scriptures and is called ellipsis by the grammarians, that is, the omission of necessary wording, as there is in the psalm, *Because neither from the east nor from the west nor from the mountains of the desert,* where there is understood, 'does a way of escape lie open', *since God is the judge* everywhere.[12] **Through the knowledge of him who has called us by his own glory and power.** This, too, belongs with what precedes, because we recognize all the mysteries of his divinity by which we are saved through the knowledge of our Lord and saviour who has called us by his own glory and power, because he did not send an angel or archangel for our salvation, he did not find in us anything of good desert for which we might be saved, rather he beheld us weak and without honor and restored us by his own power and glory. From this indeed he says, *You have not chosen me but I have chosen you.*[13]

**1:4	Through which he has given us very great and precious promises.** *Through which,* he says, through the knowledge of him, because the more perfectly anyone gets to know the Lord, the more deeply he realizes the greatness of his promises. **That through these you may be made sharers in the divine nature.** He suddenly changes the person, and from just having said of himself and his followers, *he has given us precious promises,* he immediately turns to those to whom he was speaking and says, *That through these you may be made sharers in the divine nature.* He does this not accidentally but with forethought. 'The Lord, therefore,' he says, 'has revealed all the secrets of his divine power to us who by nature have been born Jews and under the law, who were entrusted with the power of teaching by him while he was alive, to us, namely, his disciples, he has given the very great and precious promises of his spirit, for the reason that through these he

12. Ps 75:6-7 (74:7-8)	13. Jn 15:16

might give to you also who come from the gentiles, who were unable to see him while he was alive, to be sharers in his divine nature; to us, namely, teaching you what we heard from him, consecrating you through his mysteries.' Hence what he said above, *May grace and peace be fulfilled for you in the knowledge of our Lord Jesus Christ, in the manner in which all things of his divine power that [belong] to life and devotion have been given to us,* can quite properly be taken as meaning, 'May grace and peace be fulfilled for you in this, that even you may thus know our Lord Jesus Christ, just as all the promises and gifts of his divine power that lead to life and devotion have been given to us by him, that as we have either received the promised gifts from him or trust without any doubt that we shall receive them, so also by believing you may become sure of his gifts.' **Fleeing the corruption of that craving[14] which is in the world.** He does well to say that the craving of the world includes corruption and therefore must be avoided, according to him who said, *Flee from sin as from the appearance of a serpent,*[15] because there is also an incorruptible craving, about which it is sung, *My soul has craved and languished for the courts of the Lord.*[16] About this also in the book of Wisdom through a figure of speech that in Greek is called κλῖμαξ,[1] in Latin 'proceeding by steps,'[17] it is most admirably related, *The beginning,* he says, of wisdom *is the sincerest craving for discipline.*[18] The concern for discipline, therefore, is love, and love is the keeping of his laws; the keeping of the laws, however, is the completion of incorruption; incorruption, however, makes one to be near God; the craving for wisdom accordingly leads to the everlasting kingdom.

1:5 Do you, however, using all care, provide virtue in your faith. He has used virtue in this place not for courage

14. *concupiscentia*   15. Si 21:2   16. Ps 84:2 (83:3)
17. *gradatio*   18. Ws 6:17 (6:18)

or miracles but for a good way of life which must be joined to proper faith, lest without works it be worthless and dead.[19] He properly admonishes us to use all care in this, because the person who is soft and profligate in his work is brother to him who destroys his works. **In your virtue, however, [provide] knowledge**, according to that saying of Isaiah, *Learn to do what is right, seek judgment.*[20]

1:6 **In your knowledge, however, [provide] self-restraint**, so that when they have learned to do what is right, they may quickly restrain themselves from doing evil, lest the knowledge of heavenly things fall into a void if a person neglects to refrain from earthly allurements. **In your self-restraint, however, [provide] patience.** It is necessary that patience always accompany self-restraint, that whoever has learned to refrain from the pleasures of the world may also bear with adversities with a stout heart, being protected on the right hand and the left, namely, by the arms of righteousness.[21] **In your patience, however, [provide] devotion**, that one may also be devoted to those whom one bears with patiently, according to that saying of the apostle Paul, *Charity is patient, it is kind.*[22]

1:7 **In your devotion, however, [provide] love of the brotherhood**, that one may bestow the works of devotion on his adversaries for no other consideration than love of the brotherhood, seeking this, namely, with his whole purpose, that by praying and doing what is right he may convert to the disposition[23] of devotion those whom he is unable to [move] by teaching alone or by refuting. **In your love of the brotherhood, however, [provide] charity.** In this place he calls charity particularly that by which we love our creator. This is rightly joined to love of the brotherhood for those who are progressing in the steps of the virtues, because neither

19. Jm 2:17, 20   20. Is 1:17   21. 2 Co 6:7
22. 1 Co 13:4   23. *affectus*

can God be loved perfectly without one's neighbor nor one's neighbor without God. And indeed the love of God is loftier than the love of one's neighbors, because them we are ordered to love as ourselves; but God with our whole heart, our whole soul, our whole strength.[24] But nonetheless it is fitting for us to ascend to the love of God by the habit of love of the brotherhood. *For he who does not love his brother whom he sees* daily, *how can he love God whom he does not see?*[25]

1:8 For if all these things are present with you and prevail, they will render you not ineffective and without fruit. He has said, 'if they prevail', if by their more powerful strength they prove stronger against the attacks of the vices.

1:9 For he who does not possess these things is blind and groping with his hand. The eye denotes knowledge, the hand work. *He,* however, *is blind and groping with his hand* who does not have the knowledge of proper work and does whatever appears to him to be proper, and, not knowing the light of truth, as it were reaches his hand out to a work which he does not see, steps forward, on a way which he cannot foresee, and therefore suddenly falls, wretchedly, into the ruin of destruction which he was unable to foreknow. Such is everyone who does not possess these things about which Peter is speaking, however, because it is fitting that we reach fellowship with the divinity through the increase of spiritual virtues. But on the other hand Solomon, advising the wise hearer, says, *And let your eyes anticipate your footsteps,*[26] which is to declare clearly that in all our actions we should take care to foresee with earnest intent what outcome awaits us, we should examine skillfully what is done according to the will of God, what otherwise.

1:10 Wherefore, brothers, strive all the more that through

24. Mk 12:30-31   25. 1 Jn 4:20   26. Pr 4:25

good works you may make your calling and election definite.
Many are called, but few are chosen[27].[28] The calling of all
who come to the faith is definite; but those who also persis-
tently add good works to the sacraments of the faith which
they have received also make their election together with
their calling definite to those who see them; just as, on the
other hand, those who return to their wicked deeds after their
calling, when they depart from this life in these [deeds],
already make definite to all that they are condemned.
For if you do these things you will not sin at any time.
He is speaking of more serious sins. Whoever commits these
*does not have an inheritance in the kingdom of Christ and
God,*[29] and everyone who devotes himself to the virtues
mentioned above with God's help remains free from them.
Yet there are less serious sins about which it has been
written that *there is not a righteous man on earth who does
what is good and does not sin,*[30] and, *No living person will
be made righteous in your sight.*[31]

**1:11 For so there will be richly provided for you an
entrance into the eternal kingdom of our Lord and Saviour,
Jesus Christ.** With this place agrees that saying of Ezekiel
where, speaking of the building on the appointed mountain,
he says, *And its ascent was in eight steps.*[32] For here also
blessed Peter enumerates eight steps of the virtues by which,
fleeing from the corruption of worldly concupiscence, we
ought to ascend to the dwelling of the heavenly kingdon,
namely, faith, virtue, knowledge, self-restraint, patience,
devotion, love of the brotherhood, and charity. Surely, the
psalm says of these steps, *He has placed ways of ascent in his
heart,* and so on, as far as it says, *they will walk from virtue
to virtue, the God of gods will be seen in Zion.*[33]

---

27. *electi*   28. Mt 20:16   29. Eph 5:5   30. Qo 7:20 (21)
31. Ps 143 (142):2   32. Ezk 40:34   33. Ps 84:5-7 (83:6-8)

1:12 Wherefore I will begin always to remind you of these things, even though you both know them and are established in the present truth. Why does he wish always to remind those whom he says have knowledge and are established about the presence of the truth concerning their good works, unless perhaps for this reason, that they practice the knowledge that they have by works and with resolute mind guard the truth by whose presence they are established, lest at any time they withdraw from the simplicity and purity of the faith under the influence of teachers of error? He says more about these teachers, namely, in the continuation of the Letter. There coincides with this, however, the statement of blessed John in which he says, *We have not written to you as to those who are ignorant of the truth but as to those who know it.*[34] It is for this reason that the apostles write to those who know the truth and remind them to follow what they know. Hence John also in discussing these things adds a little later on, *Let what you have heard from the beginning remain in you.*[35]

1:13 For I think it right, as long as I am in this tent,[36] to stir you up by reminding you. We are accustomed to use a tent on a journey or during war, and therefore the faithful, as long as they are in the body and are straggling away from the Lord,[37] properly bear witness that they are in tents in which they pursue their journey of this life and wage a contest against the enemies of the truth.

1:14 Being convinced that the laying aside of my tent[38] is at hand. Very admirably does blessed Peter say that his departure is not death but the laying aside of his tent, because surely it is characteristic of perfect servants of God to put off the stays of the body in much the same way as

34. 1 Jn 2:21   35. 1 Jn 2:24   36. *taberculum*
37. 2 Co 5:6   38. *tabernaculum*

travelers exchange a tent for their own home when their
journey is over or those engaged in military operations
return to their fatherland when the enemy has been put to
flight and conquered. For they know that their only home,
their only city, their only fatherland is in heaven, about
which the apostle Paul also says, *We know that if our earthly*
home of this dwelling place should be destroyed, we have a
building from God, an eternal home not made by hand,
in heaven.[39]

1:16 For we did not follow learned myths when we made
known to you the power and presence of our Lord Jesus
Christ but we were made beholders of his greatness.
Here he strikes at pagans and heretics at the same time. The
former have not been afraid to call gods whatever was pleasing to them, the latter, after having received the mysteries of
the true God, from then on have been inclined not to pay
attention to the divine scriptures but rather to alter these to
their own erroneous meaning by interpreting them wrongly.

1:18 And we heard this voice brought from heaven. There
are certain persons who say that this Letter was not written
by the blessed apostle Peter. But if they would pay more
careful attention to this verse and the part of it that follows
when we were with him on the holy mountain, they would
be not at all dubious about the author of this Letter. For it is
clear that the same Peter, together with his fellow apostles
James and John, heard the aforesaid voice above the Lord
when he was glorified on the mountain, according to the faith
of the Gospels.[40]

1:19 And we have a surer prophetic sentence, that, namely,
in which he speaks in the person of the mediator between
God and men,[41] saying, *The Lord said to me, 'You are my*

39. 2 Co 5:1   40. Mt 17:1-5   41. 1 Tm 2:5

Son, today have I begotten you',[42] 'For if anyone at all,' he
says, 'does not consider our witness worthy of belief, the
fact that we beheld in secret the divine glory of our Redeemer, that we heard the voice of the Father brought to
him, at least no one will dare contradict the prophetic
sentence, no one will dare to dispute this, which already
long ago was incorporated in the divine scriptures and all
bear witness is true.' **You do well to pay attention to this as
to a lamp shining in a dark place.** The order of the meaning is,
'In paying attention to this as to a lamp shining in a dark
place you do well'. For indeed in this world's night, filled
with dark temptations, where only with difficulty is anyone found who does not offend, what should we be if we
did not have the lamp of the prophetic utterance? But will a
lamp always be required? Definitely not. **Until the day
dawns,** he says. For, *In the morning I will stand before you
and regard attentively.*[43] It belongs meanwhile to the lamp
burning during the night that *we are the children of God, and
it has not yet appeared what we shall be,*[44] and indeed in
comparison with the wicked we are the day, as Paul says,
You were formerly darkness but now light in the Lord.[45]
But if we are compared to that life in which we shall be, we
are still night and need a lamp. **And the morning star arises in
your hearts.** What is that morning star? If you say the Lord,
that is too little. The morning star is our own excellent
understanding. For if this arises in our hearts, it will be enlightened, it will be made clear. It will become love, such as
we now wish and long for yet do not possess, and we shall see
of what sort it will be in each other, just as now we see each
other's faces.

1:20 **Understanding this first of all, that no prophecy of
scripture becomes a matter for private interpretation.** This
verse follows from what he said above, *You do well to pay*

---

42. Ps 2:7   43. Ps 5:3 (5:5)   44. 1 Jn 3:2   45. Eph 5:8

attention to this. For those who pay attention to the words of the prophets certainly do well, that by means of these words they may be able to have the light of knowledge. They ought to understand this first of all, that none of the holy prophets preached the teachings of life to the people [using] his own interpretation but they handed on what they had learned from the Lord to their hearers to be put into practice by them. And they passed on the hidden heavenly mysteries which they had comprehended in secret to the people of God simply either by speaking or by writing and not like the diviners of the gentiles who brought forth to the crowds of those who were deceived as decisions of a divine oracle what they themselves had fabricated in their own heart. Therefore, just as the prophets wrote not their own but God's words, so also the reader of them cannot use his own private interpretation, lest he deviate from the true meaning, but he ought to pay careful attention to how the writer wished his words to be understood.

1:21 **For never at any time was a prophecy brought forth by the will of man, but the holy men of God spoke when inspired by the Holy Spirit.** Just as it was not in the power of those who prophesied always to have the Holy Spirit, to be able always to predict the future, but the Spirit himself filled their hearts when he willed, so also it was not within their power to teach whatever they wished, but they spoke those things alone which they had learned when enlightened by the Spirit. These things are said for this reason, that no one may dare to expound the scriptures according to his own wishes. A certain person has interpreted these words of blessed Peter absurdly, saying that just as a reed-pipe receives the breath of the human mouth to make a sound but nonetheless cannot itself understand the sound which it provides because by nature it is insensible, so the prophets, inspired by the Spirit of God, might bring forward in speech those things which the same Spirit wished but they themselves would not grasp with their mind what they were saying, according to Virgil's[2] words, *It gives forth a sound without meaning.*[46] It is clearly evident that this is a most ridiculous error. For how might they give their hearers such wise counsels about living if they themselves did not know what they were saying? Why are the prophets called seers? For what reason was it written, *The word which Isaiah saw,*[47] or some other prophet [saw], except that they perceived in secret with the clearest grasp of the mind the hidden mysteries of heavenly visions which they made known outwardly to their hearers clearly in whatever words they wished?

2:1 **There were in fact also false prophets among the people, just as even among you there will be deceitful teachers who will bring in destructive sects.** Sects in Latin are called heresies in Greek, when some one with foolish stubbornness in no way stops always pursuing eagerly[3] the error which he has once begun. Who is unaware that this is characteristic of heretics? **Denying even the Lord who bought them, they bring upon themselves swift destruction.** Paul also says about this buyer, *For you have been bought with a great price; glorify and carry God in your body.*[48] For they rightly bring upon themselves swift destruction who, denying their Redeemer,[4] refuse to glorify him by properly confessing him and to carry him in their body by doing what is right, a thing which all the heretics do. For both Arius who says that our Redeemer is less than the Father in his divinity, and Photinus who says, 'Christ is a human being, he is not God', and Manicheus who says, 'Christ is only God, he is not a true human being', and Ebion who says, 'Christ did not exist before Mary, he took his beginning from her', and Apollinaris who says, 'Christ is only God with a human body, he never took for himself a rational soul', and Pelagius who

46. Virg., *Aen.* 10:640   47. Is 2:1   48. 1 Co 6:20

says, 'Christ is not the Redeemer of children in baptism, because, having been conceived without iniquities and having been born of their mother without crimes,[49] they have absolutely no sin for which they ought to be forgiven and therefore Christ is not the saviour of all the elect,' and the rest of the heretics along with them actually deny the Lord who redeemed them with the price of his blood, because they preach him not as the truth shows him but as they make up for themselves and accordingly, having become strangers to their Redeemer, they await nothing more definite than the pit of destruction.

2:2 Because of them the way of truth will be blasphemed. The way of truth will be blasphemed because of the heretics not only in those whom they deceive and join to their heresy but also in those whom they stir up to a hatred of the christian name because of their thoroughly impure deeds and sacrifices and the detestable mysteries they perform, when the gullible think that all Christians are given up to crimes of this kind, such as the scripture says, *Because of you my name is blasphemed among the gentiles.*[50]

2:3 Their judgment [passed] already formerly, does not cease. How is there said *already formerly* it *does not cease,* however, is a verb in the present tense, except that the judgment of the destruction of the wicked began already formerly and it will never cease torturing them without end always with its presence?

2:4 For if God did not spare the angels when they sinned, and so on. Here many verses have one conclusion, *The Lord knows how to rescue the devout from temptation.*[51] *For if God did not spare the angels when they sinned,* he says, but

49. Ps 51:5 (50:7)   50. Is 52:5, Rm 2:24   51. 2 P 2:9

has handed them over to the punishments of the lower world and keeps them for greater torments on the day of judgment,[52] if he destroyed the primordial world by the flood on account of its crimes and kept the righteous Noah safe,[53] if he punished the base deeds of the people of Sodom and from the unrighteous freed Lot who was devoted to righteousness,[54] it is certainly clear that *the Lord knows how to rescue the devout from temptation* but to keep the wicked to be tormented on the day of judgment. And it must be noted in what he says about God not sparing the angels when they sinned that these evil angels were not created evil by God but became evil by sinning. **But he handed them over, dragged down by the lines of the lower world into the infernal region, to be kept in torment until the judgment.** Another translation has this verse thus, 'But thrusting them back in the prisons of the dark lower world, he handed them over to be kept for punishments in the judgment'. He shows, therefore, that the punishment of the final judgment is still due the apostate angels; concerning it the Lord says, *Go into the everlasting fire which was prepared for the devil and his angels,*[55] although by way of punishment they have already received this lower world, that is, this lower dark atmosphere, as a prison. For insofar as the lower world can be said to be space [comparable] to the height of the sky of the present atmosphere, so also to this extent can the lower world and its depth which lies beneath be understood as land [comparable] in deepness to the same atmosphere. Yet he calls this boasting of pride by which the angelic spirit became puffed up against its creator the lines of the lower world; in truth, the ropes by which sailors raise their sails that, when the breeze blows, they may leave the calmness of the harbor and entrust themselves to the ever uncertain waves of the sea are said to be lines. The attempts of the unclean spirits are fittingly compared to these lines. As soon as they were driven by the

52. Jude 6   53. Gn 7:21-3   54. Gn 19:28-9   55. Mt 25:41

blast of pride and raised themselves up against their Creator they were snatched by these very attempts at loftiness into the depths of the abyss. Certain manuscripts have, 'But he handed them over, when they had been dragged down into the infernal region, to the roarings of the lower world'. This denotes the sound either of the arrogance of pride or of the groaning in the midst of punishments. For wild beasts roar when they suffer either hunger or some other annoyance, not being able on account of the excessiveness of their arrogance to bear it if some adversity overtakes them.

2:5 And he did not spare the primordial world. This is the very same world in which the human race now lives which those who existed before the flood inhabited but it is nonetheless properly said to be the primordial world, as if it were another, because, as is found written in the following parts of this Letter, *that world [which existed] then was deluged with water and perished,*[56] namely, both the heavens that existed formerly[57] (that is, all the spaces of this present stormy atmosphere) had been destroyed by the height of the increasing waters and the land, too, had been changed to another appearance by the destructive waters. For although some mountains and valleys are believed to have been in existence from the beginning, yet they were not the same size as they are now seen to be throughout the entire world. Perhaps this could be denied except even now we see the appearance of the land changed every year by the eroding waters. This action is believed to have been all the greater then in proportion to the stronger and longer-lasting force of the waters that surged up over and washed away the land. **But he protected Noah, the herald of righteousness, as the eighth, when he brought the flood upon the world of the wicked.** It is clear to all that Noah was born in the tenth generation from Adam,[58] but he calls him the eighth,

---

56. 2 P 3:6   57. 2 P 3:5   58. 2 Gn 5:3-29

because eight persons escaped the flood;[59] he was one of
them. Yet he makes mention of the number eight for this
reason, that he may secretly imply that the time of the
flood denotes the critical moment of the final examination,
when, after all the condemned have been rejected, all the
righteous receive the glory of everlasting life. For there are
six ages[5] of the present world; the seventh age is even now
in progress in that life where the souls of the saints enjoy
the happy sabbath, that is, eternal rest; the eighth age will
come at the time of the resurrection of all and of the universal judgment. He calls Noah, however, the herald of
righteousness, because by doing righteous works he showed
to all who saw him how life ought to be lived in the Lord's
sight. For he is never found to have taught anyone by words,
in truth not one utterance of his is found made to God or
man, but what is of the greatest virtue, in the whole building
of the ark, in the coming of the flood, in the beginning of the
following age, to obey the heavenly orders with a silent
mouth indeed but with most ready affirmation of heart.

**2:6 And reducing the cities of Sodom and Gomorrah to
ashes, he rejected them by their destruction.** The fact that he
declares the cities of the wicked reduced to ashes ought to be
understood in a twofold way, because first he reduced them
with the adjacent lands to ashes by fire and, when he
covered the place of the fire later with the waters of the
Dead Sea, he wished the surrounding region still to keep the
appearance of the previous punishment. For the most admirable fruits are produced there which cause a desire to eat
them in those who see them; if you pluck them they fall
apart and dissolve into ashes and produce smoke as if they
are still on fire.[60] Hence it is said in the book of Wisdom,
She [wisdom] freed the righteous as he was fleeing from the

59. Gn 6:10,8:16
60. Aug., *De civ. Dei* 21. 5, 8; CC 48: 765, 26/28, 773, 93/99

perishing wicked, when fire came down on the Five Cities, as
a witness to whose wickedness there remains a smoke-
producing deserted land and trees bearing fruit at an inde-
finite time,[61] where there is understood: these too remain,
smoke-producing and deserted. And this is what is added
here also, **Making an example of those who are going to act**
wickedly. For the fire which once punished the people of
Sodom also plainly shows what the wicked are going to suffer without end. And the fact that their smoke-producing
land remains, that its most admirable fruits have ashes and
a bad smell within, clearly signifies to all ages that although
bodily pleasure delights the minds of the foolish for the
present, nevertheless in what concerns that which cannot be
seen it retains for itself nothing except that the smoke of its
torments rises up for ever and ever.

2:7–8 And he rescued the righteous Lot who was over-
whelmed by the wrongful way of life of the heinous; for he
remained righteous even though living in their midst and see-
ing and hearing those who tormented his righteous soul from
day to day by their wicked works. The wicked actions and
words alike of his neighbors indeed tormented the holy man;
he saw them daily without being in any way able to correct
them. But nonetheless he behaved so circumspectly that he
did not dim the vision of his pure mind on seeing or hearing
of their misdeeds but with tireless intention pressed on with
the deeds of righteousness he had begun. Or at least he was
righteous in seeing and hearing because those around him
neither saw anything in him except the works of righteousness nor heard anything except the words of righteousness;
no rumor was spread about him by those who were absent
except what was connected with righteousness, after the
example of blessed Job who says, *The hearing ear called me*

61. Ws 10:6-7

blessed, and the seeing eye gave witness to me.[62] And it must be noted that in this place blessed Peter follows the example of the Lord's teaching. For the Lord himself also, speaking in the Gospel of the day of judgment, calls to mind the sudden coming of either the flood or the fire of Sodom,[63] when the righteous are set free, but the condemned are caught in the snare of unexpected destruction. But in another place also, when he was taking care to restrain the minds of his disciples from the arrogance of pride, he held up to them the example of the angels' fall, saying, *I saw satan fall like lightning from heaven.*[64]

2:9 The Lord knows how to rescue the devout from temptation but to keep the wicked to be tormented on the day of judgment. He says that the wicked are to be held for torment on the day of judgment, not because they do not also pay the penalty in accord with their deserts when they are freed from the body before the day of judgment but because more serious tortures await them at the judgment, when those who are now tormented in their souls alone will also be tormented in their bodies which they will have received back. Hence the Lord also, when he was reproaching those cities that were unwilling to accept the word of the Gospel, ended thus, *The land of the people of Sodom will be forgiven more easily than you on the day of judgment.*[65]

2:10 But especially those who indulge their bodies in the concupiscence of uncleanness. He is speaking of those guilty of fornication who for the condemnation of their detestable corruption receive greater tortures at the judgment than those who are ordinarily wicked. **And those who boldly despise authority, pleasing themselves.** He is speaking of the proud and arrogant who will also pay a more serious penalty than ordinary persons. **Those who do not fear to**

62. Jb 29:11   63. Lk 17:26-9   64. Lk 10:18   65. Mt 11:24

create sects, blaspheming. He is speaking of the heretics who, blaspheming the faith and life of true believers, bring in sects of their own name, that is, heresies. These also, together with the former, hear that fiercer torment is in store for the fiercer.

2:11 Where the angels, although they are greater in strength and power, do not carry a dreadful judgment against themselves. What he says, Where, implies insofar as they despise authority, are bold, pleasing themselves, create sects, that is, heresies, and blaspheme. For by doing these things the angels deserved to become demons and to pay the penalty for their pride. For their spiritual nature did not allow them to be defiled by the impurity of bodily concupiscence, except perhaps that he implies that they are also to be judged for this when they entice human beings to it, just as also for the other evils they persuade humans to do.

2:12 But they, like irrational animals naturally [destined] for capture and destruction in things of which they are ignorant, blaspheming, they will also perish in their corruption. Just as it is natural for irrational animals quite often for the sake of food to fall through ignorance into capture and destruction, so the heretics, like foolish beasts,[66] in order to indulge their corrupt appetite blaspheme the incorrupt and wise teaching and life of the catholic Church and by their wicked rashness weave snares of everlasting destruction for themselves. Church history relates that heretics of this sort existed at the very times of the apostles, the followers of Simon [Magus], Menander, Basilides, Nicolaus, Marcion, Cerdonius, and a number of others. When he said about them, blaspheming, they will also perish in their corruption, he properly added:

66. Ps 49:12 (48:13)

2:13 **Receiving the reward of their unrighteousness**. For he says that the reward of unrighteousness is a punishment that the works of unrighteousness deserve, especially in the case of those who while being slaves to the corruption of the body nonetheless blaspheme the way of life of those who live pure lives, when they themselves are held bound by mad errors, they do not cease slandering those who savor what is wise. **Thinking of the delights of defilement and stain as pleasure of the day**. Pleasure is taken both in a good and a bad sense: in a good sense, indeed, when reference is made to the garden of pleasure,[67] and when there is sung in the psalm, *And you will give them to drink of the torrent of pleasure,*[68] but in a bad sense when Solomon says, *For youth and pleasure are useless;*[69] but it is accepted even in a neutral sense according to what Sarah said, *After I have grown old and my husband is an old man, shall I pay attention to pleasure?*[70] Therefore, pleasure in a good sense is properly called that of the day when all the saints take delight in the Lord, but pleasure in a bad sense is that of the night, when the condemned wrongly take delight in committing works of darkness. Therefore, it is well said of the unrighteous that they think of the delights of defilement and stains as pleasure of the day, because many persons are negligent, wrong, and shameless to such an extent that, when they devote their time to the impurest and most deplorable delights, they judge these nonetheless as the very best and, as it were, productive of light. Certain persons join the word 'pleasure' in this verse to the preceding verse, reading it thus, 'Receiving pleasure as the reward of their unrighteousness', and explaining it according to the saying of the apostle Paul, *God handed them over to the desires of their heart, to uncleanness, so that they brought harm upon their bodies in themselves,*[71] and a little bit farther along, *They committed base acts and received among themselves*

67. Gn 2:8   68. Ps 36:8 (35:9)   69. Qo 11:10
70. Gn 18:12   71. Rm 1:24

the reward, as was fitting, for their error, and just as they did not prove to have God in mind, he handed them over, filled with all iniquity, to an unseemly realization, that they would do things that are not fitting.[72] But I have considered that the distinction which I found in the works of blessed Pope Gregory[6] as the one that ought to be followed.

2:14 **Seducing inconstant souls.** Prostitutes are accustomed to be called seducers,[7] a name that has been derived from their uncleanness or from the beauty of their skin, by which they entice the unwary. Therefore, they seduce inconstant souls who, by teaching them wrongly, subject them to the erroneous sects of various teachings as if to the debaucheries of ravishers.

2:15—16 **They have followed the way of Balaam from Bosor who loved the reward of iniquity: in truth he had a reproof for his madness; a dumb beast of burden, speaking with the voice of a human being, prevented the foolishness of the prophet.** Very often heretics bring forth such foolish teachings, such detestable sacraments, that even the understanding of the slow-witted and of pagans and of those who entirely lack comprehension of divine recognition despises their madness and by discerning more soundly and wisely refutes their distorted ways contrary to God. And what is worse, because it is more frequent, many Catholics love the reward of iniquity to such an extent that even the learned are torn to pieces by the unlearned, clerics are deservedly treated likewise by the laity. These are justifiably likened to the prophet who was reproved by the words of an ass that spoke, contrary to its nature, but nonetheless he was not slowed down from the object of his wicked journey. The name of the city from which Balaam is related to have come ties in most appropriately with all these. For Bosor means 'bodily'

72. Rm 1:27-8

or 'in tribulation'.[73] The dissolute have no other reason to corrupt the word of truth through love of money and temporal desires than that they have given in to the concupiscences of the body. They are surely not worthy of the apostle's praise wherein he glorifies the true faithful and says, *But you, brothers, are not in the body but in the spirit.*[74] Hence they are also in tribulation, not indeed that which they themselves suffer for the Lord but rather in that by which they oppress the minds of the weak by the perverse examples of their works, lest they be able to move upward to salvation and repent. But even the name of Balaam himself, which is interpreted 'useless people' or 'throwing headlong to destruction',[75] is in accord with such as these. For those who willingly desert the recognized way of truth, what are they but useless people, what do they do but send their hearers (to whom they preach not salvation-giving things which may correct them but wrong things which may please them) headlong to destruction? Concerning these there is well appended:

2:17—19   These are springs without water and mists stirred up by whirlwinds, for whom the cloud of darkness is reserved; for they speak proud words of boastfulness and seduce into self-indulgent desires of the flesh those who barely manage to escape those whose way of life is wrong, promising them freedom, when they themselves are servants of corruption. Saint Jerome makes use of these verses in his book *Against Jovinian* and explains them thus:[76]

> Does not the utterance of the apostle appear to you to have depicted a new faction of ignorance? For they open, as it were, springs of knowledge, and those who have no water promise a shower of teaching, like clouds of prophecy to which the

73. Jer., *Nom. Hebr.;* CC 72:150, 27/28   74. Rm 8:9
75. Jer., *Nom. Hebr.;* CC 72:79, 20/21
76. *Adv. Iov.* 2.3; PL 23:287C

the truth of God may come they too are stirred up
by the whirlwinds of demons and vices. They speak
lofty things, and their entire utterance is pride.
*'But everyone is unclean who exalts his own
heart,'*[77] so that those who have just managed to
escape from sins return to their own error and en-
gage in self-indulgence in food and delights of
flesh. For who would not gladly hear, *'Let us eat
and drink,*[78] and we shall rule for ever'. They call
wise and prudent those evil ones whose conversa-
tion is cloying.

**2:22 For that [saying] of the true proverb has happened to
them, 'The dog has returned to its own vomit,' and, 'The sow
has washed itself in a wallow of mud.'** He says that this is a
true proverb, because he takes up a witness from the
Proverbs of Solomon which is given there with an explanation, *Like a dog who returns to its own vomit,* he says,
is the fool who repeats his foolishness,[79] and he adds on his
own, *and, The sow has washed itself in a wallow of mud.*
Therefore,

when a dog vomits, surely it spits out food that
weighed heavily on its stomach, but when it returns
to its vomit, it again is burdened with what it was
relieved of. Those also who bewail their wickedness by confessing surely cast forth the wickedness
by which they were evilly satiated and which
weighed heavily on the innermost part of their
mind; but when they repeat this after confessing it,
they take it up again. But when a sow washes
itself in a wallow of mud, it comes out filthier
still. He also who weeps for what he has committed
and yet does not give it up subjects himself to the
punishment for a more grievous fault. He despises

77. Pr 16:6 (LXX) 16:5 (Vulg.)   78. 1 Co 15:32   79. Pr 26:11

that pardon which he could have obtained by weeping, and wallows, as it were, in muddy water, because when he withdraws cleanness of life from his tears, he makes even his very fears filthy before the eyes of God.[80]

3:1 Look, dearly beloved, I am writing this second Letter to you, in [both of] which I am stirring up your sincere mind in admonition. When he says, *in which,* he means either in both Letters or in those to whom he is writing the Letters.

3:3–4 Scoffers will come in the last days in deceit, scoffing, namely, at the faith and hope of Christians, because they promise in vain that the time of resurrection will come for them. **Walking according to their own concupiscences, saying, 'Where is the promise of his coming?'** The apostle Paul, writing to the Thessalonians, says, *I ask you by the coming of our Lord Jesus Christ and our being gathered together in him not to be shaken from your understanding or terrified either by a spirit or an utterance or a Letter sent even by us as if the day of the Lord is approaching.*[81] Blessed Peter, therefore, reproves and calls scoffers those who maintain that the coming of the Lord and his promises are slow, Paul restrains those who assert that the day of the Lord is approaching. Hence it is clear to all *who love his coming*[82] that the mind must be controlled rather moderately in this conjecture so that we surmise neither that the aforesaid day of the Lord is near and will come quite quickly nor again that it is coming too slowly, but we should be diligent in seeing to this alone: that whether it comes sooner or later it may find us ready when it does come.

3:5 For it escapes the notice of those who wish for this,

80. Greg., *Reg. past.* 3.30; PL 77:110A-B
81. 2 Th 2:1-2   82. 2 Tm 4:8

that by the word of God the heavens existed formerly as did the land formed from water and through water. The land was formed from water, because at the beginning of his creation God said, *Let the water be gathered together in one place and let dry land appear, and so it was done.*[83] The same land was formed through water by the word of God, because by divine providence the whole of it is full within of veins of water, just as we see the body of living things copiously supplied with veins of blood, lest namely it should become dry and lifeless if the supply of water failed. Accordingly, once the moisture has gone we see fields dried up by the heat of summer and soon turned into dust which the wind drives away.[84] Another manuscript has, 'The heavens existed formerly made up from water and through water'. This means that part of the air which is set and stormy. For the scripture is accustomed to call this sky also the heavens. Hence it has been written, *The hawk in the heaven knows its time.*[85]

3:6 Throughout these then that world was deluged with water and perished. *Throughout these,* he means the heavens and the land which he had just named. For it was throughout these that the world which was made up of them perished. For the flood did not touch the upper parts of the world at all. Therefore the land which was overturned and covered with water not only lost for a long time its natural condition of producing fruit but also, as we have pointed out above, in a number of places took on an appearance unlike that which it had at first had. The heavens also perished, as Saint Augustine says,

> according to the extent and breadth of this air. For the water increased and occupied the entire space where the birds fly. And so the heavens that are

83. Gn 1:9   84. Ps 1:4   85. Jr 8:7

near the land, which people refer to when they
say, 'The birds of heaven', certainly perished.
There are, however (he says) also the higher
heavens of heavens in the firmament. But as to
whether these also will perish by fire or only those
that also perished in the flood is a question that is
somewhat more carefully disputed among the
learned.[86]

**3:7 But the heavens and the land which now exist have
been set aside by the same word, being kept for fire on the
day of judgment and destruction of wicked persons.** The
thought, therefore, of blessed Peter is evident, because he
maintains that that land and those heavens which perished in
the flood and after the flood were restored are the ones that
are finally to be destroyed by fire.

**3:8 Let this one thing not escape your notice, dearly be-
loved, that with the Lord one day is as a thousand years and
a thousand years as one day.** Certain persons consider that
this statement must be understood to mean that the day
of judgment will have the same length as the space of a
thousand years. They do not advert to the fact that he does
not say simply, 'One day will be as a thousand years,' but
says, *With the Lord a day is as a thousand years,* because
undoubtedly in the divine power's knowledge both past
and future and present are equally present, and the move-
ments of time which appear long and short to us with the
creator of times are certainly of equal duration, according to
that saying of the psalmist, *Since a thousand years in your
sight are as yesterday which has passed, and their years will
be as a watch in the night which is counted for nothing.*[87]
For just as it is clear that the psalmist makes a thousand
years equal in the sight of the Creator not to the future day

86. Aug., *Enarr. in ps.* 101.2.3; CC 40:1448,6-13   87. Ps 90 (89):4-5

of judgment but to yesterday which has passed, indeed he likens all our years, that is, the entire time of this world, to a watch in the night, which is a fourth part of the night, so blessed Peter compares each single day of the present world to a thousand years and a thousand years to a single day with the Lord; that is, he maintains that they are the same length, because namely He beholds all things both small and great equally. And indeed if Peter wished this to be understood only about the day of judgment, that it was truly of the same length as are a thousand of our years, he could certainly have expressed his thought more clearly and would have had no need to add, *with the Lord,* because when that final day arrived it would be evident even to all people that it was of such great length. But the apostle recounts these things in order to refute those whom he had just referred to as saying, *'Where is the promise of his coming?'*[88] He shows that the Lord is not at all forgetful of his promise or his coming to judge the living and the dead. But when he so includes each single day of our world in his eternal memory as the passing of a thousand years, so includes a thousand years that he regards them without difficulty as the space of one day, it must be clearly understood that he most definitely also knows the end of these days and of all years, and without any doubt also knows beforehand when the glory of his coming is to be revealed, when the promised rewards are to be given to the saints. Hence there is properly also added:

3:9 The Lord does not delay his promise but for your sake waits patiently, not wishing that anyone perish but that all turn back to repentance. Therefore, he who knows all times, the most recent and the past,[89] does not delay the promise of his retribution but certainly shows it in the time which he predestined before all times to be, and he still postpones it for this reason, that he may first fill up the total number of

88. 2 P 3:4   89. Ps 139 (138):5

the elect which he with the Father decreed before time began. Hence too in the Apocalypse the souls of the martyrs which thirsted for the day of judgment and of the resurrection to come quickly heard, *That they might rest still a little while until their fellow servants and their brothers might be complete.*[90] Those however who so understand the aforesaid thought of blessed Peter as if he were saying that the day of judgment will be the same length as a thousand years relate it to the necessity that those have who depart from the body with some sins and yet have been predestined to the lot of the elect of being cleansed through fire for this length of time and so finally coming to life when all their sins have been forgiven. But they do not see how shameless it is to believe that so great a multitude of the perfect and righteous, having received back their blessed and immortal bodies *in the twinkling of an eye,*[91] ought to wait for the end of the judgment in the air or on the earth for the space of a thousand years and then at last, when their comrades have been fully made ready, to hear the long-desired sentence, *Come, you blessed of my Father, receive the kingdom.*[92]

3:10 For the day of the Lord will come as a thief; on it the heavens will pass away with great violence. He is undoubtedly speaking of those heavens that passed away in the flood, that is, this air nearest the earth which is to be destroyed by fire, and which occupies only so much space, as is properly believed, as the water of the flood occupied. Otherwise, if anyone maintains that the upper heavens where the sun and the moon and the stars are located will pass away, how does he wish to understand that thought of the Lord wherein it is that then *the sun will be darkened and the moon will not give its light and the stars will fall from the heaven?*[93] For if the place of the constellations, that is, the heaven, has passed away, by what reason can it be said that on the same day of

90. Rv 6:11   91. 1 Co 15:57   92. Mt 25:34   93. Mt 24:29

the Lord constellations are either darkened or fall and that
the place of these constellations where they are held in place
has passed away because of the consuming fire? **The elements,
in fact, will be dissolved by heat.** There are four elements
from which this world is formed, fire, air, water, and earth.
That very great fire will lay waste all these. But yet it will not
consume them that they will completely cease to exist, but
it will consume two entirely, two in fact it will restore to a
better appearance. Hence it is said in what follows:

**3:13 But we wait for new heavens and a new earth and his
promises.** For he did not say other heavens and another
earth, but the old and ancient one to be changed for the
better, according to what David said, *In the beginning, Lord,
you founded the earth, and the heavens are the works of
your hands; they will perish, but you will remain, and they
will all grow old as a garment, and you will change them as a
piece of clothing, and they shall be changed.*[94] As for the
things, therefore, that will perish, grow old and be changed, it
is definitely clear that once they have been consumed by the
fire they resume a more pleasing appearance as soon as the
fire goes out. *For the shape of this world passes away*[95] not
its substance, just as with our bodies too, the shape will be
changed, the substance does not perish when what *is sowed
as a physical body rises as a spiritual body.*[96] But we read
nothing of this sort about the fire and the water. Rather we
have in the Apocalypse, *And the sea is now no longer,*[97] and
in the prophets, *And the light of the lamp shall shine for you
no more.*[98] **And we wait for his promises,** he says, **in which
righteousness dwells.** Righteousness dwells in the future age,
because then the crown of righteousness will be given to
each of the faithful in accord with the measure of his
struggle. This is a thing that cannot at all happen in this life,

94. Ps 102:25-6 (101:26-7)   95. 1 Co 7:31   96. 1 Co 15:44
97. Rv 21:1   98. Jr 25:10, Rv 18:23

according to the saying of Solomon, *I have seen beneath the sun wickedness in place of judgment and iniquity in place of righteousness and I said in my heart, 'God will judge the righteous and the wicked, and there will be a time for everything,*[99] and again he says, *I saw the deceit that goes on beneath the sun and the tears of the innocent and that there was no comforter nor were those deprived of the help of all able to resist their power, and I praised the dead rather than the living.*[100] For he praised the innocent dead rather than the living because the latter were still engaged in the struggle but the former had been given their reward of everlasting happiness; he complained that he had seen deceit beneath the sun because he knew that above the sun there is a just judge *who dwells on high and looks down upon humble things,*[101] above the sun there are dwelling places in which the righteous receive due rewards for their righteousness. What he says, *in which righteousness dwells,* can also be understood according to the saying of the psalmist, *This is the gate of the Lord, the righteous will enter through it;*[101] and in the Apocalypse John says of the city on high, *Nothing unclean will enter it nor what brings about abomination and a lie, but only those who have been written in the book of life of the Lamb.*[103]

3:14 Wherefore, dearly beloved, while you are waiting for these things, strive to be found stainless and unblemished and in peace before him. These are the holy watches about which the Lord says, *Blessed are those servants whom, when the Lord comes, he finds watchful.*[104] For he is watchful who keeps himself free from the dregs of vices, who as far as he can is at peace with all people,[105] who makes use of a very happy peace within himself to subject all the allurements of the body to the rule of the spirit. And after he had said,

---

99. Qo 3:16-17
100. Qo 4:1-2
101. Ps 113 (112):5-6
102. Ps 118 (117):20
103. Rv 21:27
104. Lk 12:37
105. Rm 12:18

Strive to be found stainless and unblemished, he did well to add, *in his sight,* that is, the Lord's, because he alone is perfectly clean who is clean at the divine judgment. Hence in praise of good married couples it is said, *For they were both righteous in the sight of God,*[106] It is well said, *in the sight of God,* because human judgments are often mistaken.

3:15 And consider the forbearance of our Lord salvation. Do not think that the Lord delays his promises but understand that he waits with forbearance, that more persons may be saved. **Just as our dearly beloved brother Paul has also written to you according to the wisdom that was given him.** He recalls that Paul had written to them, because what the same Paul wrote particularly to certain churches he is proven to have written generally to all the churches which are throughout the world and which make up the one, catholic Church.[107] And it must be noted that Peter here praises the wisdom of Paul, whereas Paul says of himself, *For I am the least of the apostles, who am not worthy to be called an apostle, since I persecuted the Church of God.*[108] See how Paul, mindful of his former unfaithfulness, humbles himself and extols the integrity of the other apostles. See how the prince of the apostles, as if forgetting his own primacy and the keys of the kingdom that had been given him,[109] stands in admiration of the wisdom given Paul, because it is customary surely for the elect to be more in admiration of others' virtues, by which they stir themselves up to make progress, than of their own. And likewise it must be noted that Paul says in his Letters, *But when Cephas had come to Antioch, I resisted him to his face, because he deserved reproof.*[110] Paul, therefore, in his Letters reproved Peter, and yet Peter himself, reading through the same Letters,

---

106. Lk 1:6
107. Greg., *Moral.* 17.29.43; PL 76:30D
108. 1 Co 15:9   109. Mt 16:19   110. Ga 2:11

judges them worthy of praise, because undoubtedly the fact that he found himself rightly reproved in them he accepted not disdainfully as an insult but gladly as a sign of affirmation. Not just any human beings know how to behave in this way towards each other but only those who have learned from the Lord to be meek and humble of heart,[110] who know how to anticipate each other in showing honor.[111]

3:16 In these [Letters] there are certain things that are difficult to understand, which the unlearned and inconstant distort, as they do other parts of scripture. All heretics distort the scriptures, for there is no book either of the Old or New Testament in which they do not understand many things perversely. But they also often twist the meaning of the scriptures either by taking something away or adding or changing, whatever their faithlessness has commanded, as it is clear that the Arians have obliterated from the Gospel that the Saviour says God is a spirit,[113] that they were unwilling to believe that the Holy Spirit is omnipotent God. He properly calls them unlearned and inconstant, because they have neither the light of knowledge nor the constancy of mind to remain among the learned until they are instructed. For there is only one remedy for the unlearned, to give a hearing to the words of the learned with humble constancy. Because heretics do not have this grace of constancy, they are removed even from the Church by the wind of their pride, as if they were light straw. About them there is well appended, **To their own destruction,** because those who try to distort the sacred scriptures, to disturb and twist the catholic faith, in doing this do nothing but condemn themselves. But the Church of Christ, after having driven away the darkness of errors, enjoys its own true light. Hence at the end of the Apocalypse, which is, as it were, the summation and the seal, of the entire divine scripture, there is well said,

111. Mt 11:29   112. Rm 12:10   113. Jn 4:24

If anyone adds to these things, God will add to him the plagues written of in this book; and if anyone takes away from the words of the prophecy of this book, may God take away his part from the book of life and from the holy city and from the things that have been written in this book.[114] Yet the things which he says are difficult to understand in the Letters of Paul [and] which have been distorted by the unlearned and the inconstant are particularly those in which he speaks about the grace of God that justifies the wicked, that is, that causes them from being wicked to be righteous.[115] For he says, *Where sin abounded, however, grace abounded the more.*[116] They did not understand this and considered that he was saying, *Let us do evil that good may come.*[117] Far be it from Paul, however, to teach his hearers to do evil in order to deserve good; his whole intention is to restrain whomever he can from evils and to encourage them to do good. But when he says, *Where sin abounded, however, grace abounded the more,* he is by this recommending more strongly the gift of grace which usually remits both grave and lesser sins for those who are converted, and to the extent that anyone has committed graver sins before his conversion, to that extent he receives greater pardon from the grace of the giver after his conversion. Therefore the apostle is saying this about the sins we have already committed, lest anyone perish through despair of pardon because of the magnitude of his crimes; but he is not urging, as enemies were interpreting, that they commit more sins that through them they may receive greater good. Hence blessed Peter also properly advises and adds:

3:17 You therefore, brothers, knowing this beforehand, be on your guard lest you be led astray by the error of the unwise and fall away from your own steadfastness, *knowing beforehand* that the silly will bring in various kinds of errors,

114. Rv 22:18-19   115. Rm 4:5   116. Rm 5:20   117. Rm 3:8

some of them denying future judgment, some altering divine
oracles, some interpreting them wrongly, some relaxing the
bridles on self-indulgence, others deceiving the hearts of
the unfortunate by this and that trick of subterfuge, *be on
your guard,* lest you fall from the steadfastness of your
faith by some cunning of those who mislead.

**3:18 Increase, therefore, in grace and in the knowledge of
our Lord and saviour, Jesus Christ,** according to that saying
of the psalmist, *They will walk from strength to strength,
the God of gods will be seen in Zion.*[118] **To him be glory
both now and on the day of eternity.** Glory always to God
and the Lord our Saviour both now, when amidst the daily
pressures of adversities we still live in the body and are
straggling away from him, and particularly then, when the
long *desired of all nations*[119] will have come and deigned to
enlighten us with the presence of his vision. Meanwhile we
deserve to sigh for him and earnestly sing, *Because one day in
your courts is better than thousands [elsewhere].*[120]

118. Ps 84:7 (83:8)   119. Hg 2:8   120. Ps 84:10 (83:11)

1.   *Climax* is a rhetorical figure of speech in which there is a gradual progression from a weaker to a stronger manner of expression.

2.   Latin *Maronis*—the *cognomen* or surname of Publius Virgilus Maro.

3.   Latin *sectari*. Again, it is almost impossible to render in English the nuances of the Latin. The English word 'sect' comes from the Latin *secta* which means literally 'a way or manner of life' and in turn is derived from the past participle—deponent, the passive form has an active meaning—of the Latin verb *sectari*, 'to pursue eagerly'. This verb is an intensive form of a more frequently found verb, *sequor*, 'I follow'. Bede seems not to have known that the Latin noun *heresis*, 'heresy', is derived from the Greek verb αἱρέω, *haireō*, 'I take', in the middle voice in Greek, 'I take for myself, I choose'.

4.   The Latin word for 'redeemer', *redemptor*, has as its base the Latin verb *emo*, 'I buy', as in the Latin tag, *caveat emptor*, 'Let the buyer beware'. The prefix *re-*, indicates 'back', and so the compound means 'redeemer'.

5.   Bede elsewhere enumerates these six ages of the world, corresponding to the six days of creation, as 1) from Adam to Noah, 2) from Noah to Abraham, 3) from Abraham to David, 4) from David to the Babylonian Captivity, 5) from the Babylonian Captivity to Christ, 6) from Christ to the end of the world. (*Hom.* I.14; *CC* 122: 99, 136-102, 240) The seventh age, corresponding to the seventh day on which God rested or the sabbath, is the time when the saints are at rest in the afterlife, awaiting the day of the final or general judgment. The eighth age or day is the time of the general judgment and eternal rest. See note 14 on 1 Peter.

6.   I have not been able to find among the writings of Saint Gregory the Great the particular division of the words in 2 P 2:13 which Bede seems to prefer.

7.   Bede has here engaged in a bit of galloping philology by attempting to relate three Latin words that are similar in appearance but etymologically unconnected, viz., the verb *pellicio*—also spelled *pelliceo*—meaning 'seduce', the noun *pellex*—also spelled *paelex*—meaning 'mistress' but here translated 'seducer', and the noun *pellis* meaning 'skin'.

157

COMMENTARY ON 1 JOHN

1:1   **WHAT WAS FROM the beginning, what we heard, what we saw with our eyes.** The blessed apostle John wrote this Letter about the perfection of faith and charity, praising the faithfulness of those who were persevering in the unity of the Church, demonstrating moreover the wickedness of those who were disturbing the peace of the Church with their wild doctrines, particularly the followers of Cerinthus and Marcion who argued that Christ did not exist before Mary. On their account, too, he wrote his Gospel. There, indeed, he declared in his own and in the Lord's very words that the Son is consubstantial with the Father, but here he brought forward what he learned from the Lord by his own utterances and refuted the foolishness of the heretics by his apostolic authority. Hence he quickly points at the outset of the Letter to the divinity and to the true humanity of the same God and our Lord Jesus Christ, saying, *What was from the beginning, what we heard, what we saw.* For the Son of God was from the beginning,[1] but the disciples heard the same Son of God when he appeared as a human being and saw him with their eyes, a fact which he explained more fully in his Gospel. For what he says here. *What was from the beginning,* is what he says in his Gospel, *In the beginning was the word, and the word was with God, and the word was God, this was in the beginning with God,*[2] and what he appends here, *what we heard, what we saw with our eyes,* is what he appends there more fully, *And the word was made flesh and dwelt among us, and we*

1. Aug., *In Ioh. ep.* 1.1; PL 35:1978   2. Jn 1:1-2

saw his glory, the glory as of the only-begotten of the Father.[3] And lest he might appear to say too little in what he said, *what we saw with our eyes,* he added, **What we observed, and our hands touched concerning the word of life.** In truth, they not only saw the Lord with their bodily eyes, just as the rest did, but they also observed him and beheld his divine power with spiritual eyes, particularly those who saw him glorified on the mountain, among whom John himself was one.[4] For what he says, *And our hands touched concerning the word of life,* overcomes the madness of the Manicheans who deny that the Lord took to himself a true body. The apostles could not doubt that this was a true body, inasmuch as they proved its genuineness not only by seeing but also by touching it, particularly John himself who, being accustomed to recline on his lap at supper,[5] touched his members more freely as he was nearer. But also after his resurrection from the dead their hands touched concerning the word of life when they knew without doubt that he had received a true body, although now incorruptible, hearing from him in person, *Feel and see that a spirit does not have flesh and bones, as you see that I have.*[6] It is well said, however, *And our hands touched concerning the word of life,* because when they proved the genuineness of his body raised from the dead by examining it even with their hands, they knew for certain that he was the word of life, that is, true God. Hence Thomas,[7] who more especially was ordered to feel him, also confessed as soon as he felt his body, saying, *My Lord and my God.*[8]

1:2 And the life was made manifest, and we saw it and bear witness. He is speaking about that life which says in the Gospel, *I am the resurrection and the life,*[9] which was made

3. Jn 1:14   4. Mt 17:1-2   5. Jn 13:23   6. Lk 24:39
7. Aug., *In Ioh. ep.* 1:3; PL 35:1980   8. Jn 20:28
9. Jn 11:25

manifest, being revealed by the divine miracles [that he worked while] in the body. And the disciples, being present, saw that to which they bore witness with unquestionable veracity to later generations, when, as the same John wrote, as he was performing signs, *he manifested his glory, and his disciples believed in him.*[10] And because the apostle John bears witness that along with his fellow apostles he saw the life made manifest, let the heretic Apelles, who argued that the same life, that is, the Lord and Saviour, showed himself to the world not as God in truth but as a man in appearance, be put to shame together with his followers. **And we make known to you the eternal life which was with the Father and showed itself to us.** He was with the Father in his eternal divinity, he showed himself to the world in time in his humanity.

1:3 **What we saw and heard we make known also to you, so that you too may have fellowship with us, and that our fellowship may be with the Father and with his Son, Jesus Christ.** Blessed John shows clearly that all those who desire to have fellowship with God ought first to be united to the fellowship of the Church and in addition to learn that faith and to receive its sacraments, which the disciples received from the truth himself while he was living in the body. Nor do they who believe through the teaching of the apostles belong less to God in any way than those who believed through the Lord himself while he was preaching in the world, except insofar as the quality of their faith or works sets them apart. Hence the Son himself, also entreating the Father for this fellowship of the saints which they have in the Father and the Son, says, *Holy Father, keep those whom you have given me in your name, that they may be one, even as we;*[11] and a little bit further on, *But not for these only do I ask but for those also who will believe in me through their*

10. Jn 2:11   11. Jn 17:11

word, that they all may be one, even as you, Father [are] in me and I in you, that they also may be one in us.[12]

1:4 And we have written these things to you that our joy may be full. The joy of teachers becomes full when by preaching they lead many to the fellowship of the holy Church and to the fellowship of him through whom the Church is strengthened and increases, God the Father and his Son, Jesus Christ. Hence Paul also says to those whom he was instructing in the faith, *Make my joy full, that you may savor the same thing, having the same charity, being of one mind, savoring together.*[13]

1:5 And this is the message which we have heard from him and make known to you, that God is light, and there is no darkness in him. By this statement blessed John both shows the excellence of the divine purity which we also are ordered to imitate when he says, *Be holy, because I also, the Lord your God, am holy,*[14] and demonstrates the mad teaching of the Manicheans which claimed that the nature of God was overcome in war by the prince of darkness and was corrupted.

1:6 If we say that we have fellowship with him and walk in the darkness, we are lying and not telling the truth. He is calling sins heresies and hatred darkness. Therefore, the confession of faith alone is not at all sufficient for salvation when it lacks the witness of good works. But neither is the uprightness of works of any avail without faith and the simplicity of love. For whoever is beset in any way by darkness cannot have fellowship with him in whom no iniquity exists. For *what fellowship does light have with darkness?*[15]

12. Jn 17:20-21   13. Ph 2:2   14. Lv 19:2   15. 2 Co 6:14

1:7 But if we walk in the light, as he also is in the light, we have fellowship with one another. The difference in words should be noted, because he says that God is in the light but we ought to walk in the light. For the righteous walk in the light, when observing the works of the virtues, they advance to better things; whereas the divine holiness, to which there is said, *But you are the same,*[16] properly is recalled as being in the light, because full goodness, always existing, does not find [a place] where it can advance. For to the faithful is said, *Walk as sons of the light, for the fruit of the light is in all goodness and righteousness and truth,*[17] but God, without any advancing, is always good, righteous, true. Therefore, *if we walk in the light, as he also is in the light, we have fellowship with one another.* In this, namely, he gives clear evidence that we advance by walking in the way of the light, if we rejoice in the tie of fraternal fellowship with which we equally may reach the true light. But even if we are seen to do the works of light, to keep undefiled the rights of mutual love, yet not even thus ought we to consider that we can be cleansed from our sins completely by our own advance or effort, for there follows: **And the blood of Jesus his Son cleanses us from all sin.** For the sacrament of the Lord's passion has equally both freed us from all sins in baptism and the grace of our same redeemer forgives whatever we have committed through daily frailty after baptism, particularly when in the midst of the works of light which we do with humility we daily confess our errors to him, when we receive the sacraments of his blood, when after forgiving our debtors we entreat that our debts be forgiven us,[18] when, mindful of his passion, we gladly put up with all adversities. Wonderfully, however, when he speaks of God does he say, *And the blood of Jesus his Son.* In truth, the Son of God could not have blood in the nature of his divinity, but because the same Son of God also became the

16. Ps 102:27 (101:28)   17. Eph 5:8-9   18. Mt 6:12

son of man, properly, on account of the unity of his person, he calls it the blood of the Son of God, that he may show that He took on a true body, truly shed his blood for us, and may refute the heretics who deny either that a true body was taken by the Son of God or that the Lord Jesus truly suffered in the body which he took on. What Paul says is similar to this, *The Holy Spirit has set you, the bishops, to rule the Church of God which he acquired by his blood.*[19]

1:8   If we say that we have no sin, we deceive ourselves, and the truth is not in us. This statement prevails over the heresy of Pelagius which claimed both that all children are born without sin and that the elect, as they be without sin, are able to advance in this life. But let him say also with the prophet, *For see, I have been conceived in iniquities and my mother has borne me in profligacy.*[20] We who have come into the world with fault cannot exist in the world without fault, but *the blood of Jesus, the Son* of God, *cleanses us from all sin,* that our sins may not keep us under the authority of the enemy for the reason that *the mediator between God and men, the man, Jesus Christ,*[21] gave up for our sake what he did not owe. For he who for our sake gave the death of his body, which he did not owe, freed us from the death of the soul, which we owed.

1:9   If we confess our sins, he is faithful and just to forgive us our sins. Because we cannot be without sin[22] in this life, the first hope of salvation is confession, lest anyone consider himself righteous and rear up stiff-necked before the eyes of God; then [comes] love, *Because·charity covers a multitude of sins.*[23] Wherefore, in the following parts of this Letter he recommends [love] to us with manifold praise. He admirably links both together, however, because

19. Ac 20:28   20. Ps 51:5 (50:7)   21. 1 Tm 2:5
22. Aug., *In Ioh. ep.* 1:6; PL 35:1982   23. 1 P 4:8

we both ought to ask God's pardon for our sins and succeed in obtaining his pardon when we do ask. Therefore, he said that the Lord is also faithful in forgiving sins and keeps faith with his promise, because he who taught us to pray for our debts[24] and sins promised that his fatherly mercy and pardon would follow. He also maintains that he is righteous, because he righteously grants forgiveness for a true confession. **To forgive us our sins,** he says, **and to cleanse us from all iniquity.** In this life he forgives the elect their daily and trivial sins, without which we cannot live in this life; after they are freed from the body he cleanses them from all iniquity, bringing them into that life in which they neither wish to sin further nor can. Now those who pray he forgives greater temptations, so that these may not overcome them, he forgives the smallest ones, so that these may not harm them, then he cleanses them from everything, so that no further iniquity may exist for the blessed in the everlasting kingdom.

1:10 If we say that we have not sinned, we make him a liar, and his word is not in us. For he himself said through a man filled with his spirit, *There is not a righteous person on earth who does good and does not sin,*[25] and he himself also taught that we cannot be free from profligacy when he admonished us to pray, *And forgive us our debts as we also forgive our debtors.*[26] Let no one, therefore, believe, as Pelagius teaches, that he can live without sins and debts, when he sees the apostles praying earnestly for their own transgressions, as the Lord teaches. And there is also written elsewhere, *The righteous falls seven times and rises again.*[27] For it is impossible that some of the saints do not occasionally incur guilt in very small sins which are committed through talk, thought, ignorance, forgetfulness, necessity, will, surprise. But still they do not cease being righteous, because

24. Mt 6:12   25. Qo 7:21   26. Mt 6:12   27. Pr 24:16

with the Lord's assistance they rise again more quickly from
their guilty act.

**2:1 My little children, I am writing these things to you that
you may not sin.** He is not contradicting himself when,
having proposed that we cannot live without sin, he now says
that he is writing to us that we may not sin. But there he
warned us of necessity, with foresight, for our salvation, of
our weakness, lest anyone congratulate himself as if he were
innocent and, by praising himself for his deserts, perish all
the more; here he consequently urges that if we are unable to
be without all fault, we nonetheless do our best not to abet
the weakness of our condition by acting carelessly but strive
vigorously and watchfully against all vices, particularly the
more serious and open ones which we can more easily overcome or be wary of with the Lord's help, that, according to
what Paul says, *No temptation may lay hold of us, except
that which is human,*[28] that is, the one alone which human
weakness is completely unable to avoid. **But even if anyone
sins, we have an advocate with the Father, Jesus Christ, the
righteous.** See to what an extent John himself observes the
humility he teaches.

> Surely he was a righteous and great man, who drank
> in the secrets of the mysteries at the breast of the
> Lord.[29] And yet he did not say, 'You have me as
> an advocate with the Father,' but he said, *'we have
> an advocate';* and he said, *'we have',* not, 'you
> have'. He preferred to place himself among the
> number of sinners, that he might have Christ as an
> advocate, rather than place himself as an advocate
> instead of Christ and be found among the con-
> demned proud.[30] (And yet it must not be said that)

28. 1 Co 10:13   29. Cf. Jn 13:23-5
30. Aug., *In Ioh. ep.* 1.8; PL 35:1983-4
• Words in parentheses have been added by Bede to Augustine's text.

bishops and officials do not make requests for the people. (For) the apostle prays for the people, the people pray for the apostle (who says), *'Praying at the same time also for us, that God may open for us the door of the word'*.[31]

The Church prayed also for Peter when Peter was in chains and it was heard,[32] just as Peter too prayed for the Church, because all the members pray for each other. The head intercedes for all, concerning whom it has been written, *Who is also at the right hand of God and who also intercedes for us*.[33] For the only-begotten Son's interceding for humankind is his showing himself as a human being in the sight of his co-eternal Father, and his having asked on behalf of human nature is his having undertaken the same nature in the elevated rank of his divinity. Therefore, the Lord intercedes for us not with his voice but by having mercy, because what he was unwilling to have condemned in the elect he saved by undertaking. And when he said that *we have an advocate with the Father, Jesus Christ,* he did well to add, *the righteous.* For a righteous advocate does not undertake unrighteous cases, but he defends us who are righteous at the judgment if we both perceive and accuse ourselves as unrighteous. For why is he not righteous who already rages against his unrighteousness by his tears?

2:2 **And he is the propitiation for our sins.** He who through his humanity intercedes for us with the Father is the same one who through his divinity makes propitiation for us with the Father. **Not, however, for our sins only, but also for those of the whole world.** The Lord is the propitiation not only for those to whom John was writing and who were then living in the body but also for the whole Church which is spread abroad throughout the whole breadth of the world,[34]

---

31. Col 4:3   32. Cf. Ac 12:5   33. Rm 8:23
34. Greg., *Moral.* 17.29.43; PL 76:30D

extending from the first elect, undoubtedly, 'to the last
person to be born at the end of time'.[35] By these words he
condemns the schism of the Donatists who said that the
Church of Christ was enclosed within the boundaries of
Africa alone. The Lord, therefore, intercedes for the sins of
the whole world, because the Church which he procured with
his blood[36] exists throughout the whole world. Nor does this
contradict what he says further on, *And the whole world is
under the power of the evil one,*[37] because throughout the
whole world there are also those who serve the evil one, that
is, the ancient enemy.

**2:3 And in this we know that we have perceived him, if we
keep his commandments.** 'Which commandments'[38] he may
be talking about he discloses further on; it is charity.[39]

**2:4 He who says that he knows him and does not observe
his commandments is a liar, and the truth is not in him.**
Christ is called the truth. He says, *I am the way and the
truth and the life.*[40] In vain, therefore, do we applaud him
whose commandments we do not keep. Nor should we consider it a big thing to know the one God, when the demons also
believe and tremble.[41] But he shows what is truly to know
God in what follows, saying:

**2:5-6 He, however, who keeps his word, truly in him the
charity of God has been made perfect.** He truly knows God
then who proves that he has his charity by keeping his commandments. For this is what it is to know God, to love. For
anyone who does not love him shows clearly that he does not
know how lovable he is, that he has not learned to taste and
see how gentle and sweet the Lord is,[42] when he does not

---

35. Greg., *Hom. ev.* 1.19.1; PL 76:1154B   36. Ac 20:28
37. 1 Jn 5:19   38. Aug., *In Ioh. ep.* 1.9; PL 35:1984-5
39. 1 Jn 2:5   40. Jn 14:6   41. Jm 2:19   42. Ps 34:8 (33:9)

strive to be pleasing in his sight by continual exertion. **And in this we know that we are in him.** He who says that he **remains in him ought himself also to walk as he walked,** that is, through a love as full as possible to pray even for one's enemies, saying, *Father, forgive them,*[43] but also to despise all the prosperous things of the world, to put up with mockery and insults gladly, as he himself also says, *If anyone wishes to come after me, let him deny himself and take up his cross and follow me.*[44]

2:7-8 Dearly beloved, I am not writing you a new commandment but an old commandment which you had from the beginning; the old commandment is the word which you heard. Again I am writing you a new commandment. The same charity is both an old commandment, because it was ordained from the beginning, and a new commandment, because after the darkness has been driven away it infused a desire for the new light. Hence there is properly appended: **Which is true both in him and in you, since the darkness has passed away and the true light now shines.** See whence it is new, because the darkness pertains to the old man but the light to the new man. Accordingly, the apostle Paul says, *Put off from yourselves the old man and put on the new;*[45] and again, *You were once darkness but now light in the Lord.*[46]

2:9 He who says that he is in the light and hates his brother is still in darkness. The Lord admonishes us to love our enemies.[47] Therefore, he who says that he is a Christian and hates his brother is still in sin. And he did well to add, *still,* because surely all human beings are born in the darkness of vices, they all remain in darkness until they are enlightened by Christ in the grace of baptism. But anyone who comes

43. Lk 23:34   44. Lk 9:23   45. Eph 4:22,24, Col 3:9-10
46. Eph 5:8   47. Mt 5:44

hating his brother to the font of life where he is to be re-born, to the cup of that precious blood whereby he is to be redeemed, even though he may think he is enlightened by the Lord, is still in darkness and cannot in any way have put off the darkness of his sins when he did not take care to put on the fundamentals[48] of charity. For this is the reason that Simon, even though just bathed with the water of baptism, heard from him who had the keys of heaven,[49] *You have no part or lot in this utterance,*[50] *for I see that you are in the gall of bitterness and the bond of iniquity,*[51] because namely he neglected the covenant of brotherly relationship and wished to buy with money the gift of the spirit by which the unity of the Church is preserved, and to have it for himself.

2:10 He who loves his brother remains in the light, and there is in him no stumbling block, that is, offensiveness. For 'he who loves his brother puts up with everything for the sake of the unity'[52] of charity. For *there is great peace for those who love your law,* that is, [love] charity, *and in them there is no stumbling block.*[53] And Paul says, *Bearing with one another in charity, being eager to keep the unity of the spirit in the bond of peace.*[54]

2:11 But he who hates his brother is in darkness and walks in darkness and does not know where he is going, since the darkness has blinded his eyes. For he is going unawares into the lower world, being unwitting and blind he is being thrown to punishment, withdrawing namely from the light of Christ who advises and says, *I am the light of the world; he who follows me will not walk in darkness but will have the light of life.*[55]

2:12 I am writing to you, little children, since your sins

48. Col 3:12: *uiscera caritatis*   49. Cf. Mt 16:19   50. Ac 8:21
51. Ac 8:23   52. Aug., *In Ioh. ep.* 1.12; PL 35:1987
53. Ps 119 (118):165   54. Eph 4:2-3   55. Jn 8:12

will be forgiven for his name's sake. He honors all his hearers whom he had gone before in Christ with the name children, because namely they had been reborn of water and the spirit[56] and had received forgiveness of their sins. And that you may not doubt that all the faithful can properly be called children of the fathers gone before, hear the prophet singing about the Church, *All the glory of that daughter of kings is from within,*[57] and likewise to the same, *In place of your fathers sons have been born to you.*[58]

2:13 I am writing to you, fathers, for you have perceived him who is from the beginning. He calls them fathers not because of age but as being greater and mature in wisdom. *For a venerable old age is not length of time nor reckoned by the number of years; but the understanding of a person is grey hair and a stainless life the time of old age.*[59] For it is the duty of fathers to recall and know the past to reveal it to the younger generation. Hence it has been written, *Ask your fathers, and they will make it known to you.*[60] And therefore he properly calls those fathers who learned to know him who is from the beginning, that is, the Lord Christ, together with the Father and the Holy Spirit, and to preach him faithfully to their hearers. **I am writing to you, young men, since you have overcome the evil one.** The time of young manhood is difficult to control on account of the urgings of the body and also contentions on account of the energy of this age-group. Hence John is writing to those young men who have overcome the temptations of bodily urgings through love of the word of God. He is writing also to those who, when faced with persecution on account of the word of God, because of their greater perfection have bravely rejected all the tricks of the malicious enemy.

2:14 I am writing to you, children, since you have

---

56. Jn 3:5 　　　　　　　57. Ps 45:13 (44:14)
58. Ps 45:16 (44:17) 　　 59. Ws 4:8-9 　　60. Dt 32:7

perceived the Father. He calls the humble in spirit children, who, the more they assent to being humbled beneath the mighty hand of God,[61] the more deeply do they perceive the hidden things of his eternity, as the Son says of such as these to the same Father, *You have hidden these things from the wise and prudent and have revealed them to the little ones.*[62] **I am writing to you, fathers, since you have perceived him who is from the beginning.**

> He hands on and repeats this. Remember that you are fathers. If you forget him who is from the beginning, you have lost your right to be called a father.[63]

I am writing to you, youths, because you are strong, and the word of God remains in you, and you have overcome the evil one.

> Advert again and again to the fact that you are youths, fight that you may overcome, overcome that you may be crowned, be humble lest you fall in the fight.[64]

2:15 Do not love the world or those things that are in the world. He is writing this generally to all the children of the Church, both to those, namely, who are fathers through the maturity of prudence and teaching, and to those who are children through their devotion to humility, and to those who are young men or youths because they have overcome the conflicts of temptations. All of these he commands equally to use the world, indeed, for what they need but not to love it for what they want over and above that; as Paul also says, *And do not have concern for the body to fulfil its desires.*[65] **If anyone loves the world, the charity of the Father is not in him.** Let no one deceive himself. One heart does not contain two loves so opposed to each other. Hence

61. 1 P 5:6   62. Lk 10:21 63. Aug., *In Ioh. ep.* 2.7; PL 35:1993
64. *Ibid.*   65. Rm 13:14

the Lord also says, *No one can serve two masters;*[66] and again, *You cannot serve God and mammon.*[67] But as the charity of the Father is the source and beginning of all the virtues, so love of the world is the root and tinder of all the vices. Hence there follows:

2:16 Since all that is in the world is the concupiscence of the body and the concupiscence of the eyes and the pride of life. When he says, *All that is in the world,* he means all who live in the world in mind, who dwell in the world[68] in love, as those who have their way of life in the heavens,[69] whose hearts are above, live in heaven although in their bodies they walk on earth. Therefore, all that is in the world, that is, all the lovers of the world, have only the concupiscence of the body, the concupiscence of the eyes and the pride of life. In truth, in these names for the vices he includes all the kinds of vice. For concupiscence of the body is everything that belongs with yearnings and delights of the body, among which are particularly food, drink and sleeping together, about which Solomon says, *The leech has two daughters who say, 'Come on, come on'.*[70] Concupiscence of the eyes is all the curiosity which comes about in learning abominable practices, in beholding base and useless shows, in acquiring temporal things, in picking out and even picking up the vices of one's neighbors. The pride of life occurs when one is puffed up by honors. Yet by these three things human cupidity is tempted.[71] By these Adam was tempted and overcome; by concupiscence of the body, namely, when the enemy showed him the forbidden food of the tree and persuaded him to eat it,[72] by concupiscence of the eyes when he said, *'You will know good and evil',*[73] and, *'Your eyes will be opened',* by the pride of life when he said, *'You will be like gods'.*[74] By these the

66. Mt 6:24　　67. Lk 16:13
68. Aug., *In Ioh. ep.* 2.12-14; PL 35:1996　　　69. Ph 3:20
70. Pr 30:15　　71. Cf. Greg., *Hom ev.* 1.16.2: PL 76:1136AB
72. Gn 3:1-7　　73. Gn 3:5　　74. *Ibid.*

Lord was tempted and overcame; by the concupiscence of the
body, that is food, when it was suggested to him, *'Command
these stones to become loaves of bread'*,[75] by the concupiscence of the eyes, that is, curiosity, when he was advised
to cast himself down from the height of the temple in order
to test whether he would be taken up by angels,[76] by the
pride of life, that is, empty boasting, when he was set upon a
mountain and all the kingdoms of this earth were shown him
and promised him if he would adore [the enemy].[77]
Which is not from the Father but from the world. Our struggle against the vices has not been naturally implanted in us by
God our Father and creator but is proved to have befallen
us from our love of this world, which we preferred
to our creator. For God made human beings upright, and they
have involved themselves in endless questions,[78] as Solomon
bears witness. Hence James also says, *Let no one, when he is
tempted, say that he is tempted by God. For God is not the
instigator of evil, for he himself tempts no one. Each one, in
fact, is tempted, drawn on and lured by his own concupiscence.*[79]

2:17   **And the world and its concupiscence will pass away;
but he who does the will of the Lord remains for ever.**
The world will pass away when on the day of judgment it will
be changed into a better shape by fire,[80] so that there may be
a new heaven and a new earth.[81] Its concupiscence will also
pass away, because there will be no further time for pamper-
ing self-indulgences or committing any other sin. For,
On that day all their thoughts will pass away,[82] those certainly by which they were intent on the desires of this world.
But as for him who does the will of the Lord, his thoughts do
not pass away at all when the world does but because he

75. Mt 4:3   76. Mt 4:5-6   77. Mt 4:8-9
78. Qo 7:29 (Vulg. 30)   79. Jm 1:13-14
80. 2 Pt 3:7,10   81. 2 Pt 3:13   82. Ps 146 (145):2

desired heavenly and eternal things they remain for ever unchangeable, because he attains from on high the rewards he had wished for. Hence the Lord also says about the faithful woman, nay rather about every soul which perfectly follows his will, *Mary has chosen the best part, which shall not be taken away from her.*[83] Therefore, he who desires to remain unshaken and quiet for ever should embrace those things that do not know how to pass away, he should follow the will of the God who is for ever.

2:18 **Little children, it is the last hour.** He calls the last age of the world which is now in progress the last hour, according to that parable of the Lord in which he tells of the workers having been hired at the first, third, sixth, ninth, and eleventh hours.[84] For those who served the will of their Creator either by teaching or living properly from the beginning of the world cultivated the vineyard of the Lord from the first hour; those who lived from the time of Noah did so from the third hour; those who lived from the time of Abraham did so from the sixth hour; those who lived from the time of the giving of the law did so from the ninth hour; those who obey the heavenly commands from the time of the Lord's incarnation to the end of the world do so from the eleventh hour.[1] In this [eleventh] hour, namely, it was foretold by the prediction of the prophets that there would be both the coming of the saviour in the flesh and that there would follow the plague of the antichrist, which would assail the heralds of salvation. Hence there follows: **And as you have heard that the antichrist is coming, now many antichrists have appeared.**[85] He is calling the heretics antichrists. But those who by their wrongful actions destroy the faith of Christ which they profess are also justifiably called antichrists, that is, opposed to Christ. All these give

83. Lk 10:42   84. Mt 20:1-7
85. Aug., *In Ioh. ep.* 3.4; PL 35:1999

witness to that greatest antichrist who will come at the end of
the world as to their head. Hence Paul also says of him that
the mystery of iniquity is already at work.[86] **From this we
know that it is the last hour.** From what? From the fact that
many antichrists have appeared. What he says about it being
even then the last hour can also be understood thus, however,
that the persecution which was being waged at that time by
the heretics had great similarity to that final persecution
which is to come just before the day of judgment, although
the former smote the Church only with savage tongues, the
latter will also smite it with injurious swords.

**2:19   They went out from us but they were not from among
us.** It appeared that we should weep as for a loss when we
heard, *They went out from us,* but quickly consolation is
offered us when there is appended, *But they were not from
us.* For it is clear that

> only the antichrists are able to go forth, whereas
> those who are not opposed to Christ are not able
> to go forth, for the one who is not opposed to
> Christ stays in his body. (But) there are those like
> this who are within, in the body of Christ when his
> body is being cured, and there will be perfect
> health only at the resurrection of the dead; they
> are in the body of Christ in the same way as evil
> humors, and when they are vomited out then the
> body is relieved. So also when the evil go out then
> the Church is relieved.[87]

They went out from us, he says, but do not be sad, *they
were not from among us.*

> From what do you prove this? **For if they had
> been from among us certainly they would have
> remained with us.** (It must be seen) from this,
> therefore, that many who are not from among us

86. 2 Th 2:7   87. Aug., *In Ioh. ep.* 3.4-5; PL 35:1999

receive the sacraments (of Christ. But) temptation
proves that they are not from among us. When
temptation comes upon them as if by the consequence of a wind, they fly forth, because they were
not grains. But all will then fly away when the
Lord's threshing-floor begins to be winnowed on
the day of judgment.[88]

If any went out by sinning but return by repenting, surely
they are proved to be not antichrists but in Christ if the
end of their present life finds them remaining in the Church.
But that it may be clear that they are not all from among us.
With the Lord's permission, certain persons go out from the
Church even before the final dismissal, showing that they
were not members of the Church and did not belong to the
body of Christ; this is so that by this it may become clearly
obvious that all are not from among us who are set with us
within and receive the sacraments of Christ, but only those
who perform works worthy of the same sacraments in the
unity of the Church of Christ.

2:20 **But you have the anointing from the holy one and
know all things.**

The spiritual anointing is the Holy Spirit himself,
whose sacrament is in a visible anointing. He says
that all who have this anointing of Christ perceive
good and evil and do not need to be taught, because the anointing itself teaches them.[89]

And he did well, when he was speaking about heretics, to
turn abruptly to his hearers and say that they have an
anointing from the holy one, in order to show them that
heretics and all antichrists on the contrary are deprived of
the gift of spiritual grace and do not belong to the Lord who
is accustomed to be called holy by the prophets; nay rather,
they hold a place of perdition among the ministers of Satan,

88. *Ibid.* 3.5; 2000   89. *Ibid.*

who has no trace of holiness.

2:21 We have not written to you as to those who are ignorant of the truth but as to those who know it. For you know the truth of the faith and of life, having been taught by the anointing of the spirit, and you do not need to be taught, except so that you may carry through what you have begun. **And that no lie is from the truth.** This verse belongs with the preceding one, and the meaning is, *We have not written to you as to those who are ignorant of the truth but as to those who know it, and* to those who know this also, *that no lie is from the truth.* But

> see, we have been advised how to perceive the antichrist. Christ said, '*I am the truth*'.[90] But *no lie is from the truth.* Therefore, all who lie are not yet from Christ. He did not say, 'Some lie is from the truth and some lie is not from the truth'.[91]

Let no one deceive himself, let no one delude himself. *No lie is from the truth.*

2:22 Who is the liar but he who claims that Jesus is not the Christ? He had just said that no lie is from the truth. But because there are many kinds of lies differing greatly from each other, now he puts the lie of the denial of Christ as if in the singular, because surely this is so abominable and detestable a lie that in comparison to it the rest seem either small or nonexistent, just as it was said to Jerusalem when she was sinning. *Sodom has been made righteous in your place.*[92] This denial is characteristic of the Jews, so that they say that Jesus is not the Christ. /[93] But the heretics who believe wrongly about Christ also claim that Jesus is not the Christ, because they do not have a correct sense of Christ

90. Jn 14:6   91. Aug., *In Ioh. ep.* 3.6; PL 35:2000   92. Ezk 16:25
93. / Cf. Aug., *In Ioh. ep.* 3.7-8; PL 35:2001-2. /

and they confess him to be not such as divine truth teaches but as their superficiality invents. Bad Catholics as well, who scorn to obey the commands of Christ, deny that Jesus is the Christ, for they do not pay the service they owe of fear and love to Christ as Son of God but according to their own wishes they are not afraid to contradict him as a man of no power. And therefore all these are proven heretics and anti-christs, that is, adversaries of Christ, the apostle bearing witness that *They confess that they know God but deny him by their deeds.*[94] / **This is the antichrist, he who denies the Father and the Son.** With this statement he strikes at both the heretics and particularly the Jews who denied that Jesus was the Christ, the Son of God, and yet said that they had God as their Father, showing that those who deny the Son in vain confess God as their Father. Hence even the Lord himself disowns them when he says, *If God were your Father, you would certainly love me; for I have proceeded and come from God.*[95]

2:23 No one who denies the Son has the Father; he who confesses the Son has the Father also. He is here searching for the sort of confession of heart, voice, and deed that Paul sought for when he said, *And no one can say, 'Jesus is Lord', except in the Holy Spirit,*[96] which is to say clearly, 'No one can serve Christ the Lord with perfect profession and action save by the gift of grace of the Holy Spirit.'

2:24 Let what you have heard from the beginning remain in you; if what you have heard from the beginning remains in you, you also will remain in the Son and in the Father. Follow with all your heart, he says, that faith, those teachings which you received from the earliest time when the Church was being born by the voice of the apostles. For

94. Tt 1:16   95. Jn 8:42   96. 1 Co 12:3

these alone are the things that make you sharers in the divine grace. *And if anyone says to you, 'See, here is the Christ, see he is there,' do not believe him; for there will arise false christs and false prophets.*[97] *You also,* he says, *will remain in the Son and in the Father,* putting the Son first, because as the Son himself says, *No one comes to the Father except through the Son,*[98] no one will see the glory of the divine eminence save he who has been reborn through the sacraments of the humanity which the Son undertook. Or at least he named the Son first and then the Father so that the Arians might not say that the Son must be believed to be less than the Father for the reason that he is never found named before the Father.

2:25 And this is the promise which he has made to us, eternal life. As if you were to ask about the reward and say, 'See, in my case, I keep and obey what I have heard from the beginning, I bear with dangers, labors, temptations, for that dwelling place; what fruit, what reward, what will he give me later?' he says, *And this is the promise which he has made to us, eternal life.* 'Let the remembrance of the promised reward cause you to persevere in the work.'[99]

2:26 I have written these things to you about those who deceive you. The deceivers whom he names are to be understood as being not only the heretics who seek to turn people aside from the faith by their perverse teaching but also those who by the allurements and adversities of the world withdraw the minds of the weak from the promise of eternal life by wrongly coddling or terrifying them.

2:27 And let the anointing which you have received from him remain in you, and you have no need for anyone to

97. Mk 13:21-22   98. Jn 14:6
99. Aug., *In Ioh. ep.* 3:11; PL 35:2003

teach you. See to it, he says, with the Lord's help that you keep the grace of the Holy Spirit which you obtained in baptism unblemished in your heart and body, according to that saying of the apostle Paul, *Do not suppress the Spirit.*[100] And so it comes about that with the Spirit teaching you inwardly you have less need of the external instruction of men. The anointing of which he speaks can be understood of charity of God which is *poured in our hearts by the Holy Spirit who has been given to us,*[101] and which very quickly sets the heart it fills on fire to observe the commandments of God. **But as his anointing teaches you about everything.** He rightly adds, *about everything,* in the same way as the Lord, speaking in the Gospel about the same Spirit, says to his disciples, *He will teach you everything.*[102]

> because unless the same Spirit is present in the heart of the hearer, the utterance of the teacher is worthless. Therefore, let no one attribute to the person teaching what he understands from the mouth of the teacher, because unless the one who is teaching is within, the tongue of the teacher toils externally in vain.'[103]

Yet a teacher ought not cease from doing what he can, according to what Paul says, *I planted, Apollos watered, but God gave the increase.*[104] **And it is true and not a lie.** He very carefully emphasizes with frequent repetition that the things which he preaches are true and quite clean of all stain of untruth, that he might restrain those who had presumed to teach otherwise and might also earnestly advise us that we cannot find everlasting life otherwise than by following that purity of faith and work which was given to the early Church by the apostles and by remaining to the end of this life in following and keeping the same [purity]. Similar to this is that saying of the apostle Paul, *Let no one deceive you*

100. 1 Th 5:19   101. Rm 5:5   102. Jn 14:26
103. Greg., *Hom. in ev.* 2.30.3; PL 76:1222A.   104. 1 Co 3:6

*with empty words; for it was on this account that the anger
of God came upon the children of unbelief.*[105] But what is
said in another translation, 'And he is truthful and not a
liar,' belongs with the previous verse where it is said,
But as his anointing teaches you about everything, meaning
that the same anointing is truthful, 'that is, the Spirit himself who teaches men cannot lie.[106] **And as he has taught
you, remain in him**. Do not be led astray by various and out-
landish teachings; by that faith, by that observance which he
taught, remain in him. For *the person who perseveres to the
end will be saved.*[107]

**2:28 And now, little children, remain in him, that when he
shows himself we may have confidence and not be disconcerted by him at his coming.** He who in the midst of persecutions by unbelievers and mockery by his sensual neighbors
remains with the Lord has confidence in his coming, knowing that *the patience of the poor will not perish to the
end.*[108] But anyone who is ashamed or afraid to offer the
other cheek to the one who strikes him[109] or to endure
patiently the reproach given by his neighbor or the other
things of this sort which the Lord has ordered us to observe,
or at least in a time of persecution to profess publicly that
he is a Christian, he surely cannot have confidence in the
coming of the Lord, because he has neglected to preserve
confidence in his profession [of faith] in this life. Yea,
rather, he will be disconcerted by him at his coming. For in
this matter he says, *He who is ashamed of me and my
utterances, this one will the son of man put to shame when
he comes in his majesty and that of his Father and of
his holy angels.*[110]

2:29 If you know that he is righteous, know that everyone

105. Eph 5:6   106. Aug., *In Ioh. ev.* 4.2; PL 35:2005
107. Mt 10:22   108. Ps 9:18 (9:19) 109. Lk 6:29 110. Lk 9:26

who behaves righteously is born of him.

Our righteousness now comes from faith. Perfect righteousness exists only in the angels, and scarcely in the angels, if they are compared to God. Yet, if there is any perfect righteousness in souls and spirits and those whom God created, it is in the holy, righteous, good angels driven away by no pride but always remaining in attentive regard to the word of God and holding nothing else sweet except him by whom they are created. Perfect righteousness is in these. But in us it began to exist according to the Spirit in faith. (Hence the psalmist says,) *Make a beginning*[2] *for the Lord by confessing.*[111] Make a beginning, he says. The beginning of our righteousness is the confession of our sins. You have begun not to defend your sin, you have already started [on the path] towards righteousness. It will be perfected in you, however, when it will delight you to do nothing else, when death will be swallowed up in victory,[112] when no concupiscence will appeal to you, when there will be no struggle against flesh and blood,[113] when there will be the crown of victory and triumph over the enemy, then there will be perfect right-eousness. (Therefore) *If you know that he is righteous,* he says, *know that everyone who behaves righteously is born of him,* of God, of Christ. And because he said, he *is born of him,* he is encourag-ing us. Therefore, because we have already been born of him, we are perfect.[114]

Accordingly, listen to what follows:

3:1 See what kind of charity the Father has given us, that

---

111. Ps 147:7 (146:7)   112. 1 Co 15:54
113. Eph 6:12   114. Aug., *In Ioh. ep.* 4.3; PL 35:2006-7

we are called and are the children of God. The grace that our
Creator has given us is great, so that we both know how and
are able to love him, and to love him as children love their
father, when it would have been a great thing if we were able
to love him in the way faithful servants love their masters, in
the way lowly, faithful hired servants love their masters. But
the same John bears witness in his Gospel how we ought to be
made children of God, saying, *He came to his own place, and
his own people did not receive him; but he gave power to as
many as received him, who believe in his name, to become
children of God.*[115] By joining both witnesses, therefore, it
becomes clear that we are made children of God through
faith and love. But the teachings of both Pelagius and Arius
are condemned by this. The heresy of Pelagius, indeed, who
had dared to say that human beings can be saved without
the grace of God, is condemned in that it is said that the charity and the power by which we receive the adoption of sons[116]
is given to us by God. Arius, moreover, who said that
the Son is less than the Father and unlike him, is refuted
from what the same John says both here to the effect that
charity by which we are called and are the children of God
is given to us by the Father and also in his Gospel through
the Lord our Saviour says that the power to become children
of God is given to those who believe. For it is clear that they
have one substance and the same power who bestow
heavenly gifts on men equally and without distinction.
**It is for this reason that the world does not know us, that it
does not know him.** By the world in this place he means the
lovers of the world. And this is why at the judgment, when
these same persons have seen the glory of the saints whose
faith they had despised, *they will say to one another, groaning and repenting, 'These are they whom we once held in
derision and, as it were, a byword for taunts; witless we
judged their life madness and their end without honor. How*

115. Jn 1:11-12   116. Ga 4:5

have they been numbered among the children of God, and is their lot among the saints?'[117]

3:2 Dearly beloved, we are now children of God, and it has not yet appeared what we shall be. Paul also says, *For you have died, and your life has been hidden with Christ in God,*[118] died, namely, by snuffing out your former life which was in sins, and having a new life in Christ through faith, whose depth has not yet visibly appeared to us. **We know that when he appears we shall be like him.** And Paul also explains this in other words, saying, *When Christ, your life, appears, they you also will appear with him in glory.*[119] *We shall be like him,* he says, because when we shall enjoy with attentive regard[120] his unchangeable and eternal divinity, we also shall be immortal and like him indeed, because we shall be happy. And yet, we shall not be like our Creator, because we are creatures. For, *Who among the children of God shall be like God?*[121] Although this can also seem to be said about the immortality of the body and in this we shall indeed be like God, but [in fact we will be] only like the Son who alone among the persons of the Trinity received a body, in which he died, rose and brought it to the heavenly heights. **For we shall see him as he is.** For God to be means to be eternal and to remain unchangeable. Hence he says to Moses, *I am who am,* and, *You shall say to the children of Israel, 'He who is sent me to you.'*[122] Therefore, we shall see him as he is when we regard him attentively in the very substance of his deity, a thing which is granted to absolutely none of the elect in this life, when even the lawgiver himself entreated the Lord, whom he was accustomed to regard attentively in his appearance as an angel, and said, *Lord, show me yourself that I may see you,*[123] and heard from the same Lord, *No one shall see my face and live.*[124] Still, in

117. Ws 5:3-5   118. Col 3:3   119. Col 3:4
120. *contemplatio* 121. Ps 89:6 (88:7) 122. Ex 3:14
123. Ex 33:13   124. Ex 33:20

return for the merit of his great holiness, he said to him, *I shall show you all goodness.*[125] Hence Paul also says, *Now we see in a mirror in obscurity, but then face to face.*[126]

> Hence the reply that Moses received is true, because no one can see the face of God and live, that is, no one living in this life can see him as he is. For many have seen, but what the will (of God) chose, not what his nature presented. And this is what John says, *For we shall see him as he is,* not as human beings have seen him, when he wished, in the appearance that he chose, not in that nature in which he is hidden within himself even when he was seen, but as he is. This was what was being requested from him (by Moses) when it was said to him, '*Show me yourself,*' by him who spoke with him face to face, for no one has ever grasped the fullness of God with the eyes of his body let alone with the mind. For it is one thing to see, another to comprehend by seeing, because a thing is seen whenever it is sensed as present, but it is comprehended totally by sight because it is seen in such a way that none of it is hidden from the one seeing it or a complete view of its outline can be made out, as nothing of your present intention is hidden from you but you can have a complete view of the outline of your ring. I have included two things as examples, one pertaining to the gaze of the mind, the other to the physical eyes, for sight must be referred to both, that is, both to the eyes and to the mind.'[127]

3:3 And everyone who has this hope in him makes himself holy, as he also is holy. Many say that they have hope of the

---

125. Ex 33:19   126. 1 Co 13:12
127. Aug., *ep.* 20-21; CSEL 44:294,9-295,9

heavenly life in Christ but they make this confession ineffective by living carelessly. He who is eager to strive vigorously to perform good actions gives clear evidence in his case of his hope from on high, being convinced that no one will arrive at the likeness of God in the future except by making himself holy with the holiness of God in the present, that is, unless he imitate [this holiness] by rejecting *wickedness and worldly desires,* however, and by *living soberly and righteously and faithfully.*[128] For thus are we ordered to imitate the purity of divine holiness in accord with the capacity of our nature, as we are admonished to hope for the glory of the divine likeness in accord with our own, that is, created, measure. For the teaching of Pelagius which says about human beings, 'They make themselves holy as if someone can make himself holy by his own free choice without divine help,' must not be believed to be of assistance. But he who has hope in the Lord makes himself holy, as far as he can, by striving himself and in everything requiring the grace of him who says, *Without me you can do nothing,*[129] and by saying to him, *Be my helper, do not forsake me.*[130]

3:4 **Everyone who commits sin also commits iniquity.** Let no one say, 'Sin is one thing, iniquity another.' Let no one say, 'I am a sinner but I am not wicked.' (For,) *Everyone who commits sin also commits iniquity,* **and sin is iniquity.**[131]

The force of this thought is grasped more easily in the Greek language in which this Letter is written, since in that language iniquity is called ἀνομία, which implies something done, as it were, against the law or without the law, since in Greek νόμος means law. When John says therefore, *Everyone who commits sin also commits iniquity,* that is,

128. Tt 2:12   129. Jn 15:5   130. Ps 27:9 (26:9)
131. Aug., *In Ioh. ep.* 4.8; PL 35:2010

ἀνομίαν, *and sin is iniquity,* he clearly suggests that by every single sin we commit we act against the law of God, according to that saying of the psalmist, *I have counted all sinners on earth as transgressors.*[132] For all who commit sin are guilty of transgression, that is, not only those who reject the known precepts of the written law which have been given them but also those who whether through weakness or negligence or even ignorance destroy the innocence of the natural law which we all received in the first-created man. But the Latin word is also in agreement with this same explanation, for iniquity means 'what is opposed, as it were, to equity'.[3] And he *who commits sin also commits iniquity, and sin is iniquity,* because whoever commits sin surely becomes opposed, by sinning, to the equity of the divine law. Nonetheless, lest we who are entirely unable to be without sins and iniquities should absolutely lose hope about salvation, let us see what follows about the Lord:

3:5   **And you know that he appeared in order to take away sins, and there is no sin in him.** John the Baptist also bears this witness concerning the Lord, saying, *Look, the lamb of God, look, he takes away the sins of the world.*[133] But the Lord was able to take away sins because *there is no sin in him.* Many great and perfect persons have come into the world, but none of them was able to take away the sins of the world, because none was able to be in the world without sin. Therefore let not Pelagius glory, let not Julian,[4] his follower, exalt himself when he hears, *Everyone who has hope in the Lord makes himself holy.* For no one takes away sin, because not even the law, although holy and righteous and good,[134] was able to remove it, no one [can] except he in whom there is no sin. He takes them away, however, both by forgiving those that have been committed and by helping that they may not be repeated and by bringing us to the life

132. Ps 119 (118):119 133. Jn 1:29   134. Rm 7:12

where they are completely unable to be committed.

3:6 Everyone who remains in him does not commit sin. 'Insofar as one remains in him, to that extent one does not commit sin.'[135] **And everyone who commits sin has not seen him or perceived him.** He is speaking of the vision and perception of faith by which the righteous even if this life take pleasure in seeing God, until they come to that view of clear vision of him to come of which it is said above, *For we shall see him as he is.* Therefore, *Everyone who commits sin has not seen him or perceived him.* For if he had tasted and seen that the Lord is sweet[136] he would never by sinning separate himself from seeing his glory. And insofar as the righteous call up the memory of the abundance of his sweetness and spring up in his righteousness,[137] to that extent do they strive by keeping themselves free from sins to be in harmony with his unchangeable and incomparable righteousness.

3:7 Little children, let no one deceive you. He who acts righteously is righteous, as he also is righteous. *He is righteous,* he says, *as he also is righteous,* and above, *he makes himself holy, as he also is holy,* not that our righteousness and holiness can be equal to the divine righteousness or holiness, since it is written, *There is no one holy as is the Lord.*[138] But as there is a great difference between the face of a person and his image in a mirror—because the image is an imitation, the body the truth, and yet

> as the eyes are here, so also are they there, as the ears are here, so also are they there, the reality is different. But as it is (related) to the likeness, (so indeed) we also bear the image of God, but not that which the Son, equal to the Father, has. (For) we also, if we were not as he is, according to our

135. Aug., *In Ioh. ep.* 4:8; PL 35:2010   136. Ps 34:8 (33:9)
137. Ps 145 (144):7   138. 1 S 2:2

limited capacity, would not be said to be like him.
Therefore (he makes) us (holy,) as he also is (holy,)
but he is (holy) from eternity, we are (holy) by
faith; we are righteous, as he also is righteous, but
he in unchangeable duration, we are righteous by
believing in him whom we do not see, that we may
someday see.[139]

3:8 He who commits sin is of the devil, not by deriving the
origin of his body from the devil, as Manicheus believes most
wickedly about all human beings, but by taking the example
and suggestion of sinning from him, just as we also have
become children of Abraham by imitating the faith of Abraham, and on the contrary the Jews have not become the
children of Abraham by abandoning the faith of Abraham, as
the Lord said to them, *You are of your father, the devil.*[140]
Since the devil sins from the beginning. Although he began
by saying, *from the beginning,* he added a verb in the present
tense, *he sins,* because from the time when in the beginning
the devil began to sin he has never ceased, being deterred
namely, neither by the immensity of his present punishments nor by fear of future ones. Hence anyone neglecting
to turn away from sinning is justifiably said to be of him.
But *from the beginning the devil sins,* from that time certainly from which he was made, from which also he was the
beginning of all created things. Now, it should not be
doubted that the angels were formed among the first
created beings, but while the rest [of them] referred the
glory of their condition to the praise of their Creator, he
who was formed first, as soon as he beheld the height of his
honor, puffed up proudly with his followers against the
Creator and sinning because of the same pride from the
beginning was changed from an archangel into the devil.
The Son of God appeared for this reason, that he might

139. Aug., *In Ioh. ep.* 4.9; PL 35:2010   140. Jn 8:44

destroy the works of the devil.
> All sinners, to the extent that they are sinners, are born of the devil. Adam was made by God, but when he consented to the devil he was born of the devil and begot all his progeny to be as he was. That birth cast down to death, the second birth, (that is, of baptism,) raised up to life; that birth drags sin along with it, the second birth liberates from sin. For Christ came as a human being to take away the sins of the human race.[141]

About this taking away there is properly appended:

3:9 Everyone who is born of God commits not sin since His seed remains in him and he is not able to commit sin since he is born of God. But he says this, not about every sin—for, *If we say that we have no sin, we deceive ourselves*[142] —but about the violation of charity which he who has within himself the seed of God, that is, the word of God by which he is reborn, cannot commit.[143] For he makes this clear in what follows by saying:

3:10 In this the children of God and the children of the devil are clear. Everyone who is not righteous and does not love his brother is not of God. Love alone, therefore, distinguishes between the children of God and the children of the devil. Those who have charity are born of God; those who do not have it are not born of God.[144]
> Have whatever you wish, if you do not have this alone[145] nothing is of any good to you; if you do not have other things, have this and you have fulfilled the law. *For he who loves another has fulfilled the law,*[146] *and the fullness of the law is charity.*[147]

---

141. Aug., *In Ioh. ep.* 4.11; PL 35:2011   142. 1 Jn 1:8
143. Aug., *In Ioh. ep.* 5:3; 2013-14   144. *Ibid.* 5.6; 2015
145. *Ibid.,* 5.7; 2016   146. Rm 13:8   147. Rm 13:10

3:11 For this is the message that you have heard from the beginning, that we should love one another, as the Lord says, *This is my commandment, that you should love one another.*[148]

3:12 Not like Cain who was of the evil one and slew his brother. And why did he slay him? Because his works were evil but his brother's righteous. He explains how Cain was of the evil one, because namely he also did evil deeds. 'Therefore, where there is envy there cannot be brotherly love.'[149] But the sin of the evil one, that is, the devil, is in the heart of such a person, because the devil also cast man out through envy.

> Therefore, in speaking of the righteous works of Abel he means only charity, in speaking of the evil works of Cain he means only hatred of one's brother. It was not enough for him to hate his brother, he also envied his good works. (Therefore) it is by this that persons are distinguished. Let no one pay attention to words but to deeds. If a person's heart does not prompt him to do good for his brothers he shows what is within him. People are put to the test by temptations.[150]

3:13 Do not wonder, brothers, if the world hates you. The world means 'those who love the world'. Nor should we wonder that those who love the world are not able to love their brother who is separated from the love of the world and attentive only to heavenly desires. For religion is abomination to the sinner, as scripture bears witness.[5]

3:14 We know that we have been brought over from death to life because we love our brothers. Let no one falsely exalt

148. Jn 15:12   149. Aug., *In Ioh. ep.* 5.8; PL 35:2016
150. *Ibid.,* 2017

himself because of his virtues, let no one needlessly be afraid of his lack of strength; anyone who is filled with love for his brother gives clear evidence that he belongs to the lot of the elect, because he has deserved to have his portion in the land of the living.[151] **He who does not love remains in death.** He is speaking of the death of the soul. For, *The soul that commits sin is the one that will die.*[152] The life, in truth, of the flesh is the soul, the life of the soul is God; the death of the body is to lose its [life-giving] spirit, the death of the soul is to lose God. Hence it is clear that we are all born into this light [of life] dead in soul, deriving original sin from Adam, but by the grace of Christ to the faithful in giving them new life it is brought about that they can be alive in soul. Truly the mystery of baptism and of faith is the only thing of advantage to them; this brings those who love their brothers with a sincere mind from death to life. And therefore it must be noted that he does not say, 'He who does not love will come to death', as though he were speaking of the everlasting punishment that awaits sinners in the future, but he says, *He who does not love remains in death,* in that death surely from which he could arise even in this life if he would love his brothers perfectly. For indeed from this it is said in the Apocalypse, *Blessed and holy is he who has a part in the first resurrection; the second death has no power over these.*[153]

3:15 Everyone who hates his brother is a murderer. If someone makes light of hating his brother, isn't he going to make light of murder in his heart, too? Even though he does not lift a hand to slay someone he is already held by God to be a murderer. The one is alive, and the other is already an adjudged killer. **And you know that no murderer has life remaining in him.** Although such a person is perceived to live by faith among the saints, he does not have

151. Ps 142:5 (141:6)   152. Ezk 18:20   153. Rv 20:6

everlasting life remaining in him. For when the time of retribution comes near, even he who is held in thrall by this kind
of murder, that he is at discord and variance and does not
keep peace with his brothers, will be condemned with
Cain who was of the evil one.[154] For it must be noted that
he does not say unconditionally, 'A murderer does not have
life remaining in him', but he says, *no murderer,* namely, not
only he who attacks his brother with a sword but also he who
attacks him with hatred.

**3:16 In this we have come to know his charity, that he laid
down his life**[155] **for us.** What sort of perfect charity ought to
be in us we have learned from the Lord's passion. For,
*Greater love than this no one has, that someone should lay
down his life for his friends.*[156] Hence Paul also says, *But
God manifests his charity for us, since when we were still
sinners Christ died for us.*[157] Blessed Peter was advised to
have this [kind of love] when the Lord said, Peter, *do you
love me? feed my sheep;* he answered that he did love him
and immediately he heard, *But when you grow old, you will
reach out your hands and another will gird you and lead you
where you do not wish; but he said this,* says the evangelist,
*implying the kind of death with which he was going to honor
God.*[158] For he was teaching him to whom, as he was confessing his love, he had handed over his sheep to lay down his
life for these same sheep in witness of his perfect love.
He laid down his life for us, he says, **and we ought to lay
down our lives for our brothers.** But perhaps someone says:
And 'when' am I able 'to have that kind of charity; Do not
quickly despair about yourself, perhaps [charity] is born
but has not yet been made perfect; foster it, lest it be
choked out.' And 'by what,' you say, 'do I know' that the
charity which I may foster is born in me?[159] Listen to what
follows:

154. 1 Jn 3:12   155. *anima*   156. Jn 15:13   157. Rm 5:8
158. Jn 21:17-19   159. Cf. Aug., *In Ioh. ep.* 5.12; PL 35:2018

3:17 He who has worldly substance and sees his brother in need and closes his heart against him, how does the charity of God remain in him? 'See from what charity begins. If you are not yet able to die for your brother, be able to give your brother of your possessions.'[160] For if you will not share the suffering of your brother who is suffering difficulty, certainly the charity of the Father from whom you have both been reborn does not remain in you.

3:18 Little children, let us love not in word or with the tongue but in deed[161] and truth, *in deed,* namely, that when our brother and sister are naked and need daily food we may give them the things necessary for their bodies; likewise when we behold them in need of spiritual gifts we may provide for their necessity as far as we can; *in truth,* however, that we may bestow these benefits on them with a simple intention and not for the sake of human praise, not through vainglory, not to the prejudice of others who, though endowed with greater means, do not do anything of this sort. For the purity of truth cannot dwell in any mind tainted like this with flaws, although it appears to perform the deeds of love for its neighbors.

3:19 By this we know that we are of the truth, that is, when we perform the works of devotion in truth, it is evident that we are of the truth which God is, inasmuch as we imitate his perfection according to our capacity. **And we convince our hearts in his sight.** This thought follows from what precedes, because when we love our neighbor in deed and truth we clearly perceive that we persuade our hearts in the sight of the highest truth. All persons, when they decide to do something, persuade their hearts to turn themselves to a consideration of the deed. But those who plot evils would like to conceal these from God if they could, as he bears witness when

160. Aug., *In Ioh. ep.* 5.12; PL 35:2018   161. *opera*

he says, *For everyone who commits evil hates the light and does not come to light, so that his deeds may not be made manifest.*[162] But in fact those who consider doing good most easily persuade their hearts so that they desire to be open to the sight of the godhead, a thing that is usually evidence of the highest perfection, when each one rejoices to have his deeds and thoughts seen by God. Hence he says in what follows, *But anyone who acts according to the truth comes to light, that his works*[163] *may be made manifest, because they have been wrought in God.*[164] Therefore, through true love we perceive that we are from the truth and that we persuade our hearts in the sight of the same truth, that is, we persuade our hearts to have the kinds of thoughts which may be worthy of divine sight.

3:20 But if our heart accuses us God is greater than our heart and knows everything. If our conscience accuses us within because we have not performed our good deeds with that spirit in which they ought to have been performed, how can we be hidden from the knowledge of him to whom it is sung, *Behold you, O Lord, know everything,*[165] and, *Because the darkness will not be concealed from you, and the night will be illumined as the day.*[166]

3:21 Dearly beloved, if our heart does not accuse us, if

> it truly answers us that we love and that in us is brotherly love, not feigned but sincere, seeking the salvation of our brothers, expecting no advantage from one's brother except his salvation,

likewise *if our heart does not accuse us,* namely, when we say in prayer, *Forgive us our debts as we also forgive our*

---

162. Jn 3:20   163. *opera*   164. Jn 3:21
165. Ps 139:4 (138:5)   166. Ps 139 (138):12

debtors,[167] **we have confidence before God,**

> not in the sight of men but where God himself
> sees, in the heart.[168]

3:22   And we shall receive from him whatever we ask, since we keep his commandments and do the things that are pleasing in his sight. This great and desirable promise has been given to the faithful. But if anyone is so senseless and foolish as not to be delighted by the heavenly promises let him at least take fright at what wisdom on the contrary thunders, saying, *The prayer of someone who turns away his ear so as not to hear the law will be detestable.*[169] The fact that / Paul asked the Lord three times that the angel of Satan might depart from him and was not able to obtain his request, but instead it was said to him, *My grace is sufficient for you, for virtue is perfected in weakness,*[170] ought not to appear contrary to this thought of blessed John. /[171] For although we do not always receive what we wish when we pray, nonetheless we receive for our salvation the reward of our faithfulness, as the same Paul, when he prayed to the Lord, received not what he sought but what he held to be useful. But on the other hand the condemned are often listened to for their wishes, they are not listened to for wishes, they are not listened to for their salvation. Hence even their head, 'the devil,' in order that he might tempt blessed Job,[172] 'was listened to for what he wished but for what was for his condemnation. For it was granted that that man was to be tempted for the reason that when the latter had been tested the former was to be torture.' /[173] Therefore, when John had said, *We shall receive from him whatever we ask, since we keep his commandments,* as if you had asked, 'What commandments,' he immediately appended:

167. Mt 6:12   168. Aug., *In Ioh. ep.* 6.4; PL 135:2021
169. Pr 28:9   170. 2 Co 12:9   171. Cf. Aug., *In Ioh. ep.* 6.6; 2023
172. Jb 1:12   173. Aug., *In Ioh. ep.* 6.7; 2023.

3:23 And this is his commandment, that we believe in the name of his Son, Jesus Christ, and that we love one another. At first he wrote *commandment* in the singular and then subsequently added two commandments, namely, faith and love, because undoubtedly these cannot be separated from one another. For without faith in Christ we are not able to love one another properly nor can we truly believe in the name of Jesus Christ without brotherly love. **And that we love one another,** he says, **as he gave us commandment,** that is, with an irreproachable love, not as thieves and as perpetrators of any other type of crimes, who certainly love one another but not purely. For thus he gave us his commandment when he said, *This is my commandment, that you love one another as I have loved you.*[174] For what is, *as I have loved you,* if not, 'Love for the reason that I have loved you, namely, that you may reach the heavenly kingdom'? And what is the reward for keeping these commandments of faith and love? There follows:

3:24 And anyone who keeps his commandments remains in him and he in him. Therefore, 'Let God be your house and you be the house of God; abide in God and let God abide in you. God abides in you that he may surround you, you abide in God that you may not fall.'[175] Keep his commandments, hold on to charity, do not be separated from faith in him, that you may glory in his presence, and you will abide secure in him now through faith, then through sight. And he will abide in you always, according to what the psalmist chants to him, *They will exult for ever, and you will dwell in them.*[176] **And by this we know that he abides in us, by the spirit which he has given us.** In the earliest times the Holy Spirit fell upon believers and they spoke in tongues which they had never studied.[177] But nowadays, because the holy Church does not

174. Jn 15:12   175. Aug., *In Ioh. ep.* 9.1; PL 35:2045
176. Ps 5:11 (12)   177. Ac 2:1-4

need external signs, whoever believes in the name of Jesus Christ and has love for his brother gives witness to the Holy Spirit abiding in him. For the Holy Spirit brings it about that charity may be in man, *for charity has been poured in our hearts,* Paul says, *by the Holy Spirit who has been given to us.*[178] But because many do not have charity and destroy the unity of the Church by their perverse teaching and neverthe-less argue that they have the Holy Spirit in them, properly there is appended:

4:1 **Dearly beloved, do not believe every spirit, but test the spirits [to see] if they are of God, since many false prophets have gone forth into the world.** And who it is that tests the spirits and how they can be tested the Lord teaches in the Gospel where he foretold that such things would come to pass as John related had already come in his time. He said, *Beware of false prophets who come to you in sheep's cloth-ing but inwardly are greedy wolves; you will recognize them by their fruits. Do people gather graves from thorns or figs from thistles?*[179] Therefore, these are fruits by which the evil spirits who speak in false prophets can be discerned, namely, the thorns of schism and the dreadful thistles of heresies by which, by wounding their faith, they defile those who approach them heedlessly, just as on the contrary the fruits of good [works], namely, charity, joy, peace in the Holy Spirit, are appropriately signified by the pleasant odor of grapes and the sweetness of figs.

4:2 **By this is the Spirit of God perceived: every spirit which confesses that Jesus Christ has come in the flesh is of God.** In this place he is demanding a confession not only of the catholic faith but also of good action which is brought about through charity. Otherwise, quite a few heretics, many schismatics, many false catholics confess that Jesus Christ has

178. Rm 5:5   179. Mt 7:15-16

come in the flesh but they negate their confession by their deeds, by not having charity. In truth,

> charity brought (the Son of God [to take]) a body, (and therefore) whoever does not have charity denies that (he) has come in the body (and such a one is proven conclusively not to have the Spirit of God. But) that is the Spirit of God which says that Jesus (Christ) has come in the body, which says this not with the tongue but by deeds, not by speaking but by loving.[180]

4:3 And every spirit which rejects Jesus is not of God. He rejects Jesus who denies either his divinity or his soul or his flesh, which the catholic faith truly teaches that he had. He also rejects Jesus who falsifies the commandments and words of Jesus either by living perversely or by more perversely interpreting them. But he also strives to reject Jesus as hard as he can who upsets the unity of the holy Church which Jesus came to bring together. Nor is it to be wondered at that such are not of God when they nullify the works and words and sacraments of God. For they are so far from being of God that certain of them, who wished by their warped teaching to separate the divinity of Christ from his appearance as a human being also eradicated this verse in which it is said, *And every spirit which rejects Jesus is not of God,* from this Epistle, lest their errors, namely, be proven conclusively [to be wrong] by the authority of blessed John. Accordingly, Nestorius put forward that he did not know that this statement was contained in genuine copies and therefore he did not fear to reject Jesus and by this to make himself a stranger to God, saying that the blessed Virgin Mary was the begetter only of a

180. Aug., *In Ioh. ep.* 6.13; PL 35:2028

human being, not of God, so that he made one person of the man, another of his divinity. He did not believe that Christ was one in the word of God and in his body and soul but preached that he was separately one [being] as Son of God, another as son of man. **And this is the antichrist, of whom you have heard that he is coming and even now is in the world.** He is coming as the day of judgment draws near, since that one, the son of iniquity, far more wicked than the rest, has been born into the world, and he is even now in the world in the minds of those who fight against Christ, by their declaration or by their work, without the remedy of repentance.

4:4 **Little children, you are of God and you have overcome him.** You have overcome the antichrist by confessing that Jesus Christ has come in the flesh, that is, by having the charity which Jesus Christ taught when he came in the flesh, which he also recommends in the Gospel, saying, *Greater love than this no one has, that someone should lay down his life for his friends.*[181] For

> how was the Son of God able to lay down his life
> for us except by clothing himself with flesh in
> which he could die? Therefore, anyone who vio-
> lates charity, whatever he may say in words, by his
> life denies that Christ has come in the flesh, and
> he is an antichrist. 'And you have overcome him,'
> (he says. But) how have they overcome him?[182]

Is it by the power of their free will? Certainly not. Let Pelagius be silent, let John himself say, **Since he who is in you is greater than he who is in the world.** He teaches them therefore to maintain their humility, lest they credit their victory to their own strength and be overcome by the arrogance of pride. He teaches them always to have confidence and the hope of overcoming in the midst of adversities, keep-

181. Jn 15:13   182. Aug., *In Ioh. ep.* 7.2; PL 35:2030

ing in mind that the Lord is stronger in protecting them than the devil in attacking them.

4:5 They are of the world; so they speak of the world, and the world hears them. The antichrists, that is, the heretics, although they invoke the name of Christ and make the sign of Christ on themselves, are nevertheless of the world, that is, of the number of those who savor worldly things, who seek the lowest, who ignore the heavenly, and thereby speak of the world, namely, by reason of their worldly wisdom. They oppose the christian faith by saying that it cannot be that the Son is coeternal with the Father, that the chaste virgin brings forth a child, that flesh rises immortal from the dust, that man sprung from the earth receives a dwelling place in heaven, that a newly-born small child is held bound by the guilt of the first man unless he is reborn in Christ by the water of baptism and set free. *And the world hears them*, because they are not able to call the hearts of the spiritual back from the simplicity of faith to worldly and bodily senses. But also all catholics who hear that statement of the Lord, *Love your enemies, do good to those who hate you and pray for those who persecute and slander you*,[183] and again, *If you forgive people their sins, your heavenly Father will also forgive you your transgressions, but if you do not forgive other people, your heavenly Father will not forgive you your sins*,[184] and say that in no way can they forgive unavenged injuries, these surely are proven conclusively to be of the world and therefore to speak of the world. And because they do not have fundamentals of charity, in vain do they keep the mysteries of the faith inviolate. But those also who are proven to oppose the commandments of Christ are to be included under the name of antichrists.

183. Mt 5:44   184. Mt 6:14-15

4:6 We are of God; anyone who knows God hears us, anyone who is not of God does not hear us. For, *physical man does not comprehend the things which are of the spirit of God, for to him they are foolishness.*[185] Therefore, someone who does not wish to hear the preachers of charity is clearly perceived as one who does not know God or is not of God, because he has neglected to imitate the charity which God practised towards men. **By this we know the spirit of truth and the spirit of error,** *by this,* surely, because he who hears us has the spirit of truth, he who does not hear us has the spirit of error. And this is the discernment of spirits about which he advised above, saying, *Test the spirits [to see] if they are of God.*[186] But

> Let us see what he is going to advise, on which we ought to hear him:[187]

4:7–8 Dearly beloved, let us love one another, since charity is of God.

> He greatly recommended charity, because he said, *'It is of God'.* He is going to say more; let us listen attentively:

And everyone who loves is born of God and perceives God, he who does not love does not know God, because God is charity.

> What could he have said more? *'God is charity.'* (Therefore) to act against (charity) is to act against God. Let no one say, 'I am sinning against a human being when I do not love my brother, and a sin against a human being is unimportant; only let me not sin against God.' How do you not sin against God when you sin against (charity? *God is charity.'*)

---

185. 1 Co 2:14   186. 1 Jn 4:1
187. Aug., *In Ioh. ep.* 7.4-5; PL 35:2031

4:9 By this has the charity of God appeared among us, that he sent his only-begotten Son into the world, that we might live through him.

> As the Lord himself says, '*Greater love than this no one has, that someone should lay down his life for his friends.*'[188] And there the love of Christ for us was proven, because he died for us. Whereby was the love of the Father for us proven? Because he sent his only Son to die for us, as the apostle Paul also says, '*He who did not spare his own Son but handed him over for us all, how did he not also give us everything with him?*'[189]

4:10 And in this is charity, not that we loved him, but that he loved us. 'We did not love him first; for it was for this that he loved us: that we might love him.'[190] Grace, in truth, precedes man, that he might love God with that love by which he might do what is good. Hence the psalmist says, *His mercy will precede me.*[191] **And he sent his Son as an expiation for our sins.** And this is the greatest evidence of the divine charity towards us, because when we ourselves did not know how to entreat him for our sins, he sent us his Son who might gratuitously give pardon to us who believed in him and call us to the fellowship of the Father's glory. This verse in certain manuscripts is read thus, 'And he sent his Son as an acceptable offering for our sins.'[192] But one who makes an acceptable offering[193] is one who makes a sacrifice.[194] For the Son of God for our sins made a sacrifice by offering, not victims from flocks, but himself. Hence Paul well advises us by saying, *Therefore, be imitators of God as dearly beloved children and walk in love, as Christ also loved us and handed over for us as an offering and victim to God in the odor of sweetness.*[195] With this statement there also agrees what John

---

188. Jn 15:13   189. Rm 8:32, Aug., *In Ioh. ep.* 7.7; 2032
190. Aug., *In Ioh. ep.* 7.9; 2033   191. Ps 59:10 (58:11)
192. Aug., *In Ioh. ep.* 7.9; 2033   193. *litator*
194. *sacrificator*   195. Eph 5:1-2

adds here by way of exhortation, saying:

4:11 Dearly beloved, if God so loved us, we ought also to love one another. But what follows,

4:12 No one has ever seen God, needs further discussion, since the Lord both promises that God is to be seen by persons who are pure of heart[196] and says of the saints that their angels in heaven always see the face of the Father.[197] But the same John also has this statement in his Gospel where he goes on to add, saying, *The only-begotten Son who is in the bosom of the Father has himself described [him].*[198] Blessed father Ambrose has explained this thus:

> And no one has even seen God for the reason that no one has beheld that fullness of divinity in which God dwells,[199] no one has grasped him with his mind or eyes; for, *has seen,* must be referred to both. Accordingly, when there is added, *The only-begotten Son who is in the bosom of the Father has himself described [him],* a sight is being asserted of the mind rather than of the eyes, for an appearance is seen but power is described; the former is grasped with the eyes, the latter with the mind.[200]

Likewise blessed Augustine, discussing the same question, says in his book on seeing God,

> Therefore, when the only-begotten Son who is in the bosom of the Father describes him in an unutterable description, the pure and holy rational creature is filled with an unutterable sight of God which we shall then obtain when we have been made like the angels;[201] because no one has ever seen God in his distinctive quality, as the

196. Mt 5:9   Mt 18:10   198. Jn 1:18   199. Col 2:9
200. Ambr., *Exp Luc.* 1.25; CC 14:19, 396/403
201. Lk 20:36

visible things of the body, known by the senses,
are seen—since if he was ever seen in this way he
was not seen, as it were, in his own nature but by
his will he was seen under the appearance that
he wished, appearing with his own nature hidden
and remaining unchangeable within himself. But in
that way in which he is seen as he is,[202] he is seen
now, perhaps, by certain of (his holy) angels; yet
he will then be seen thus by us when we have been
made like them.[203]

And after a little bit, explaining the thought of Saint Ambrose, he says,

For, *No one has ever seen God,* either in this life
as he is or even in the life of the angels, as those
visible things which are beheld by bodily sight,
because *the only-begotten Son who is in the bosom
of the Father has himself described [him].*[204]
Hence what he describes is said to belong to the
sight not of the eyes but to that of the mind.[205]

Likewise after quite a gap he says,[206]

He has reminded us that our hearts must be purified[198] for that sight by which we shall see God as
he is. For because bodies in our manner of speaking are called visible, God is accordingly said to be
invisible, lest he be believed to be a body; not that
he will deprive pure hearts of the attentive regard
of his substance, since this great and highest
reward is promised to those who worship and love
the Lord, as the Lord himself said when he
appeared visibly to bodily eyes and promised that
he was to be beheld invisibly by pure hearts:
*He who loves me is loved by my Father, and I will
love him and show myself to him.*[207] In truth, his

202. 1 Jn 3:2   203. Aug., *Ep.* 147.22; CSEL 44:296,17-297,2
204. Jn 1:18   205. Aug., *Ep.* 147.28; CSEL 303,4/9
206. *Ep.* 147.48; 323, 8/20   207. Jn 14:21

nature is equally invisible as the Father, just as it is equally incorruptible. This the apostle immediately declared, saying,[208] *But to the invisible, incorruptible king of the ages,*[209] manifesting the divine substance to men in what preaching he was able.

God, therefore,

> in a thing invisible and must not be sought after by the eye (but by the mind). But in the same way, if we wish to see the sun, we should cleanse the eye of the body by which light can be seen, let us who wish to see God cleanse the eye (of the heart) by which God can be seen. For, *Blessed are the pure of heart, for they will see God.*[210]

But because this vision is hoped for in the future, what must we do while, still existing in the body, we are at a distance from the Lord, what consolation must we make use of when we are not yet allowed to enjoy the divine sight? He says, **If we love one another, God remains in us.** But let no one consider that this love by which God remains

> is kept by a kind of languid and slothful meekness, nay rather, not meekness but half-heartedness and negligence. That is not charity but laziness. Let charity be eager to correct, to emend. And if there are good habits, let them please you, if there evil ones, let them be emended, corrected.[211]

Therefore, if we love one another with a sincere and intelligent charity, God remains in us, manifested by the works of that charity, although not yet visibly appearing. **And his charity has been perfected in us.** We must ask, however, how he says that the perfection of divine charity[212] consists in

---

208. Aug., *Ep.* 147:37; CSEL 44:311, 11/12   209. 1 Tm 1:17
210. Aug., *In. Ioh. ep.* 7.10; PL 135:2033-34, citing Mt 5:8
211. Aug., *In Ioh. ep.* 7.11; 2034
212. Aug., *In Ioh. ep.* 8.4,10; 2037-38, 2042

mutual love, when the Lord proclaims in the Gospel that it is no great thing if we love those who love us unless the same love also reaches to our enemies,[213] about whom he seems here to be almost entirely silent, unless perhaps [he means] we ought also to love our enemies within the compass of our brotherly love, namely, so that they may not always remain enemies but may come to their senses and be allied to us in a fraternal compact. *If we love one another,* he says, *God remains in us, and his charity has been perfected in us.*

> Begin to love, you will become perfect. You have begun to love, God has begun to dwell in you, that by dwelling more perfectly he may make you perfect.[214]

4:13 By this we know that we remain in him and he in us, that he has given us of his spirit.

> From what do you perceive this very thing, that he has given you of his spirit? Question your heart. If it is full of charity you have the spirit of God, (Paul bearing witness when he says,) *Because the charity of God has been poured forth in our hearts by the Holy Spirit who has been given us.*[215]

4:14 And we have seen and bear witness that the Father sent his Son the saviour of the world. Let no one despair of salvation, because although there are great diseases of crimes which oppress us, the physician who may save is omnitent. Only let everyone remember that the same Son of God who came as a meek person to save is going to come as a very strict one to judge.

4:15 Whoever confesses that Jesus is the Son of God, God remains in him, and he in God. He is speaking of the perfect

---

213. Mt 5:44-46   214. Aug., *In Ioh. ep.* 8.12; PL 35:2043
215. Rm 5:5, cited by Aug., *ibid.*

confession of the heart which can neither be corrupted by the deceit of evilly persuasive heretics nor shaken by the tortures of persecutive pagans nor waver by the example of sensual brothers nor by the sloth of one's own frailty. Indeed there are those who even deny by words that Jesus is the Son of God, such as the many who are alleged to have existed at the very time when John was writing these words; there are likewise those who 'confess him in words (and) deny him by their deeds.'[216] Hence he does well to say now, *Whoever confesses that Jesus is the Son of God, God remains in him, and he in God,* when he just previously said, *If we love one another, God remains in us,*[217] suggesting indeed that everyone who has love for his brothers truly bears witness that Jesus is the Son of God.

4:16   And we have perceived and we believe in the charity which God has for us. We know that Jesus is the Son of God and that the Father sent him as the saviour of the world and we believe in the charity which God has for us, because, namely, when he had but one Son, he was unwilling that he be his only one, and, that he might have brothers, he adopted *for him* those who might possess eternal life with him. **God is charity.**

> He already said that previously;[218] see, he says it again. (Charity) could not be recommended to you more highly than that it should be said to be God. Perhaps you were going to reject the gift of God. Do you also reject God?

And he who remains in charity remains in God and God in him.

> They dwell together, he who surrounds and he who is surrounded. You dwell in God, but that you may be surrounded; God dwells in you, but

216. Aug., *In Ioh. ep.* 8.14; PL 35:2044   217. 1 Jn 4:12
218. 1 Jn 4:8

that he may surround you lest you fall, because
the apostle speaks thus about this very charity,
Charity never falls.[219] How does he fall whom
God surround?

**4:17 By this has charity been perfected with us, that we
may have confidence on the day of judgment.**

He tells how everyone may prove to himself how
much he has become perfect in Him. Anyone who
has confidence in the day of judgment, charity has
been perfected in him. What is it to have confidence in the day of judgment? Not to fear that
the day of judgment is coming.[220]

For when someone has first turned away from his evil
actions to repent, he begins to fear the day of judgment,
namely, that when the righteous judge appears he may
himself be condemned as unrighteous. But when he is
enlivened by his progress in a good way of life, he will learn
not to fear what he did fear but rather to wish for the coming of him who is *the desired of all nations,*[221] hoping that
he will be crowned with the saints because of the merit of his
good actions. But on what basis we can have confidence in
the day of judgment he shows clearly by appending more
fully: **Because as he is, so also are we in this world.** But

can a human being be as God?' (But we should
recall what was also said previously) that 'as' is not
always said [to imply] equality but it is said [to
imply] a certain likeness, as when you say, 'As
I have ears, so my image has them, too'. Is this
entirely true? But still you say, 'as'. If, therefore,
we have been made to the image of God, why are
we not as God, not to [the point] of equality but
according to our capacity? By this, therefore,

219. 1 Co 13:8   220 Aug., *In Ioh. ep.* 8.14, 9.1-2; PL 35:2044-45
221. Hag 2:8

is confidence given us on the day of judgment,
Because as he is, so also are we in this world.[222]
by imitating, namely, the perfection of love in the world of
which he daily provides us an example from heaven. Of this
the Saviour says in the Gospel, *Love your enemies and pray
for those who persecute you, that you may be the children
of your Father who is in heaven, who makes his sun rise on
the good and evil and rains on the righteous and the
unrighteous.*[223]

4:18 **There is no fear in charity**, in such charity, namely,
which knows how to do good even to enemies and love them
in imitation of divine goodness. **But perfect charity casts out
fear**, that fear, namely, of which it is said, *The beginning of
wisdom is fear of the Lord,*[224] by which everyone undertaking the works of righteousness fears that the very strict
judge may come and, finding him insufficiently chastened,
condemn him. That charity banishes fear which provides
confidence in the day of judgment as a reward for righteousness. But perfect charity also drives out the fear of present
adversities from the soul. This is what he was seeking to have
who besought the Lord and said, *Rescue my soul from fear
of the enemy.*[225] He had this who said, *Who will separate us
from the charity of Christ? Tribulation or difficulty or persecution or hunger or nakedness or danger or the sword?*
and so on.[226] **For fear involves punishment.**

> The consciousness of sins torments the heart;
> righteousness has not yet been attained. There-
> fore, in the psalm about that very perfection of
> righteousness, (it says) *You have changed my
> weeping into joy, you have torn off my sackcloth
> and girded me with happiness, that my glory may
> sing to you and that I may not be pierced,*[227]

222. Aug., *In Ioh. ep.* 9.3; PL 35:2047   223. Mt 5:44-45
224. Ps 111 (110):10, Si 1:16   225. Ps 64:1 (63:2)
226. Rm 8:35   227. Ps 30:11-12 (29:12-13)

> (that is), let there be nothing which may disturb
> my consciousness. Fear disturbs, but do not fear;
> charity enters and cures what fear wounds. [228]

For anyone who is afraid has not been perfected in charity,
because, surely, *fear involves punishment,* in the way in
which surgery by a physician involves punishment, although
just as the health wished-for follows upon the surgery by a
physician, so the desired charity follows upon fear. What
the psalmist says, *The fear of the Lord is holy, enduring for
ever,* [229] ought not to be considered contrary to these words
of blessed John. For there are two kinds of fear, one by
which

> people fear God in order not to be cast into hell;
> this is that fear which leads on to charity, but it
> comes only to depart. For if you still fear God on
> account of punishment, you do not yet love him
> whom you thus fear, you do not desire good but
> avoid evil. But from the fact that you avoid evil,
> you are correcting yourself and beginning to desire
> good. When you begin to desire good, there will be
> in you (that holy) fear, (namely,) that you may
> lose that good itself (not) that you may be
> cast into hell (but) that the presence (of the Lord
> which) you are embracing, (which) you desire to
> enjoy (for ever) may desert you. [230]

4:19 Therefore, let us love, for God first loved us. Let us
love, because he first loved us. 'For from what might we love,
unless he had first loved us?' [231] For from this he himself says
in the Gospel, *You have not chosen me, but I have chosen
you.* [232] For thus will we be perfect in charity if, just as he
first loved us for the sake of nothing else than our salvation,
we shall also love him for no other reason than his love for

228. Aug., *In Ioh. ep.* 9.4; PL 35:2048   229. Ps 19:9 (18:10)
230. Aug., *In Ioh. ep.* 9.5; PL 35:2049
231. Aug., *In Ioh. ep.* 9.9; 2050   232. Jn 15:16

us. But because there are those who love God in word only, advisedly there is added:

4:20 If anyone says, 'I love God', and hates his brother, he is a liar. By what do you prove that he is a liar? Listen. **For he who does not love his brother whom he sees, how can he love God whom he does not see?**

> What then? He who loves his brother loves God. It
> is necessary that he love God in order to love love
> itself.[233]

For, **God is love.**[234] And lest someone dare say, 'And what stands in the way of my loving God even if I do not love my brother?' he properly appended:

4:21 And we have this commandment from God, that he who loves God should also love his brother. For,

> How do you love him whose (commandment) you
> hate? Who is there who may say, 'I love the em-
> peror but I hate his laws?'[235]

It is not thus with the true lover of God, but he says, *See how I have loved your commandments, Lord,* and therefore he adds confidently, *In your mercy give me life.*[236]

5:1 Everyone who believes that Jesus is the Christ is born of God.

> Who is it that believes that Jesus is the Christ?
> He[237] who lives in the way that Christ com-
> manded. Let no heretic, (let no schismatic) say,
> 'We also believe (that Jesus is the Christ).' For,
> *'The demons also believe and tremble,'*[238]

and, as we read in the Gospel, they confessed, and *they knew that he was the Christ.*[239] But because they do not have love and the works of the truth, they are not of God.

---

233. Aug., *In Ioh. ep.* 9.10; PL 35:2052   234. 1 Jn 4:8,16
235. Aug., *In Ioh. ep.* 9.11; 2053   236. Ps 119 (118):159
237. Aug., *In Ioh. ep.* 10.1; 2053-54   238. Jm 2:19
239. Lk 4:41

And everyone who loves him who begot him loves him who is born of him. By his admirable skill in preaching blessed John has taken care to enflame us to love of our neighbor, first by reminding [us] that everyone who believes perfectly is born of God, then by suggesting that it is right for someone who loves God also to love him who is born of God. For if anyone is so slow-witted that he has neglected to love a human being because he is a human being, because he is undergoing the same straggling journey with him on earth, he must be advised that he should love him at least for this reason: that he is born of God, that he has been made a sharer with him of divine grace, that with him he looks forward to the same rewards of the heavenly life. This exhortation pertains especially to those who have been made brothers to us not only by their participation in our human nature but also by their profession of faith. But because there are some who love their neighbors only on account of blood relationship or on account of some temporal advantage, the holy evangelist properly makes clear who is the true lover of his neighbor by appending:

5:2 By this we perceive that we love those born of God, when we love God and keep his commandments. He alone, therefore, is proven properly to love his neighbor who is perceived also to burn with love of his Creator. And lest anyone deceive himself about his love of his Creator by professing by word only that he loves him, when he had said, *By this we perceive that we love those born of God, when we love God,* he did well to add, *and keep his commandments.*

5:3 For this is the charity of God, that we keep his commandments. The Lord himself also says this, *If anyone loves me he will keep my word.*[240]
    The proof of love, therefore, is its manifestation in

240. Jn 14:23

deed. For we truly love if, according to his commandments, we keep our self-wills in check, for he
who still wanders away through unlawful desires
does not truly love God, because he is speaking
against him in his willfulness.[241]

And his commandments are not burdensome. And he himself says, *My yoke is sweet and my burden is light.*[242] But it
ought not to appear contradictory to these words either of
the Lord or of blessed John that the Lord himself also says
elsewhere, *How narrow the gate and straight is the way that
leads to life,*[243] and that the prophet says to him, *On account
of the words of your lips I have kept hard ways,*[244] and the
apostle, *It is fitting for us to enter into the kingdom of God
by many tribulations.*[245] For the hope of heavenly rewards
and the love of Christ makes light those things which of
their own nature are hard and rough.[246] For it is hard to suffer persecution for righteousness' sake,[247] but the fact that
the kingdom of heaven belongs to those who suffer this
makes even this sweet. Hence it is well that there is appended:

**5:4 Since everything that is born of God overcomes the
world.** The divine commandments are not difficult because
all those who devote themselves to them with true faithfulness reject both the adversities of this world and its allurements, with a placid mind, loving death itself also as the
entry into the heavenly fatherland. And lest anyone trust in
his own strength in being able to overcome either the
debauchery or deeds of the world, he advisedly adds,
This is the victory that overcomes the world, our faith,
that *faith* surely *that works through love,*[248] that faith by
which we humbly request the help of him who says,
In the world you will have persecution, but have confidence,

---

241. Greg., *Hom. ev.* 2.30.1; PL 76:1220C   242. Mt 11:30
243. Mt 7:14   244. Ps 17 (16):4   245. Ac 14:22
246. RB 58:8; CSEL 75²:147
247. Mt 5:10   248. Gal 5:6

I have overcome the world.[249]

5:5 Who is he who overcomes the world but he who believes that Jesus is the Son of God? He overcomes the world who joins works worthy of the same faith to his belief in Jesus as the Son of God. But are faith in and confession of his divinity alone enough for salvation? See what follows:

5:6 This is he who came by water and blood, Jesus Christ. Therefore, he who was the eternal Son of God became a human being in time, that he who had created us by the power of his divinity might recreate us by the weakness of his humility. *He who came by water and blood,* the water, namely, of his baptismal cleansing and the blood of his passion. **Not in water only but in water and blood.** Not only did he deign to be baptized for the sake of our cleansing, that he might consecrate and pass on to us the sacrament of baptism, but he also gave his blood for us, he redeemed us by his passion, that being always restored to health by his sacraments we might be nourished for salvation.[6] **And it is the Spirit who bears witness that Jesus Christ is the truth.** When the Lord was baptized in the Jordan, the Holy Spirit came down upon him in the appearance of a dove,[250] giving witness that he is the truth, that is, the true Son of God, the true *mediator between God and men,*[251] the true redeemer and reconciler of the human race, himself truly clean from all stain of sin, truly able to take away the sins of the world.[252] The baptizer himself also understood this when he saw the coming of the same Spirit and said, *He who sent me to baptize in water said to me, 'Him upon whom you see the Spirit coming down and remaining is he who baptizes in the Holy Spirit.' And I saw and have given witness that this is the Son of God.*[253] Therefore, because the Spirit bears witness

249. Jn 16:33   250. Mt 3:16-17   251. 1 Tm 2:5
252. Jn 1:29   253. Jn 1:33-34

that Jesus Christ is the truth, he calls himself truth,[254] the baptizer proclaims him as truth, the son of thunder[255] spreads the good news about truth, let blasphemers who teach that he was a phantom be silent, let the memory of those who deny that he was either God or true man perish from the earth.[256]

5:7-8 Because there are three who bear witness, the Spirit and the water and the blood. The Spirit bore witness that Jesus is the truth when it came down upon him as he was baptized. For if he were not the true Son of God, the Holy Spirit would never have come upon him so manifestly. The water and the blood also bore witness that Jesus is the truth when they issued from his side as he was dead upon the cross.[257] This would never have been possible if he had not had the true nature of flesh. But also the fact that when he was praying before his passion *his sweat became like drops of blood running down on the ground*[258] bears witness to the truth of the flesh he had taken on. Nor must we remain silent about the water and the blood also having borne witness to him when they poured out of his side in so lifelike a manner when he was dead. This was contrary to the nature of bodies and on that account appropriate to the mysteries and apt for the witness of the truth, implying namely both that the very body of the Lord would be better [able to be] victorious after death, when he was raised in glory, and that his very death would give us life. That his blood also ran down on the ground like drops of blood by a holiest mystery bore witness to him that he cleansed the Church throughout the whole world by his blood. Therefore, **There are three who** give **witness** to the truth, **and the three,** he says, **are one.** These remain distinct, then, and none of them is severed from its connection with the other, because it must not be believed

254. Jn 14:6   255. Mk 3:17   256. Jb 18:17, Ps 34:16 (33:17)
257. Jn 19:34   258. Lk 22:44

that his humanity existed without his true divinity or his divinity without his true humanity. But these are also one in us, not by the substance of the same nature but by the operation of the same mystery. Now, as blessed Ambrose, says,

> The Spirit renews the mind, the water is of avail for [baptismal] cleansing, the blood points to the cost. For the Spirit made us children of God by adoption, the water of the sacred font washed us, the blood of the Lord redeemed us. The one an invisible witness, therefore, the other a visible, results from the spiritual sacrament.[259]

5:9 If we receive the witness of man, the witness of God is greater, since this is the witness of God which is greater, that he bore witness to his Son. Great is the witness of man which he bears of the Son of God, when he says, *The Lord said to my Lord, 'Sit at my right hand';*[260] and from the person of the Son himself, *The Lord said to me, 'You are my Son';*[261] and likewise from the person of the Father speaking of the Son, *He called upon me, 'You are my Father, my God and the one who undertakes my salvation',*[262] *my Father,* because I am the Son of God, *my God,* because I am a human being, *the one who undertakes my salvation,* because I am going to suffer and be saved from death. *And I shall place him, my first-born,* he says, *high above the kings of the earth.*[263] Great is this witness of [Christ as] man of the Son of God and it is true and entirely worthy of being received. But much greater is the witness of God that he himself bore of his Son when he addressed him from heaven and said, *'You are my beloved Son, I am well pleased with you',*[264] Great is the witness of the precursor which he bore to the Son of God when he said, *I have baptized you with*

259. Ambr., *De spir.* 3.10.68; CSEL 44:178, 83-179, 88
260. Ps 110 (109):1   261. Ps 2:7   262. Ps 89:26 (88:27)
263. Ps 89:27 (88:28)   264. Lk 3:22

water, but he will baptize you with the Holy Spirit.[265] Greater is the witness of the Father by which he sent upon him the Holy Spirit, with which he was always filled, even visibly.

5:10 Anyone who believes in the Son of God has the witness of God in himself. Anyone who so believes in the Son of God that he carries out in deed what he believes has the witness of God in himself, [the witness] certainly that he is also justifiably numbered among the sons of God, since the only Son of God himself promised his faithful ones that, *If anyone serves me, my Father will honor him.*[266] But if you deserve to have the testimony of God, if you have God as witness of your inviolate faith, how does the ignominy of men harm you, how does even persecution harm you? For, *If God is on our side, who is against us?*[267] **Anyone who does not believe in the Son makes him a liar, since he does not believe in the witness which God bore concerning his Son.** In vain do the Jews, in vain do the heretics think they believe in and reverence the Father as long as they reject Christ and refuse to believe in him. For anyone who does not honor the Son does not honor the Father who sent him. Those who do not believe in the Son—who said, *The Father and I are one,*[268] and when Caiphas interrogated him and said, *Are you the Christ, the Son of the blessed one?* answered, *I am,*[269]—but argue that he is not the Son of God or that he is not like the Father, actually make the Father a liar, because they do not believe in the testimony which God bore concerning his Son, in that testimony namely which I have also recalled above, *'You are my beloved Son, I am well pleased with you'.*[270] But neither do they believe in that testimony which he gave to him as the hour of his passion drew near, as he prayed and said, *Father, save me from this hour, but it is for this I have come*

---

265. Mk 1:8
266. Jn 12:26
267. Rm 8:31
268. Jn 10:30
269. Mk 14:61-62
270. Lk 3:22

to this hour, Father, glorify your name, and he answered
from heaven even in the hearing of the crowd, *I have both
glorified it and I will again glorify it,*[271] meaning that he was
the true God, the Father in heaven of him who was about to
suffer death on earth as true man.

**5:11 And this is the testimony, that God has given us eter-
nal life.** He has given us eternal life, he says, and he who was
speaking was still living his temporal life and in his flesh and
susceptible to death. But he gave us eternal life just as he
gave us who believe in his name the power to become sons
of God.[272] For that you may know that the power to have
eternal life has been given you by God, hear the prophet,
*Who is the person who wishes life and desires to see good
days? Restrain your tongue from evil and your lips from
speaking deceitfully,*[273] and so on, to the end of the psalm.
He has given us eternal life, therefore, but while we are still
struggling along on earth in hope, [it is the] life which he is
going to give us in heaven when we arrive before him in
reality. **And this is life in his Son,** namely, in faith and the
confession of his name, in the reception of his sacraments, in
keeping his commandments. Hence he himself also says,
No one comes to the Father except through me,[274] and
Peter says concerning him, *For there is no other name under
heaven given to mankind by which it is fitting for us to be
saved.*[275]

**5:12 Anyone who has the Son has life; anyone who does
not have the Son of God does not have life.** Lest he appear
to say too little when he says that life is in the Son, he adds
that the Son himself is life. The same Son also shows this in
glorifying the Father when he says, *For just as the Father has*

271. Jn 12:27-28   272. Jn 1:12
273. Ps 34:12-13 (33:13-14)   274. Jn 14:6
275. Ac 4:12

life in himself, so has he granted it to the Son also to have life in himself.[276] For in what way the same life which is common to the Son and the Father enlightens believers as well, the same Son implies when, praying to the Father elsewhere, he says, *As you have given him power over all flesh, that all that you have given him he may give them eternal life. For this is eternal life, that they may know you, the only true God, and him whom you have sent, Jesus Christ.*[277]

5:13 I am writing these things to you, that you who believe in the name of the Son of God may know that you have eternal life. *That you may know,* he says, that you who believe in Christ may be sure of your future happiness, that you may not be led astray by the deception of those who deny that Jesus is the Son of God and therefore maintain that there will be no advantage for those who have believed in his name. And the madness of the heretics is astonishing, for even though he is called the Son of God so often throughout this entire Letter, they contrarily affirm that the Christ of God is not his Son but a created being—something they read absolutely nowhere except where reference to his humanity is being emphasized.

5:14 And this is the confidence which we have in him, that no matter what we request according to his will, he hears us. He provides us with great confidence for hoping for heavenly goods from the Lord, because whatever we request from him even in this life concerning salvation we obtain, according to what he also promises in the Gospel to those who believe, saying, *I say to you, 'Believe that you will receive everything which you request when you pray, and it will come to you'.*[278] It must be noted, however, that when we pray we are listened to by the Lord only if we request what he has

276. Jn 5:26   277. Jn 17:2-3   278. Mk 11:24

ordered. For he himself says, **Seek first the kingdom of God and his righteousness.**[279] Hence when even John had said that we are listened to no matter what we request, he did well to insert, *according to his will.* Therefore, he ordered us to have full and unhesitating confidence in being listened to for those things which are linked, not to our own advantage and temporal consolation, but to the will of God. We are admonished to include this even in the Lord's prayer, *Your will be done,*[280] namely, not our own. For if we remember as well that saying of the apostle, *We do not know what we should pray for, according to what is fitting,*[281] we understand that we sometimes beg for things opposed to our salvation and are very appropriately denied those things which we ask for earnestly by him who discerns what is useful for us more properly than we do. There is no doubt that this happened also to the teacher of the gentiles himself.[282]

5:15 And we know that he hears us whatever we request, we know that we have requests that we beg from him. In many ways he impresses upon us the things which he had just finished saying, that he may stir us up more quickly to prayer. But there remains the addition which he made, that we request according to the will of our Creator. This can be taken in two ways, namely, that we both ask for what he wills and that we come to ask being as he desires us to be. This is to have *faith which works through love*[283] and above all to remember that Gospel commandment, *And when you stand up to pray, forgive if you have anything against anyone, that your father who is in heaven may also forgive you your sins.*[284]

5:16 Let anyone who knows that his brother is committing

279. Mt 6:33   280. Mt 6:10
281. Rm 8:26   282. 2 Co 12:7-9
283. Ga 5:5   284. Mk 11:25

a sin-not-to-death ask, and life will be given to him who is sinning not to death. These and things of this sort which have to do with the duty of love of our brothers are requested according to the Lord's will. For he is speaking about daily and trivial sins which, as they are difficult to avoid, so also are they easily cured. But James implies more openly in what order this request for one another's sins is to be carried out when he says, *Confess your sins to one another and pray for each other, that you may be saved.*[285] If perhaps you have transgressed by speech or thought or forgetfulness or ignorance, therefore, go to your brother, confess to him, beg for his intercession. If he by confessing simply makes you aware of your own weakness, you by interceding devoutly also wipe away his wrongdoing. But what has been said applies to trivial sins. But if you have committed something more serious bring in the elders of the Church[286] and be chastened at their investigation. **There is a sin to death; I do not say that anyone should ask for it.** An important question arises here, because blessed John shows clearly that there are some brothers for whom we are admonished not to pray, although the Lord orders us to pray even for our persecutors. This cannot be resolved otherwise than by admitting that there are certain sins among our brothers which are more serious than persecution of enemies. The sin of a brother to death, therefore, occurs when anyone, after the recognition of God which has been given through the grace of our Lord Jesus Christ, opposes the brotherhood and is aroused by the torches of envy against that very grace by which he has been reconciled to God. The sin not to death, however, occurs if someone does not withdraw love from his brother but through some weakness of mind does not practise the duties of the brotherhood which he should. Wherefore even the Lord on the cross said, *Father, forgive them, because they do not know what they*

285. Rm 5:16   286. Jm 5:14

are doing.[287] Not yet had they been made sharers of the grace of the Holy Spirit and entered the company of the fellowship of the holy brotherhood. And blessed Stephen prayed for those by whom he was being stoned,[288] because they had not yet believed in Christ and were not contending against that shared grace. And the apostle Paul, accordingly, did not pray for Alexander, I believe, because he was still a brother and had sinned to death, that is, by opposing the brotherhood through envy. But he did pray that those be pardoned who had not sundered their love but had succumbed to fear. For he spoke thus, *Alexander the metalworker has shown many evils towards me; the Lord will repay him according to his works. You also avoid him, for he has greatly resisted our utterances.*[289] Then he added those for whom he did pray, speaking as follows, *In my first defence no one was there to help me, but all abandoned me; may it not be reckoned against them.*[290] But the sin to death can be considered as the sin up to [the time of] death. He forbids anyone to ask [pardon] for this, because, namely, pardon for a sin that is not corrected in this life is begged for in vain after death. But if we look carefully at what follows the former explanation appears more closely linked to the general import of this lesson, for there is appended:

5:17 **All iniquity is sin and it is a sin to death.** There is such a variety of sins, he says, that everything which is discordant with reasonable moral standards is to be counted as a sin, although slight sins cannot at all take away from or lessen for the righteous the reward of their righteousness, least of all those without which they can in no way pass through this life; and likewise certain sins are so far from any portion of righteousness; they are committed with such iniquity that without any contradiction they plunge the person who

<hr/>

287. Lk 23:34   288. Ac 7:60
289. 2 Tm 4:14-15   290. 2 Tm 4:16

commits them, if they are not corrected, into eternal punishment. It has been written about them, *The soul which sins shall itself die.*[291] The absurd discussion of the Stoics is clearly rejected by this statement of blessed John. They have dared to say and to maintain against every sensibility of humankind that all sins are equal, saying that it makes no difference whether a person has stolen an ox or a chicken, because it is not the beast but the brain[292] that has constituted the crime. The heretic Jovinian has followed them, rationalizing that there is no difference between marriage and virginity, that in any grant of retribution those who do not abstain are to be preferred to those who eat frugally. Therefore, everything that is committed or thought of iniquitously must be related to sin. But there are certain sins to death of which the apostle says, *Since those who do these things shall not attain the kingdom of God.*[293]

5:18 We know that everyone who has been born of God does not [commit] sin, namely, the sin to death. This can be understood of every capital crime and particularly of that by which the brotherhood is violated, as we have explained above. But I have also said that the sin to death can properly be understood as the sin persisted in up to the time of death, because, *Everyone who has been born of God does not commit sin.* Accordingly, David committed a mortal crime. For who does not know that adultery and murder deserve everlasting death?[294] But David nonetheless, because he was born of God, because he belonged to the company of the children of God, did not sin up to [the time of] death, because by repenting quickly he won pardon for his guilt.[295] **But being of the generation of God preserves him, and the evil one does not touch him.** The grace of Christ by which we have been reborn preserves the faithful *who according to his*

291. Ezk 18:4   292. *non animal . . . sed animus*   293. Ga 5:21
294. 2 S 11:2-17   295. 2 S 12:13-17

purpose have been called to be saints[296] from committing
the sin to death and, if because of the frailty of the human
condition they have offended in any matters at all, it defends
them, so that they cannot be touched by the evil enemy. It
must likewise be said that we remain in the state of being of
the generation of God as long as we do not commit sin,
indeed those who persevere in being of the generation of God
cannot commit sin or be touched by the evil one. *For what
do light and darkness have in common, or Christ and
Belial?*[297] In the same way as day and night cannot be
mingled, he says, so [cannot] righteousness and iniquity, sin
and good works, Christ and antichrist, the evil one and those
who are the generation of God [are incompatible].

**5:19 We know that we are of God, and the whole world is
under the power of the evil one.** We are of God by his grace
and we have been reborn in baptism through faith and kept
that we may remain for a long time in faith. But the lovers
of the world are subject to the malicious enemy either
because they have never been freed from his sovereignty by
the waters of rebirth or because by sinning again after the
grace of rebirth they have been brought again under his
sovereignty. And not only the lovers of the world, but also
those newly born who do not yet possess the power of
discerning good and evil belong to the kingdom of the
malicious enemy on account of the guilt of that first
transgression, unless they are delivered from the power of
darkness and transferred to the kingdom of the Son of his
charity[298] through the grace of a benevolent Creator. Hence
he does not say simply that the world is under the power of
the evil one but with one addition, *The whole world,* he says,
is under the power of the evil one. For, as blessed Ambrose
says, 'We human beings are all born under sin, and our very

296. Rm 8:28   297. 2 Co 6:14-15
298. Col 1:13

origin is in vice'.[299] And in vain does Pelagius strive to assert that small, new-born children have no need of being reborn by the grace of baptism because they are born as clean of all filth of sin as Adam was when he was created in paradise, deriving, namely, from him no stain of original fault, being guilty of nothing until they begin to sin of their own free will. But as for us, having put aside the poisons of the antichrists which he who drank from the source of life, the breast of the Lord, condemns throughout the whole of this Letter and drives from the Church, let us hear in the summary the good word of salvation that he calls up for us;[300] let us pay attention to the works of the supreme king that he is speaking of. There follows:

5:20 And we know that the Son of God has come and has given us understanding that we may perceive the true God and may be in his true Son. Could anything clearer than these words have been said, anything sweeter, anything stronger against all heresies? Christ is the true Son of God, the Father of our Lord Jesus Christ is the true God, the eternal Son of God who was in the world and through whom the world was made[301] has come for a time into the world and for no other reason than our salvation, that is, that he might give us the understanding to perceive the true God. For no one was able to come to life without perception of the divinity, no one was able to perceive God unless he himself taught us, as he himself also says, *And no one knows the Son except the Father nor does anyone know the Father except the Son and he to whom the Son wishes to reveal,*[302] there is understood, both the Father and the Son; for the Son who appeared visibly in the flesh and deigned to make known the hidden mysteries of the godhead to the world through his Gospel revealed both. **This is the true God and eternal life.** He had said that the Son

299. Ambr., *De paen.* 1.13.3; CSEL 73:126,44/45
300. Ps 45:1 (44:2)   301. Jn 1:10   302. Lk 10:22

was true God, he repeats that he is true God again and again, he says that he is eternal life, but definitely not the eternal life which is promised to us in such a way that it will so take us up away from time that it will never remove from us the end of living happily. But the Son is life without temporal beginning, forever remaining, and forever going to remain without end.

5:21 **Little children, keep yourselves from idols.** You who perceive the true God, in whom you have eternal life, keep yourselves from the teachings of heretics which lead to everlasting death, because like those who fabricate idols in place of God, they by their wicked teachings change the glory of the imperishable God into the likeness of perishable things.[303] Keep yourselves also from *covetousness, which is the service of idols,*[304] be on guard lest you prefer the allurements of the world to the love of the Creator. For this also will be reckoned among the idols, that insofar as we have a concern with and an inclination for the truth alone we deserve to be gladdened without end at our vision of the world. For, *The world and its cravings will pass away; but anyone who does the will of the Lord abides forever.*[305]

303. Rm 1:23   304. Col 3:5   305. 1 Jn 2:17

NOTES TO COMMENTARY ON 1 JOHN

1. Bede has borrowed this enumeration of the different ages of the world from Saint Gregory the Great (*Hom. ev.* 1. 19. 1; PL 76: 1154 C). See note 5 on 2 Peter.

2. Latin *incipite*. Saint Augustine in this passage quotes the reading of what is commonly called the Roman psalter, from its usage in the Latin offices of the churches in Rome during the early centuries. The so-called Gallican psalter found in the Latin Vulgate version of the scriptures here has the variant reading *praecinite*, 'sing in the presence of', and the Latin translation made by Saint Jerome according to the Hebrew has *canite*, 'sing'. This is a good place to note that when Bede quotes the psalms he almost invariably does so from the Roman psalter, indicating that this was probably the version in use during the seventh and eighth centuries in the north of England at his twin monasteries of Wearmouth and Jarrow.

3. Latin *iniquitas* and *aequitas*, where in the former the prefix *in-* means 'not', as it frequently does in English.

4. Julian of Eclanum, a bishop during the fifth century in Italy who had Pelagian leanings. Bede mentions his writings more fully in the first book of his *Commentary on the Song of Songs* (CC 1198:167-80), where he is at pains to refute Julian's teachings in detail. It has been suggested by the editors of the *Clavis Patrum Latinorum* (Bruges, Belgium: K. Beyaert, 1961), nos. 751-2, that two of the works which Bede quotes from there and which he thought he had written by Julian—*De amore* and *De bono constantiae*—were actually works of Pelagius himself; a third work—*Epistula ad Demetriadem*—is definitely from the hand of Pelagius.

5. I have not been able to verify this as a quotation from the scriptures. It is possible that Bede borrowed it from an earlier writer and that it is a Latin translation of some verse from the Greek Septuagint.

6. Latin *salus*. Bede here is aware of the meaning of the word in later, Church Latin, (spiritual) 'salvation', and of its meaning in classical times, 'health'.

COMMENTARY ON 2 JOHN

1   **THE ELDER to the elect lady and her children whom I love in the truth.** Certain persons thinks that this and the following Letter are not by the apostle John but by a certain presbyter [named] John whose tomb is pointed out even today at Ephesus. Papias, someone who heard the apostles and was bishop of Hierapolis, even makes mention of him often in his writings. But nowadays the general consensus of the Church holds that the apostle John wrote these Letters, too, because in truth they show a great likeness in words and faith with his first Letter and condemn heretics with a like zeal. John calls himself an elder, however, either because he was already advanced in age or because the name of elder, that is, a presbyter, is also fitting for a bishop, on account of the maturity of his wisdom and his seriousness. Hence Peter also says, *Therefore I, a fellow elder and witness of the sufferings of Christ, entreat the elders among you.*[1] *The elder,* he says, *to the elect lady and her children whom I love in the truth,* that is, whom I love with a true love, one, namely, which is according to God, or at least whom I love because I regard them as persevering in the truth. **And not only I but also all who perceive the truth.** Because he is beginning to write against heretics who have fallen away from the truth, he properly recalls that there is but one love among the saints for all who have come to know the truth, so that by their unanimity together with the large number of Catholics he may startle those who have separated themselves from their company,

1. 1 P 5:1

since they are few. For in truth all Catholics throughout the world follow one canon of truth, but not all heretics and unbelievers are in unanimous agreement about their error but they impugn each other no less than they do the very way of truth.

2 On account of the truth which abides in us and will be with us for ever. We love you and yours, he says, for no other reason than the truth of the faith which lasts permanently in us and is always unassailable, because namely we have ascertained that you also guard the same faith invincibly.

3 May grace and mercy and peace be with us from God the Father and from Jesus Christ, the Son of the Father, in truth and charity. Since the heretics of that time, Marcion and Cerinthus, were denying that our Lord Jesus Christ was the true Son of God but were tracing his beginning from his human birth, John, to refute the blasphemers, properly recalls that he is the Son of God the Father. He also bears witness that grace and mercy and peace are to be given to believers by him as by God the Father, so that he may point out that he is equal and coeternal with the Father whose gifts he designates as being the same as those of the Father. In the same way the Lord himself, speaking of his consubstantiality with the Father, says, *For whatever the Father does, the Son in like manner also does.*[2]

5 And now I ask you, lady, not as if I were writing a new commandment but what we have heard from the beginning, that we love one another. By this word he censures the heretics who were trying to bring in new teachings, abandoning those which they had heard from the apostles, and in this way breaking the covenant of fraternal charity. He says

2. Jn 5:19

therefore that he is writing a commandment which is not at all new but only giving this encouragement that the ancient faith and undiminished charity may abide in all.

7 Since many deceivers have gone forth into the world who do not confess the coming of Jesus Christ in the flesh. This can be understood both of the heretics, who indeed confess, but in some part of their faith in him do not properly understand that Jesus Christ was incarnate, denying either that his flesh was real or his soul real or his divinity real or that God was his real Father or that his Holy Spirit was the real, omnipotent God, or something else which the true faith confesses. And this can also be taken as applying to the Jews, who deny utterly that Jesus is the Christ, who swear solemnly that the Christ has not yet come in the flesh for the salvation of the world but wait for the antichrist who is going to come to their destruction.

9 Everyone who strikes out ahead and does not remain in the teaching of Christ does not have God; the one who remains in [this] teaching has both the Son and the Father. Note the distinction of words and embrace the truth of faith. He says that the one who does not remain in the teaching of Christ does not have God, but he says that the one who remains in his teaching has both the Son and the Father, so that he may show that the Father and the Son are the one true God and convict those of lying who maintain that the Son is either not God or posterior to or less than the Father.

10–11 If anyone comes to you and does not bring forward this teaching, do not receive him in the house or speak a greeting to him; for the one who speaks a greeting to him shares in his malicious works. John put into practice also through his actions these things that he taught in words about abominable schismatics and heretics. For someone who heard him, the most holy and brave martyr Polycarp,

bishop of the people of Smyrna, tells that at one time
    When he entered the baths at Ephesus to wash and
    saw Cerinthus there, he immediately leapt up and
    departed without washing, saying, 'Let us flee from
    here, lest the very baths in which Cerinthus, the
    enemy of truth, is washing fall down.'[3]
When the same Polycarp had also on one occasion chanced
to meet Marcion, who said to him, 'Acknowledge me', he
answered, 'I acknowledge [you], I acknowledge the first-
born of satan.'[4] The apostles and their disciples then used
such great caution in religion that they would not allow
anyone to have even the contact of a word with any of those
who turned aside from the truth, just as Paul also says,
Avoid the heretical person after the first and second reproof,
knowing that such a one is wrong and commits sin, since he
is self-condemned.[5]

14 The children of your elect sister greet you. Just as he
forbids greeting the opponents of truth, so on the contrary
does he greet the elect in the person of the elect, both that
unbelievers may be abominated by all the good, if perhaps
they may thus wish to be corrected, and that the peace and
charity of believers towards one another may always
increase.

3. Eusebius/Rufinus, *Hist. eccl.* 3. 28; GCS 9:335,1/4
4. Jer., *Vir. ill.* 17; TU 14:18,26/28   5. Tt 3:10-11

1   **THE ELDER to the dearly beloved Gaius whom I love in the truth.** Who and what sort of person this Gaius may have been is shown in the course of the Letter, because namely by his good deeds he increased the faith in Christ that he had received and if he was not at all in a position himself to preach the word he nonetheless rejoiced in supporting from his resources those who did preach. Now we think that this is the Gaius whom Paul mentions in his Letter to the Romans, *Gaius my host and that of the whole Church greets you.*[1] For because both he who receives and he who is received are usually called the host,[1] he was a host of the entire Church because he kindly received all who came to him, namely, both preachers and hearers of the word, as the following parts of this Letter clearly explain. Hence John also loves him in the truth, that is, not for the sake of temporal advantages but only in the consideration of the everlasting goods which he sees he loves. Gaius, however, appears to have been at Corinth, from the fact that Paul was staying in that city when he wrote his Letter to the Romans, whom he also greeted in his person. But he also makes mention of Gaius as if he were a citizen of Corinth in his Letter to the Corinthians, saying, *I give thanks to my God that I baptized none of you except Crispus and Gaius, lest anyone should say that you were baptized in my name.*[2]

2   **Dearly beloved, I make it my prayer for you to begin to prosper in everything, as your soul does prosperously.**

1. Rm 16:23   2. 1 Co 1:14-15

I earnestly long for this, he says, from the Lord in my
frequent prayers, that you bring to a good end what you are
doing well, and as your soul, that is, the inward intention of
your mind, now does favorably, that is, makes progress in
your works of almsgiving, since you are rich both in the goodness of a generous spirit and in resources of money, that you
bestow these on the needy and so with the Lord's help
always be able to lead a life full of virtues.

4 **I am thankful for nothing more than these, when I hear
that my children are walking in the truth,** that is, when I perceive those whom I have begotten for God by preaching and
baptizing keeping to the truth both of the proper faith and
good action.

5 **Dearly beloved, you are doing faithfully whatever you
perform for your brothers and also for strangers.** When he
says, *You are doing faithfully,* he means, 'You are doing this
as one who is truly faithful by making your faith clear by
your works'.

7 **For they have departed for the sake of the name and have
received nothing from the gentiles.** When he says, *For the
sake of the name,* there must be understood, of the Lord
Jesus Christ. The ancients were accustomed to speak this
way. For they departed for the sake of the name of the Lord
for two reasons, namely, either by coming to preach his
name of their own free will or after having been driven from
their native land by their fellow-citizens or fellow-tribesmen
on account of their faith in and confession of the holy name.

8 **We ought, therefore, to receive such as these, in order to
be fellow-workers of the truth.** Blessed John, who had left
everything on account of Christ, joins himself to these
individuals of the wealthy faithful that he might thus make
them more ready to take pity upon the poor and stragglers.

And he must not be disbelieved to have been truly able to say what we read that Paul said, *You yourselves know that these hands of mine ministered to my own necessities and to those who were with me. I have shown you in every way that by so laboring it is fitting to sustain the weak and to remember the word of the Lord, as he said, 'It is more blessed to give than to receive.'*[3] He speaks of them as being fellow-workers of the truth, however, because

> anyone who bestows temporal means on those who have spiritual gifts is a fellow-worker in those very spiritual gifts. For since there are few who have amassed spiritual gifts and many who abound in temporal possessions, the wealthy in this way become sharers in the virtues of the poor when they provide relief for these same holy poor from their riches.[4]

For thus indeed it was that the Lord said, *He who receives a prophet in the name of a prophet will receive the reward of a prophet, and he who receives a righteous person in the name of a righteous person will receive the reward of a righteous person.*[5]

9 Perhaps I would have written to the Church, but he who loves to hold the first place among them, Diotrephes, does not receive us. Diotrephes, it appears, was some proud and arrogant heresiarch of that time who preferred teaching new things and laying claim to primacy of knowledge for himself to listening humbly to the ancient commandments of the holy Church which John was preaching. Hence [his name] Diotrephes is well interpreted as [meaning] 'distinguished fool or tasteless elegance',[6] that he might express the faithlessness of his heart even by his name.

10 For this reason, if I come I may remind you of his works,

3. Ac 20:34-35   4. Greg., *Hom. ev.* 1.20.12; PL 76:1166A-B
5. Mt 10:41   6. Jer., *Nom. Hebr.*; CC 72:151,10

that is, by censuring him more overtly I may bring them forward to everyone's notice, according to that saying of the apostle Paul, *What do you wish? Shall I come to you with a rod?*[7] **The things that he is doing by babbling against us with his evil words.** It must be noted that as we ought not by our own fault to stir up against us the tongues of slanderers, lest they themselves perish, so we ought to bear calmly those stirred up [against us] by their own malice, that our merit may increase. But occasionally we ought also to restrain them, however, lest in spreading evil about us they pervert the hearts of those innocents who might have heard us to their good. Hence it is that John refuted the tongue of his detractor, for fear that those who might have heard would not hear his preaching and remain in their evil ways.

11 Dearly beloved, do not imitate evil but what is good. He makes clear what good he wanted him to imitate by going on and saying:

12 Witness is being given to Demetrius by all, namely, because he was sustaining the weak and supporting the needy for the sake of the truth. He proposes him to Gaius, therefore, as an example to be imitated, that he might himself be able to be worthy of like praise from all.

15 Peace be to you. The friends greet you. Greet the friends in the name. He bestows the grace of peace and salvation on the friends, that through them he might show that Diotrephes and the other enemies of the truth are cut off from salvation and true peace.

7. 1 Co 4:21

NOTES TO COMMENTARY ON 3 JOHN

1.   The Latin *hospes* may mean both 'host' and 'guest'. Cf. French *hôte*.

COMMENTARY ON JUDE

1   **J**UDE, **a servant of Jesus Christ, a brother, however, of James, to those who are loved in God the Father and preserved and called for Jesus Christ.** The apostle Jude, whom Matthew[1] and Mark[2] in their Gospels call Thaddaeus, writes against the same perverters of the faith whom both Peter and Paul condemn in their Letters.

3   **Dearly beloved, having every concern of writing to you concerning your common salvation.** He speaks of their common salvation, of that salvation which was shared by him and them. For indeed the salvation, faith, and love of Christ are one and common to all the elect. **Pleading for you to struggle hard for the faith which was once handed down to the saints,** pleading for you to learn no other faith than that which was once handed down to you by the apostles and to struggle always on its behalf to death.

4   **For certain wicked persons have entered in secretly, who were long ago designated for this judgment.** He says, *for this judgment,* for this condemnation which they deserve by acting wickedly; as the Lord says, *And those who have done what is right will go forward to the resurrection of life, but those who have behaved evilly to the resurrection of judgment,*[3] that is, of condemnation. **Transmuting the grace of our Lord into self-indulgence.** The grace of our Lord softened the harshness of the law, because when it said, 'If anyone does this or that let him be stoned, if anyone does

1. Mt 10:3   2. Mk 3:18   3. Jn 5:29

241

this or that let him be consumed by flames', the Lord mitigated the stringency of the law and by the grace of the
gospel gave permission to cleanse by repentance and the
fruits of almsgiving the acts of wickedness that had been
committed. But they transmute his grace into self-indulgence
who sin more permissively and freely the more they see that
they are less likely to be called to account by the strictures
of the law for the crimes that they have committed. **And
denying the only sovereign and our Lord Jesus Christ.**
The only sovereign is our Lord Jesus Christ together with
the Father and the Holy Spirit, as the only sovereign is the
Father together with the Son and the Holy Spirit, as also
the only sovereign is the Holy Spirit together with the Father
and the Son, the only sovereign is the entire Trinity, Father
and Son and Holy Spirit. For whichever person you name in
the same holy and undivided Trinity is the only God, and
when you name the entire Trinity together, you name the
only true God. Hence it must be properly understood that
any heretics who deny that the Father of Christ is the good
and righteous true God deny the only sovereign and our
Lord, any who deny that Jesus Christ is the true Son of
God also certainly deny the only sovereign and our Lord,
any who diminish the power of the Holy Spirit also
speak against the majesty of the only sovereign and our
Lord, because undoubtedly the same Father and Son and
Holy Spirit is the only sovereign and our Lord.

5 **But I wish to remind you who once knew all things,**
namely, knew all the hidden mysteries of faith, and had no
need to hear novelties from new teachers as if they were more
holy, **that Jesus saved the people from the land of Egypt and
afterward destroyed those who did not believe.** He is referring
not to Jesus the son of Nun[1] but to our Lord, showing first
that he did not have his beginning at his birth from the holy
virgin, as the heretics have wished [to assert], but existed as
the eternal God for the salvation of all believers, according

to the mystery of his name;[4] then implying that he so graciously saves those who believe that he might justly condemn unbelievers. For in Egypt he first so saved the humble who cried out to him from their affliction that he might afterward bring low the proud who murmured against him in the desert. He stresses this so much that we may remember even now that he so saves believers through the·waters of baptism, which the Red Sea foreshadowed, that he demands a humble life of us even after baptism and one separated from the filth of vices, such as the hidden way of life of the desert quite properly pointed to. If anyone actually profanes this life either by departing from the faith or by acting evilly, being turned away in heart, as it were, to Egypt, he will deserve not to reach the promised fatherland of the kingdom but to perish among the ungodly. Alternatively: *He afterward destroyed those who did not believe,* because the righteous judge both now and later strikes some persons, if their faults require it. Punishment, in truth, sets free from [paying the] penalty those alone whom it changes. For present evils lead those whom they do not correct to future ones.

6 **In fact, the angels who did not maintain their place of leadership but abandoned their dwelling place has he kept in eternal chains in darkness for the judgment of the great day.** First, it must be remembered in this statement also, as in the preceding one, that Jesus our Lord punished the angels who transgressed. For he who was born of the virgin as a human being at the end of the ages received the name of Jesus at the message of an angel,[5] having been born God of the Father before all ages, he with the Father provided for every created being when he willed, and from the beginning so condemned the proud angels in the darkness of this air that he might keep the same for greater punishment on the day of judgment.

4. Mt 1:21   5. Lk 1:31, 2:21

And therefore they are justifiably to be condemned who argue that Jesus Christ is not true God but was only a human being and the offspring from the two sexes. Then, there must be brought in the fact that he who did not spare the angels when they sinned does not spare proud human beings, but will condemn them also both severely before the judgment and more severely in the universal judgment when they have not maintained their place of leadership, namely, that by which they were made sons of God through the grace of adoption, but have abandoned their dwelling place, that is, the unity of the Church in which they were reborn to God, or at least their seats in the heavenly kingdom which they would have received if they kept their faith.

7 **Just as Sodom and Gomorrah and the neighboring cities in like manner committed fornication,** and so on. Because he had given the example of condemnation against those who denied the only sovereign and our Lord Jesus Christ by recalling the destruction first of the people who murmured and were unbelieving in the desert and then of the wicked angels who raised themselves up against their Maker, so by recalling the conflagration of the people of Sodom he gives the example of those who exchange the grace of our Lord for self-indulgence.

8 **These also in like manner who indeed defile their flesh or despise the sovereignty or blaspheme the majesty,** here must be understood, they also are to be condemned like the people of Sodom who defiled their flesh, like the unbelieving people who blasphemed the majesty of the divine power, like the angels who despised the sovereignty of their Creator.

9 **When Michael the archangel quarreled with the devil and contended over the body of Moses, he did not dare to bring a judgment of blasphemy but said, 'May God order you.'** It is not entirely obvious from what scriptures Jude took

this witness. But nonetheless we should know that we find something like it in the prophet Zechariah. For indeed he says that, *The Lord showed me Jesus the priest standing before the angel of the Lord, and satan was standing at his right hand, that he might oppose him. And the Lord said to satan, 'May the Lord rebuke you, satan, and may the Lord who chose Jerusalem rebuke you.'*[6] But in this place it is very easily understood that Jesus the priest desired that the people of Israel be freed from the captivity of Babylon and return to their fatherland, but satan resisted him, unwilling for the people of God to be freed, but instead sold to the enemy, and these gentiles, and therefore the angel who was the peoples' helper, rebuked him and removed him from doing further injury to the same people. But we remain uncertain when Michael had a struggle with the devil over the body of Moses. But nevertheless there is no lack of those who say that the same people of God have been called the body of Moses from the fact that Moses himself was part of that people, and therefore that Jude was properly able to say that what he had read had been done to the people had been done to the body of Moses. But wherever and whenever this contention of the angel with the devil occurred, we must carefully consider that if Michael the archangel was unwilling to bring a charge of blasphemy against the devil who opposed him, but restrained him with a mild word, how much more ought all blasphemy be avoided by human beings, and especially lest they offend by a careless word the majesty of the Creator.

11   **Woe to them, because they have gone in the way of Cain and been led astray through [hope of] reward by the error of Balaam and have perished through rebellion [like that] of Korah.** Those go in the way of Cain who, on account of their envy of better teachers, appropriate to themselves a name by

6. Zc 3:1-2

which they may be honored. Those perish by the error of
Balaam who for the love of earthly advantages assail the
truth which they themselves know. Those perish through
rebellion [like that] of Korah, who went down alive to
the lower world, whoever by their yearning for an undeserved
place of leadership cut themselves off from the unity of the
holy Church and, knowing and foreseeing how much evil
they do, nonetheless go down to the underworld of
viciousness. And the Lord indeed reproved Cain when he was
thinking of killing his brother, but his envy did not allow him
to be saved.[7] The Lord forbade Balaam from making the
journey against the people of God, but his love of money
prevented him from obeying.[8] Moses, through the Lord
speaking in him, took care to soothe Korah as he was acting
proudly, but the arrogance with which he seethed rendered
him incurable.[9] So, truly, so do the heretics behave, who at
the reproof of the holy Church scorn being corrected, and
even more, they strive, like Cain, to kill their brothers with
the sword of evil teaching, like Balaam, to deceive them
with evil advice, like Korah, to rise up against catholic
teachers, to their own destruction.

**12 These are stains in their own feasts, reveling without
fear.** Anyone who sins has been stained; the stain is the very
viciousness which defiles the one committing it. And therefore he calls the heretics whom he is censuring stains because
not only do they themselves perish in their eatings and drink-
ings, whether bodily or spiritual, but they also destroy and
corrupt others. **Clouds without water which are carried
about by the winds.** The clouds are the holy preachers
who, having their way of life in the heavens,[10] flash with
miracles and drop down rain with their utterances; about

7. Gn 4:5-8   8. Nb 22:5-24:13
9. Nb 16:1-35   10. Ph 3:20

whom it is said to God, *Your truth [extends] to the clouds.*[11]
But the heretics are *clouds without water* who *have set their
mouths against heaven*[12] through their proud words but do
not irrigate with the water of wisdom the hearts of their
hearers, *which are carried about by the winds,* because they
are carried away at the suggestion of invisible spirits to
various errors of vices. **Fruitless trees in autumn, twice dead,
uprooted.** It is a dead tree which does not produce good
fruit;[13] but anyone who has also brought forth the fruit of
evil work is called a twice-dead tree. And if anyone who
has been unwilling to bear the fruit of good work is said to
be worthy of being cut down for his barrenness and cast into
the fire, what punishment do you think the person deserves
who either by acting perversely or perverting others has
yielded rotten fruit? Nor is it astonishing if those who are
proven to have been uprooted are said to be fruitless and
twice-dead [like] trees. For it is said of the saints, *Rooted
and grounded in charity.*[14] But those who do not fear to up-
root themselves from the firmness of charity deservedly lose
whatever good fruit they appear to have, such as these are
deservedly compared to trees in autumn, that it may be
shown that their salvation is without hope. For in autumn
not only are no fruits usually formed but even those which
were formed and are ripe fall off. To the condition of this
time, namely, are they compared who themselves both
neglect to yield the fruits of faith and are eager to root out
those good things they see any other believers producing and
to make culls of them.

**13 Wild waves of the sea, casting up as foam the things that
disconcert them.** The wild waves of the sea are the perverse
teachers who are both always restless and stirred up within
themselves, dark and bitter, and do not stop forever assailing

11. Ps 36:5 (35:6)   12. Ps 73 (72):9
13. Mt 7:17-19   14. Eph 3:17

the peace of the Church, which is like the durability and strength of a breakwall. But of such as these is it properly said, *casting up as foam the things that disconcert them,* because like surging waves, the higher they raise themselves up in their pride, the more disordered they are and broken up into frothy foam and perish. **Wandering stars for whom an onslaught of darkness has been kept for ever.** The wandering stars, which are seven,[2] never rise or set in the same place as they did the previous day but are seen now low on the horizon at the winter solstice, now high at the summer solstice, and now in an intermediate position at the two equinoxes. So, undoubtedly, so are the heretics, who promise the light of truth and never persevere in the stance they assume in their teaching, but now presenting their teaching in this way, now in that, they themselves certainly indicate how the manifestation of light which they promise is to be rejected. And indeed the best known of the planets, that is, the wandering stars, are the sun, the moon, the morning and evening stars. These are sometimes taken as indicating something good, as when the sun is understood as the Lord, the moon the Church, the morning star John the Baptist, who by his brith preceded the Lord who was about to be born in the flesh and gave witness to his light, but also as indicating something evil, as when we read about the Lord saying of the seed that had been sown on rocky ground, *But when the sun rose, it was scorched,*[15] which he himself explained by adding, *But when persecution arises on account of the word, he is at once scandalized.*[16] The heat of the sun, therefore, points to the fierceness of persecution. The moon indicates something evil, when we read, *The fool is changed like the moon,*[17] the morning star something evil in, *How have you fallen from heaven, O morning star,*[18] [3] which can be understood not only of the first fall of the devil but also of his members, who by their heresy fall from the

15. Mt 13:6   16. Mt 13:21   17. Si 27:12   18. Is 14:12

Church. The evening star indicates something evil in, *And you make the evening star rise over the children of the earth,*[19] because although both the antichrist and his servants transform themselves into angels of light,[20] nevertheless they do not bear witness to the divine light as the morning star does to the sun but they show instead the works of darkness to their followers, like the star which is called evening-star and which appears in the west at dusk and is the forerunner of the night that is about to follow. *Wandering stars,* he says, *for whom an onslaught of darkness has been kept for ever.* For those who bring the darkness of errors into the Church of God in the name of light will properly be sent into the eternal darkness of torments; those who disturb the peace of the faithful after the manner of storms at sea will rightly be struck with an onslaught of tortures.

14–15 For Enoch, the seventh from Adam, prophesied of them, saying, 'Look, the Lord comes amid his holy thousands to pronounce judgment against them all.' He does not say against all human beings but against all the wicked, leaving none of them unpunished. There is appended about them, **'and to censure all the wicked.'** He does well to say that Enoch who prophesied these things was the seventh from Adam in order to substantiate by an example what he said previously, that wicked persons who snuck in to undermine the faith of the devoted had long ago been consigned to such a judgment.[21] **'And to censure all the ungodly,** he says, **for all their works of godlessness which they godlessly performed and for all the harsh words which all the ungodly spoke against him.'** This statement is true indeed, because when the Lord comes in judgment he will censure and judge the ungodly not only for the works of iniquity which they have performed but also for their iniquitous words. But nevertheless we must know that the book of Enoch from which he

19. Jb 38:32   20. 2 Co 11:14-15   21. Jude 4

took this is classed by the Church among the apocryphal scriptures,[22] not because the sayings of so great a patriarch in any way can or ought to be thought worthy of rejection but because that book which is presented in his name appears not to have been really written by him but published by someone else under his name. For if it were really his, it would not be contrary to sound truth. But now because it contains many incredible things, such as the statement that the giants did not have human beings for fathers but angels,[23] it is deservedly evident to the learned that writings tainted by a lie are not those of a truthful man. Hence this very Letter of Jude, because it contains a witness from an apocryphal book, was rejected by a number of people from the earliest times. Nonetheless because of its authority and age and usefulness it has for long been counted among the holy scriptures, particularly because Jude took from an apocryphal book a witness which was not apocryphal and doubtful but outstanding because of its true light and light-giving truth.

16 These are grumblers, complainers, walking according to their own desires. The more anyone grumbles and complains of the present labors of the Church, the less he has suppressed the desires of the flesh within himself. But on the other hand, holy Daniel and the other men with heavenly desires,[24] reject with greater contempt all transitory things which appear to be adverse the more steadfastly they desire only the things on high.

19 These are they who separate themselves, animals, not having the Spirit. The condemned separate themselves this way from the lot of the righteous, they are physical, that is, they follow the cravings of their own soul, because they have not deserved to have the Spirit of unity by which the Church

22. Jer., *Vir. ill.* 4; TU 14:9,11/15　　　　23. Enoch 6-7
24. Dn 9:23

is gathered together, by which it is made spiritual. Therefore they spread apart, because they do not have the glue of charity.

20–21 But you, dearly beloved, build yourselves up on your most holy faith, pray in the Holy Spirit, keep yourselves in the love of God. We pray in the Holy Spirit when pierced by divine inspiration we request help from on high to receive the good things which we are unable [to acquire] of ourselves. Blessed Jude, therefore, advises us so to build ourselves up on the foundation of our holy faith, so to join ourselves as living stones to the house of God which is the Church, so to keep ourselves in the love of God, that we may never presume on our own strength but may hope in the help of divine protection, lest anyone, according to the teaching of Pelagius, declare that he can be saved on his own, but all may request the coming of the Holy Spirit to us, that inspired by him we may be able to pray more earnestly, lest we perhaps be separated from the company of the holy Church with those who do not have the Spirit and therefore persist in being physical.

22–23 And censure some, indeed, who are judged, but save others, snatching them from the fire, have mercy on others with fear. What he says, *with fear,* must be joined to all three that he had mentioned, because when anyone censures those who are apostates and shows that they are worthy of condemnation, he ought to act with fear, lest perhaps something of this sort happen to him or those close to him whom he loves, and also anyone who chastises another and snatches him from the fire of his vices ought to look to himself, for fear he himself may also be tempted,[25] and anyone who has mercy on a neighbor who repents ought of necessity to act in his case, circumspectly too, lest he be perhaps either

25. Ga 6:1

severe or devoted more than is just. **Hating even that stained garment which is fleshly.** He calls our body our fleshly garment. We ought not, however, to hate our body but we ought to hate it in every way it is stained and see to it, as far as we are able, that we render it stainless, so that from being fleshly it may deserve to be made spiritual. Because this must be accomplished not by the power of our free will but by the grace of God, there is properly added:

24 **But to him who is able to keep you without sin and establish you stainless in rejoicing before the sight of his glory.** He does well to say that we whom he previously advised to serve God with fear are to be established in rejoicing before the sight of his glory, because the more anxious we are about our actions in the present, the more joyful shall we be in the future about the reward we have received.

25 **To the only God our saviour through Jesus Christ be glory, splendor, lordship and power before all ages both now and for ever. Amen.** This summary bestows coequal and coeternal glory and the kingdom both on the Father and Son through all and before all ages and refutes the error of those who believe that the Son is less or later than the Father, when it says that glory, splendor, lordship, and power belong to God the Father through Jesus Christ our Lord, and this not from some beginning in time but before all ages both now and for ever. Amen.

NOTES TO COMMENTARY TO JUDE

1. Bede here equates the Old Testament name Joshua with Jesus, which is the case in Hebrew, which was originally written only with consonants. Joshua is mentioned as the son of Nun in Dt 31:23 and Jos 1:1, and the Latin has the same form for his father's name as is here given in English. However, the Latin of Bede in this particular passage has the spelling *Nave,* which is to be found instead of Nun in Si 46:1.

2. The 'wandering stars' are the planets, as Bede says a bit further on. At his time they were thought to be seven in number, including the sun and the moon.

3. Latin *lucifer.* This literally, 'morning star', but in English, as a proper noun, Lucifer has come to be used as one of the names for the devil.

CISTERCIAN PUBLICATIONS INC.

TITLES LISTING

THE CISTERCIAN FATHERS SERIES

THE CISTERCIAN STUDIES SERIES

Temporarily out of print   † Forthcoming

* *Temporarily out of print*   † *Forthcoming*

THOMAS MERTON

THE CISTERCIAN LITURGICAL DOCUMENTS SERIES †

FAIRACRES PRESS, OXFORD

Distributed in North America only for Fairacres Press.

DISTRIBUTED BOOKS

* Temporarily out of print   † *Forthcoming*